Peers Inc

Peers Inc

*How People and Platforms Are
Inventing the Collaborative Economy
and Reinventing Capitalism*

R OBIN C HASE

PUBLICAFFAIRS
New York

To the heroes: the entrepreneurs, change makers, and nurturers building us all a sustainable world.

CONTENTS

Introduction

BACK IN 2000, sleepless at night during the early months of building Zipcar, I had a recurring nightmare. Lying in bed next to my husband, I imagined the mafia—the rental car mafia—bursting through the door, black machine guns bearing down on us. I understood clearly that we were on a path that was going to break a hundred-year-old industry.

What I failed to appreciate back then was the much larger movement made possible by the Internet. Zipcar was a trailblazer. When you can connect and share assets, people, and ideas, everything changes, not just how you rent a car. Google, eBay, Facebook, OK-Cupid, YouTube, Waze, Airbnb, WhatsApp, Duolingo—all are part of this transformation of capitalism. Web 2.0, the sharing economy, crowdsourcing, collaborative production, collaborative consumption, and network effects are simply terms we've created along the way in an effort to capture what is going on. Attributing all this to "the Internet" misses the building blocks and therefore the ability to replicate this type of activity in a more controlled way. There is one structure that underlies all these—excess capacity + a platform for participation + diverse peers—and it is fundamentally changing the way we work, build businesses, and shape economies. I call it Peers Inc.

Peers Inc combines the best of people power with the best of corporate power. One can think of it as using every resource and every stakeholder efficiently. The "Inc" delivers only on industrial strengths (that require significant scale and resources), and the "Peers" deliver on their individual strengths (localization, specialization, customization). When Incs and peers focus only on what they do best, each handling what is difficult, annoying, or just plain impossible for the other, the resulting collaboration is compelling and sometimes miraculous.

In a world of scarcity, Peers Inc organizations create abundance. Harnessing resources we already have—physical assets, skills, networks, devices, data, experiences, processes—these organizations grow efficiently, and sometimes exponentially. Peers Inc redefines our understanding of assets—proprietary versus in common, private versus public, commercial use versus personal use—and requires a rethinking of regulations, insurance, and governance. Tapping into a diversity of peers, these organizations are creative and have the potential to learn exponentially. Peers Inc rewrites the rules for value creation: Shared resources unlock the greatest efficiencies, shared minds the greatest innovation.

Peers Inc is driving the transition from the industrial to the collaborative economy. The old economy was built upon the idea that wealth is created by hoarding assets and selling them off bit by bit. This is why we invented patents, copyrights, trade secrets, certifications, and credentials. It is also why I owned my own car and why I bought hundreds of records. We all hoarded stuff, kept it close, and locked it up, because we believed that this was the way we (individuals, corporations, institutions, governments) would reap the most value. The result was an enormous loss of potential—excess capacity just yearning to find the light of day. When we look deeply into the whys and hows of Peers Inc accomplishments, we see again and again that open and connected assets and minds result in the greatest value.

In our volatile world, Peers Inc collaborations can create change with a pace, scale, and quality we previously thought impossible. Creativity, innovation, resilience, and redundancy are intrinsic to every Peers Inc endeavor. This is the structure for our times: With it we can experiment, iterate, adapt, and evolve, quickly. We can solve large problems cost-effectively and rapidly. We can scale globally yet adapt to the very local. The old industrial model cannot solve climate change. It is too slow, too inefficient, too exclusive. Peers Inc is driving the rapid transformation of our economy and will also provide an answer to the conundrum of disappearing jobs, escalating income inequality, and devastating resource scarcity.

What we do now will have profound and lasting effects on our future. We are at the end of the old fossil-fuel-saturated, consumption-based industrial economy. We are at the beginning of the new collaborative economy, which thrives on sharing, openness, and connectedness. What we choose to leave behind and how we prepare for the new will determine whether we make this transition in time and how many people we help cross the chasm. It's an all-hands-on-deck moment.

HOW TO READ THIS BOOK

Entrepreneurs, businesspeople, the digerati, the revolutionaries, policymakers, and the naturally curious should all find novel, thought-provoking ideas within. The arc of the book runs like this:

Part I: The Building Blocks

Chapter 1: Zipcar start-up story, where it all started. Then the three components of Peers Inc: excess capacity (**Chapter 2**), platforms for participation (**Chapter 3**), peers (**Chapter 4**). **Chapter 5** (the three miracles): This is one of my favorite chapters and the fulcrum on which this book pivots.

Part II: Execution

Chapter 6 (building your own Peers Inc), **Chapter 7** (government's role), and **Chapter 8** (legacy institutions) provide concrete ways to act on this new paradigm, and, of course, lots of stories. Chapter conclusions propose unconventional policy recommendations that build on each other. I was surprised where writing this book led me!

Chapter 9 is all about the power of money and funding. If you are looking to stir up the revolution, this chapter has the seeds for how to work around the status quo.

Chapter 10 is one of the reasons I wrote this book. It lays out the case for how the Peers Inc structure is the only way we are going to meet the speed, scale, and local adaptation requirements to address climate change in time to prevent the catastrophic change that we've set in motion. This chapter is both sobering and optimistic.

Chapter 11: The conclusion is really a beginning. I make a strong case that transition to the collaborative economy is inevitable.

PART I

The Building Blocks

ONE

"Hello, Zipcar. This Is Robin."

My Three Theses

AFTER I CO-FOUNDED ZIPCAR, a national magazine described Antje Danielson and me as "two moms" from Cambridge, Massachusetts.[1] While it's hard to see this statement as anything except condescending, it named pieces of my life experience that absolutely made me the most qualified person to run Zipcar—namely, being a mother of three. But let me start at the beginning.

My father was an American diplomat. I lived in seven countries and went to thirteen schools before graduating from high school in Alexandria, Egypt. This upbringing made me resourceful, adventurous, and independent, and I learned quickly how to navigate new cities and be pragmatic about transportation. From an early age I'd been given the freedom to go where I wanted by foot, push scooter, and bike, exploring Damascus (Syria), Jerusalem, Mbabane (Swaziland), and Arlington (Virginia), and getting out of my mom's hair—she had six children and a laundry list of responsibilities. While most American teenagers were pining for their driver's license and the freedom it would bring, when we moved to Alexandria, Egypt, for my senior year of high school, my transportation options gloriously expanded to include very cheap taxis and trolleys.

After all those years of movement and a life of constant novelty, as an adult I ended up in Cambridge, Massachusetts, for twenty years. Twenty whole years! How could I feel a similar independence in Cambridge, finding the fastest and most convenient ways to move

myself and my three young children through the busy and complicated dance of day care, work, food shopping, time in the park,
playdates, and after-school activities? In our urban environment, this
usually meant traveling by foot (no car seats, no seat belts, no search
for parking) or by public transit. But having occasional access to a
car would have simplified rather than complicated things.

My self-reliant, resourceful, adventurous, and impatient attitude
came into play in those early months of building Zipcar. Much
later—post-Zipcar—I learned in conversation with a friend, Karim
Lakhani, whose meticulously researched PhD thesis was on innovation platforms, that the best solutions and the most creative practices
usually come from people as far removed as possible from those
who are "experts" in a field.[2] I would be such a person. By contrast,
the people with the money, prospective angel investors and venture
capitalists that Zipcar needed to make the company work, were car
owners and daily drivers. Our idea of sharing cars, rentable by the
hour and by the day, went against what they knew about people,
status, lifestyle, technology, operational difficulty, financing, and
women as founders of car companies.

Zipcar started on a bright back-to-school day in September 1999.
September has always felt like the month when, no matter my age, I
think about the future, change, and the promise of the year stretch-
ing ahead. Perhaps this is because I live in a northeastern university
town where herds of young people arrive with full backpacks just as
the leaves change and the wind picks up. That September Antje and
I were in Ras Café, a few blocks from our children's elementary
school, with a couple of hours before school let out. Her son and my
youngest daughter had been best friends the year before in kinder-
garten, two active rapscallions who had recognized a partner-in-
crime. Antje described what she had seen on a recent vacation to her
hometown in Germany. Sitting in a café in Berlin, she had seen a
shared car parked across the street. She had investigated and found
it was available for rent by the hour and by the day. She was smitten
by the idea. What did I think? Would it work in Cambridge?

Mine was the perfect ear to hear this: the right person at the right
place at the right time. I'd recently attended a reunion at MIT's

Sloan School of Management and had listened to my classmates' stories of start-ups and successes. Metro Boston was a hotbed of technology start-ups at the time. Raytheon, DEC, Data General, Wang, and EMC had all been founded here—it was the East Coast equivalent of Silicon Valley. The current dot-com boom, enrapturing investors and entrepreneurs alike, reached its peak a year later, in March 2000, with the NASDAQ at an all-time high.

Not only was I ready to do a start-up, I also was the target market for car sharing. My husband drove our car out to his suburban office every morning, where it would sit in a parking lot all day. And while I definitely needed a car sometimes, there was absolutely no way I wanted to buy another, park it on the street in our city neighborhood, maintain it, and shovel it out after snowstorms. I didn't want to deal with remembering the monthly alternate-side-of-the-street-cleaning days and dashing out to move the car when I heard the garbled 7:00 a.m. warning from the tow truck loudspeaker. For me, as for most people who live in a city and don't need a car to get to work, the costs of car ownership are far greater than the potential benefits. Once, maybe twice, and under duress, I'd borrowed a neighbor's car. But asking to borrow it regularly would make me feel like I was a moocher. I needed Zipcar.

Two months after incorporating, we got our first angel investment, $50,000, from Jeannie Hammond, an MIT classmate. The bulk of that money went to one engineer, Jim Lerner, who worked closely with me to build Zipcar's first website, the member application page, the car reservation and payment processes, the basic fleet management system, and the database integration that underpinned these. A significant but smaller amount went to logo and website design. Four months later, Zipcar had $68 in its bank account and three days before going live. The plan was to place four cars in four reserved parking spaces, one near each of four consecutive subway stops in Cambridge and Boston. We already had a new lime-green Volkswagen Beetle that we had named Betsy. I had bought the car myself, using my house as collateral, and was paying it off in installments of $299 per month. Three additional cars, all Volkswagens—a Beetle, a Golf, and a Passat—were scheduled to be delivered the next morning.

Then I got a call from the vice president of the leasing company. He informed me that he would feel "more comfortable" with a $7,000 security deposit for each car before he would release the vehicles to us. You'd think I might have panicked. Instead, I just felt tired. Nothing had come easily. Here was just another hurdle.

It was late afternoon and I didn't have the brainpower to think through options, so as a distraction, and because it was on my calendar, I went to a 6:00 p.m. launch party for another start-up. The reception was in a barely renovated factory building: cement floor, walls newly painted white, long catering tables covered with white paper tablecloths against one wall. I had just walked in when Juan Enriquez, an angel investor I'd been in touch with, came over. I would get to know Juan later, but on that June day we had a remarkably short and direct conversation.

"Hi, Robin. How's Zipcar going? What can I do for you?"

"I need $25,000 by tomorrow morning."

"Done," he said.

And indeed, by nine o'clock the next morning, when I called the bank, the money had been wired in. I gave the lessor the money, we got the cars, and Zipcar launched.

But I still had to raise real money. In 2000, the online networks and marketing portals that connect would-be funders with would-be innovators had yet to be invented, so peer lending, crowdfunding, and one-stop shopping for angel investors were not options.

My first tip-off that venture capitalists and I might not see eye to eye was at my third meeting with one of Boston's founding fathers of venture capital. We were eating together in the office building lunchroom after our more formal meeting. I learned that he had children too—nine! I am fifth in a family of six. I told him that my favorite movie as a child was *Peter Pan*, and that after I saw the movie for the first time on TV, when I was five or six, I had climbed up on to the top of the dresser in my shared bedroom and had jumped off with the hope of flying. I landed on the floor with a hard thud.

He told me that he had put one of his children, at age two, on top of the dresser in the bedroom. Holding out his arms to his child, he told him, "Jump! Jump!" The child hesitated. "Jump! I'll catch you," he repeated. The child jumped, and he stepped away and let him fall. "I had to teach him at an early age that you can't trust anyone."

That story stayed with me on the subway ride back home to my house, and when I went to pick up my six-, nine-, and twelve-olds from school. It ricocheted through my head all afternoon. And I repeated it to my husband once my children had been put to bed. It seemed that venture capitalists and I had completely different worldviews. I thought you could trust people. That the vast majority of people were good. That I could count on my father, and even a stranger, to catch me if I fell within arm's reach. Every day, perhaps naively, I try to find and build the world I want to live in. From the outset, I saw Zipcar as an example of a different way of thinking about business, in which assumptions about trust, responsibility, and collaboration were changed.

MY THREE THESES

My three most fundamental beliefs, which gave me faith Zipcar would work, gave most investors and business reporters pause.

Robin's Thesis #1: People are willing to "share" cars instead of owning them because the economics make sense.

Investors' response: The American psyche is tuned toward consumption and ownership. Americans have a special relationship with their cars and our status is bound up in our cars. We don't want to use cars. We want to own them.

Robin's Thesis #2: A technology platform leveraging the Internet and wireless technology makes sharing effortless.

Investors' response: The technology hurdles are too high, too complex. It's never been done before. You aren't an engineer.

Robin's Thesis #3: The company can trust people to pick up and drop off the cars without supervision, fill them up with gas using the company credit card, and take their trash when they go.

Investors' response: The people doing it in Europe are Swiss! We Americans will never treat cars so well.

There are quotation marks around the word "share" in that first thesis because I learned that about 40 percent of the people I surveyed in the fall of 1999 had really negative associations with that word. To them, sharing implied "dirty," "poor quality," "having to wait," and "hippie-ish"—all qualities that were far from the service we intended to build. As a result, I abandoned use of the word *sharing*, but not the idea. We believed that technology would transform sharing into a seamless and efficient transaction. Zipcar would provide a high-quality service, and our customers wouldn't have to coordinate with other people or wait for a turn.

As it turns out, my belief in the potential for sharing foretold what would unfold in social media over the next decade. Facebook and other social media companies have since thoroughly rebranded the word *sharing*. Fortunately, my prediction that people were willing to share was accurate. Hardly a minute after the Zipcar website went live (but before the launch), the phone rang.

"Hello, Zipcar. This is Robin. How may I help you?"

"Hi, I'd like to rent a car."

"Are you kidding me? We just went live! This is incredible! Sure!"

And so Craig Kleffman became the first Zipcar member. He rented our cars by the hour to transport his drum set to gigs he played at, and rented them by the day to get himself to the out-of-town triathlons he participated in. For people like Craig, who live in cities and don't need a car to get to work, both car ownership and car rental mean getting more car than they actually want to use. People chose Zipcar because sharing was the financially smarter choice—and we were cool, smart, fun, urban, convenient, and reliable as well. Upon its sale to Avis in 2013, thirteen years after its founding, Zipcar had 760,000 members sharing 10,000 cars across the United States,

Canada, and the United Kingdom. Recent purchases of local car-sharing providers in Spain and Austria, and a launch in Paris in 2014 continue to extend Zipcar's reach.

Zipcar's goal was to make renting a car as easy and convenient as getting cash from an ATM. We needed to deliver simple, convenient, reliable access to cars that were available—just like ATMs—throughout the city. Users needed to be able to reserve and unlock cars in seconds, at any time, and with no one standing between them and the vehicle.

It took me six months to come up with this simple ATM metaphor for what we were trying to do. Today I think we were successful not because we made renting a car as easy and convenient as getting cash from an ATM but because we made renting a car easier and more convenient than owning one. The "Wheels when you want them" tagline foreshadowed the movement toward giving consumers access rather than ownership. Why own (and store, manage, and pay for) the whole thing when you can be assured of having it at hand only when you need it? That said, delivering on this new way of consuming took a lot longer than half a year.

I knew that nobody would rent a car for an hour if it took fifteen minutes to pick it up—finding a service location, standing in line, and filling out the requisite forms—and almost as long to return it. The logic for a very low transaction effort (and cost) was compelling from our business perspective as well: For Zipcar to work, we needed to be indifferent between eight 1-hour rentals and one 8-hour rental. Getting our transaction costs as close to zero as we could was absolutely necessary. When our fleet grew and I needed to hire a VP of operations with big-fleet experience, the candidates from the car rental industry would ask me, "So what's Zipcar's transaction cost?" At that time, almost all of our hard-won investment dollars were being poured into technology. Our development costs were huge. But the result was zero marginal cost for each transaction.

"What is *your* transaction cost?" I'd prompt. I learned that in the rental industry the cost was between $8 and $12 per transaction!

Yikes. No wonder they required a one-day minimum for every rental and extension.

What was good for us was also exactly what the customer wanted. To make the transaction cost zero, to make sharing effortless, we needed technology that had several parts:

1. *Customer-facing software.* Initially customers used the website to join Zipcar, reserve cars, pay their bills, and manage accounts (smartphones didn't exist yet).
2. *Back office:* The web pages—that only we could see—allowed us to manage customers, cars, and parking locations.
3. *In-vehicle hardware.* The Zipcard reader under the windshield allowed customers to walk up and unlock the car they had reserved. An antenna enabled communication with the reservation system, and a small black box let us physically unlock the doors, enable the ignition, know what distance had been driven, and understand why the check-engine light might be on.

When Craig, our first member, reserved a car, it would go something like this. Say he wanted to do a big grocery store run on Tuesday night and needed a car from 7:00 to 9:00 p.m. At Zipcar.com he could see the schedule by calendar week for "Betsy," an eye-catching lime-green Beetle (Volkswagen had only just introduced the new Beetle months before Zipcar's launch). If Betsy was booked until 7:30 p.m. on that Tuesday night, Craig could decide whether he wanted to leave half an hour later or preferred to go on Wednesday night, when the car was free.

In an old-school car rental company, the schedule would be visible to employees only.

CRAIG: I want Beetle Betsy Tuesday from 7:00 to 9:00 p.m.
OLD SCHOOL: Not possible. It is booked. Do you want a more expensive car?
CRAIG: No.

OLD SCHOOL: Do you want to go Wednesday night?
CRAIG: No.
OLD SCHOOL: Do you want to walk to a car that is ten blocks
away?
CRAIG: No, never mind.

Craig alone knew what mattered most to him, and putting the decision into his hands instead of the company's was faster, cheaper,
and smarter. He could rapidly and effortlessly make the trade-offs
inside his head.[3]

Zipcar's service was a little more than six months old when we
got incredible outside validation for our scrappy start-up. It was a
weekday morning in early 2001, and our new VP of operations, Mark
Heminway, was in safari mode, leaning against the cool concrete
wall of a downtown Cambridge parking lot waiting to observe our
proof-of-concept moment "in the wild."

Mark had worked at Hertz Car Rental for the previous fifteen
years, eventually heading their North American fleet operations.
Where he once would call up Ford and GM and order 300,000 cars
over the course of a year, now with Zipcar he'd call up those same
colleagues and say, "Hey, I'd like to buy . . . two." Mark understood
the seasonal patterns of car use and the car rental industry's business model. He and his colleagues had worked their way up, living
through industry fluctuations, mergers and acquisitions, layoffs and
rehiring, so they all had a network of friends dispersed throughout
the industry.

Mark's good friend Jay Inslee stood by his side in the parking
garage. Many years earlier, Jay had been Mark's boss. Now he was
the COO at Dollar/Thrifty. Jay had flown in from Tulsa to get an up-
close look at Zipcar's technology and customer service innovations.
Earlier in the office, Mark had shown him how a member quickly
signs in to the website and is presented with the calendar for his favorite car. He could book that one or any other car in the network in
about twenty seconds. Reservations were sent wirelessly to the cars,
so the right car would open only to the right person at the right

time. Switching to see inside Zipcar's virtual back office, Mark had noticed there was a rental scheduled for 11:00 a.m. in a parking garage just a block away.

As the two men waited in the municipal garage, anonymous and unnoticed, a young man in a business suit walked rapidly toward the Zipcar parked in its reserved space on the garage's ground level. He held a briefcase in his left hand; his right was up at his ear with a cellphone. As he approached the driver's-side door, he removed Zipcar's proximity membership card from his breast pocket and held it over a small gray box tucked beneath the inside corner of the windshield. Both Mark and Jay were too far away to hear the click as the door unlocked, but the member wasn't. He put the Zipcard back in his pocket and opened the car door. Still talking on the phone, he dropped his briefcase onto the passenger seat, shut the door, and put on his seatbelt. He started the car with the keys that were dangling from the steering column, backed out, and pulled away.

Jay's response was just one word: "Wow." I glowed when Mark debriefed me.

My three theses had proved true. Zipcar had taken fundamental car industry beliefs and turned them on their head. People were happy to share a car rather than own it (Thesis #1). And amazing wireless technology could make renting a car a completely do-it-yourself experience, reducing the cost of the rental transaction from around $10 to zero (Thesis #2). Customers could in fact be our collaborators, trusted to pick up and return a rental car without supervision (Thesis #3).

PEERS INC

The more I've thought about it, I've come to understand that sharing is actually figuring out how to tap into existing excess capacity. Zipcar thrived by leveraging the opening provided by the wasteful economics of current car consumption models—the fact that personally owned cars sit idle 95 percent of the time.[4] But we weren't the only ones leveraging idle capacity: The U.S. government similarly shared its R&D and satellites with everyone for global positioning systems (GPS), and the city of Bogotá, Colombia, took advantage of the fact that its thoroughfares were relatively car-free on Sunday mornings by turning the streets over to pedestrians, runners, bicyclists, and skaters and featuring performances throughout the city. Examples of exploiting the hidden value in idle assets abound once you start to look for them. Recognizing the role of excess capacity was the first of my epiphanies. Unpacking my Zipcar experience, seeing the commonalities with other emerging companies, and appreciating the scale of the firestorm that Zipcar helped catalyze, took many years.

When Zipcar formally launched in 2000, less than 40 percent of Boston's households had Internet access. Nobody had smartphones. Wikipedia would not be launched until 2001, followed by Facebook in 2004 and YouTube in 2005. It was important that we include the ".com" on the end of zipcar.com so anyone who saw it would know to look for us on the World Wide Web. But by 2014, investment into companies whose core assumptions mirrored the ones we pioneered in 2000 had exploded. Sharing houses and apartments, Airbnb raised $450 million in that year. Sharing travel and costs on long car trips, BlaBlaCar raised $100 million. Disrupting the status quo in urban transportation and collaborating with people driving their own cars as taxis, Uber raised $3 billion and Lyft raised $250 million. In total, companies building platforms to tap into excess capacity raised more than $5.5 billion that year, which was close to four times what had been raised by similar companies in 2013, which was again more than double what had been raised in 2012.[5]

What is happening? The Internet has eliminated a key corporate competitive advantage. In 1937, in the influential essay "The Nature of the Firm," British economist Ronald Coase wrote that the corporation was invented to do things that individuals and small companies couldn't do. In particular, small companies would choose to become larger companies whenever it was cheaper to hire than to outsource. What would make hiring cheaper than outsourcing?

Transaction costs (a term Coase invented). Finding, monitoring the quality of, and managing many discrete individuals was expensive. It was cheaper to hire them. But now the Internet has transformed that equation. Today, we see that the smartest companies and governments are using the Internet's ability to facilitate collaboration by leveraging expertise, assets, and resources outside their sphere of control.

The result is a very efficient, and often more humane, way of doing things. On one side of the collaboration, we have *industrial strengths*: companies, governments, and institutions (the "Inc") that apply significant resources, talent, and money to simplify the complex, apply standards and consistency, deliver economies of scale, and create global brands. On the other side we have *individual strengths*: individuals and small companies (the "peers") that engage in local, small-scale, customized, and specialized efforts to create just-right unique goods and services, often tapping into their own social networks.

The thirty companies included in the 2014 funding numbers I listed earlier are just the tip of the iceberg. Significant sectors of the economy are transitioning to this new approach—building platforms to unlock excess capacity and welcoming outside collaboration. My three Zipcar theses are the kernels of the Peers Inc building blocks. The first is that excess capacity (sharing an asset) makes economic sense, the second is that platforms for participation make sharing simple, and the third is that peers are powerful collaborators. This book is about the platforms and the peers, the collaboration and the synergies I first uncovered at Zipcar. Enabled by new technology, a revolution is taking place inside capitalism as we reimagine the role of consumers, producers, and even ownership. I call this new paradigm Peers Inc: a transformation of the relationship between companies and people.

Peers Inc finds abundance where there once was scarcity. It leverages the ability of individuals and small actors to experiment, adapt, iterate, and evolve. When done well, Peers Inc can create change at a pace, scale, and quality we previously thought impossible. Peers Inc is leading the transition from industrial capitalism to the collaborative economy.

INDUSTRIAL CAPITALISM	COLLABORATIVE ECONOMY
Encyclopedia Britannica (40,000 articles)	Wikipedia (32 million articles in 287 languages)
Monoculture	Diversity
Centralized	Distributed
Defends the status quo	Experiments, learns, adapts, evolves
Assets and wealth controlled by the few	Largest networks win
AT&T, Verizon	Skype, WhatsApp, and mesh networks
Seeks monopoly status	Seeks to maximize participation
Thrives on economies of scale	Thrives on the economics of free (excess capacity)
Standardization	Customization and personalization
Value created through trade secrets and patents	Value created through idea exchange and open standards
IStockPhoto (millions of photos)	Flickr (billions of photos)
Network TV (sixty years of three networks)	YouTube (one hundred hours of video uploaded per minute; one month's worth of video is the same volume as network TV in total)
Bank of America, Capital One (too big to fail)	Lending Club, Prosper (resilient and offer redundancy)
Owns the asset	Borrows the asset
Personal car	Zipcar, Car2Go
Buses and trains	BlaBlaCar
One dollar is the same as every other dollar	Intangibles are visible and valued
Mainstream media	Blogosphere, Twitter, Tumblr

In this book I delve into the right-hand column and answer many questions surrounding the collaborative economy:

- What is the economic underpinning behind this transformation?
- What is the organizational structure that powers it?
- What does it mean for employment and for how people find work and earn a living?
- What miracles does this paradigm makes possible?

- How do you build a platform from scratch?
- What is the role for government? How do big institutions transform?
- Does Peers Inc democratize power or strip people of it?
- How can we use Peers Inc to address our biggest challenges, such as climate change?
- What does our future look like?

The Peers Inc model transcends the world of business. It is my belief that it is shaping powerful change. Throughout this book, I'll provide the evidence for how the Peers Inc model can take this rapidly changing world and transform it into the one we want to live in: sustainable, equitable, thriving, and full of potential.

And now we begin.

TWO

Excess Capacity

Abundance in a World of Scarcity

ON CHRISTMAS WEEKEND in 2003, Frédéric Mazzella was trying to get from Paris to his small rural hometown. His options—trains and buses—were expensive, and they didn't even get him all the way. He knew there had to be people making that same trip who would be happy to share their costs of driving, if only he could quickly, easily, and safely find them. Mazzella, who is enterprising and tenacious, took years to turn his idea into a platform and several more to get it just right. But by the end of 2013, his company, BlaBlaCar, had more than 10 million active users. Today, more than 2 million people every month are traveling across Europe by getting rides in strangers' cars. That's more people than ride the Eurostar train between Paris and London, for which the $21 billion Channel Tunnel was built.

Frédéric's company achieved this for less than $21 billion because it made available an unused asset that every one of us sees and ignores every single day: the three or more empty passenger seats that accompany every car driver who travels alone. It's the perfect example of excess capacity, invisible until you learn to think differently . . . and then you can't help but see it everywhere.

Leveraging excess proved to be an important component of Zipcar's success. Before Zipcar, people in Boston who needed a car had just two options. They could rent in twenty-four-hour bundles, or they could own their own car, paying an average of $8,000 a year in depreciation and costs for insuring, parking, maintaining, and fuel-ing it.[1] Zipcar allowed people to book cars near them in less than twenty seconds and rent them for as little as thirty minutes. An early Zipcar member told me that he had decided to join when he real-ized he hadn't driven his own car in so many months that he'd basi-cally lost it in the downtown Boston garage where he paid $250 a month for a space.

In both cases—renting or owning—it is necessary to buy a lot more car than you really want, resulting in significant excess capac-ity. I knew that Zipcar would win on the economics if it allowed people to pay only for the amount of car they actually used. The "ex-cess" could then be purchased by other drivers. Instead of owning 100 percent of a car and using it 1 percent of the time, it was possible to align usage and cost much more closely. And instead of one thou-sand urban residents owning four hundred cars, with Zipcar these same one thousand active drivers are satisfied with just thirty cars.

I started noticing excess capacity all the time. I was obsessed. Even a lazy Sunday inspired observations about excess capacity. I'll walk you through an average morning, then teach you to start rec-ognizing the excess capacity we overlook every day.

It is a fall Sunday morning in Cambridge. I'm sitting near the win-dow, reveling in the warm sun, laptop on my lap, reading the *New York Times* online. I'm interrupted by the sound of an incoming Skype call, but the person on the other end hangs up before I find the app.

I've decided to do a long-postponed chore: listing on Craigslist a wildly uncomfortable carved wooden love seat I bought fifteen years ago. I take a few photos with my smartphone and upload them. Before I can finish, Craigslist asks me to retype a series of distorted letters that have popped up in a box on the screen. Thankfully, I'm able to decipher them on the first try. Done! I fall down a Craigslist rabbit hole when I see a section labeled "free." What kinds of things are people giving away? I browse—TV, couch, TV, cat litter (presumably unused), mattress—and then I see it: two bags of wool cloth scraps, mostly of old suits, from a grandmother's attic, used to make rag rugs. Hey! My grandmother made rag rugs too, and I've got the tool she used to cut the wool into quarter-inch strips. I'd like to try my hand at it. The gifter lives in Concord, about fifteen miles from Cambridge. It could be a beautiful drive out there given the time of year; city mouse that I am, I feel like I've been missing out on the glory of fall foliage. My husband, Roy, is game. We reserve a Zipcar for noon to 3:00 p.m. so that we can take a walk around Walden Pond while we are out there. Roy pulls out his smartphone and enters the Concord address using Waze, an app he is infatuated with.

Once in the car, we drive past the Sunday farmers market held in the tiny urban elementary school parking lot. Wanting to turn onto Memorial Drive, we encounter an unexpected roadblock: We forgot that Memorial Drive is closed to vehicular traffic Sunday mornings, opening up the space for bikes and pedestrians. We take a detour to the opposite side of the river, and off we go.

How many examples of excess capacity did you find?

I'm sitting near the window, reveling in the warm sun. Passive solar warming is the first example. The sun's heat exists, and it's already "paid for." I can choose to let it dissipate, or I can take advantage of it.

Reading the New York Times online. Online news started out as repurposed copy from the newspaper's print editions (second example). For the first few years, the *New York Times* was able to enter the online world and learn it at a very low cost, paving the way for the future reality of its dominance as the location for consuming news. Given the changes in the way we read over the last decade, we would now say that the print edition is repurposed copy from the online version. Same content, new outlet, some additional readers.

I'm interrupted by the sound of an incoming Skype call. Skype was built on the back of the excess capacity found in my computer (third example), my built-in video camera (fourth example), and my already purchased data plan (fifth example) on the Internet (sixth example). Voice calls (and now video calls) were previously brought to my house by copper cables. The trunk line on the street was hooked up to my private abode; I then had to go to a store, buy a phone, bring it back to my house, and plug it in, and the phone company would charge me a monthly fee for that service. Today, all of that communication is being done using cables, connections, and devices that are already paid for, thanks to the proceeding century of dogged investments by telephone and cable companies and leveraging my own personal equipment and monthly payment for Internet access.

Comparing Skype and the old-style phone company isn't exactly fair, but it does tell a good story about how much has changed. Starting in 1877 with Alexander Graham Bell's patents, the company that later became AT&T had to build everything from scratch. Over the next hundred years, AT&T's path to power included patent hoarding, endless lawsuits, multiple acquisitions, and becoming first an unregulated monopoly and then a regulated one. At its peak in the 1950s and 1960s, it employed over a million people.[2] Ultimately, after a ten-year battle in the U.S. courts, the Justice Department ordered it broken up into seven regional companies in 1984.

Two of the seven "Baby Bells"—AT&T and Verizon—thrived. The two companies placed eleventh and sixteenth, respectively, in the U.S. Fortune 500 in 2014, working their way back to the top and striving for monopoly status again. Today, wireless communication is central to their business: AT&T had 110.4 million wireless customers in 2013, and Verizon had 102.8 million.[3]

Skype was founded in 2003 and had amassed 633 million users by 2010. In 2013, it had 36 percent of the market in international calling.[4] Skype built its company by finding another use for our personal computers, video cameras, and data connections. Making the decision to sign up and join the Skype network takes about two minutes and costs nothing.

Listing on Craigslist. The seeds of this list are directly rooted in excess capacity. In the mid-1990s Craig Newmark had been doing a lot of evangelizing about the Internet and "saw a lot of people helping each other out." Then, he wrote, in "early 1995, I decided to give back a little via a cc list, focusing on arts and tech events in San

Francisco."[5] Craig was living in San Francisco and interested in the arts and technology events himself, and he realized that in his free time he could become a central hub. He collected and catalogued these events, wrote them down once in an email, and could now quickly share that knowledge with lots of people simply by copying them (seventh example). He formalized Craigslist into a company in 1999 so that it could grow more effectively without himself as the core.

Craigslist (and Craig Newmark himself) "is a big believer in open source software [eighth example], and relies heavily on Linux, MySQL, Perl, Apache, Sphinx, Redis, Haraka, and many others."[6] Open source software itself is being created through tapping into developers' excess-capacity work time (nights and weekends at first). Software tools allow thousands of individual coders to contribute tiny snippets of code that can be incorporated into the eventual open source software platform. The fact that people can contribute with as little as one line of code or a few minutes of effort has made for a massive long tail of contributors and almost infinite amount of excess capacity to be leveraged.

I take a few photos with my smartphone. This is an example of one of the most creative, profitable, and world-changing excess capacity opportunities the world has ever witnessed. I'm not talking about the ability to take photos with your phone—although that is indeed remarkable—but about the opening up of the phone to outside innovation. In the United States, up until the early 1980s, the telephone in your house was actually the property of that same monopoly phone company, AT&T. You paid them a monthly rental fee for it. The phone wasn't yours, and no tampering was allowed; it was simply a way to connect to their network. Needless to say, that kind of monopoly power resulted in very little innovation in customer-facing products and services.

Cell phones began their slow penetration into the U.S. market starting around 1990. Back then, they were an expensive luxury, mainly owned by the wealthy or by people whose employers were paying the bill. For many years, my father-in-law, a doctor, was the only person I knew who had a cell phone. I got my first mobile phone in 2002—after 50 percent of American adults already had one—under pressure from my Zipcar staff, who hated not being able to get in touch with me when I was out of the office.

Cell phones do transform your life, but it was Apple's announcement, about eight months after the release of the iPhone, that it would invite third-party, non-Apple applications that marked the real revelation of the potential in the phone's excess capacity. It's important to note here that in this instance, Steve Jobs does not get credit for being prescient and visionary. In fact, he was exactly the opposite. Here's how it really went down.

The many months of the iPhone pre-launch hype produced the desired results. People were lined up for days outside of stores to score one of the phones when they went on sale on June 29, 2007. Sure, the iPhone was cool. The touch screen could be pinched small and spread wide. It could handle your music, your contacts, your calendar, your phone calls, and—something that is important for this story—would let you browse the Internet with the touch-screen keyboard. Jobs's vision was that if you wanted to do other things on the phone, you would go to the Internet to do them. This gave Jobs total control over the user experience.

Software hackers had a different idea.

The iPhone could only be run on one telecommunications network—AT&T's. The months after the launch were filled with a new tension, as hackers looked for the key to breaking Apple's SIM locks so that non-AT&T users could use their own SIM cards. The frenzy and urgency behind the desire to separate the iPhone from AT&T's service area and quality of service are obvious in this headline from Engadget, an online technology news service, specifying the exact time of this occurrence: "iPhone unlocked: AT&T loses iPhone exclusivity, August 24, 2007, 12:00pm EDT."[7]

But swapping out the SIM card was just the start. What hackers really wanted to do was to get inside to manipulate the smartphone and play with its features. The tech press, blogs, and commentary thrilled with rumors, claims, retorts, promises. On September 18, Jobs offered this memorable comment to the press: "It's a cat-and-mouse game. We try to stay ahead. People will try to break in, and it's our job to stop them breaking in."[8] As a mother of three, I could have predicted the response his comment would provoke. Over the next forty-eight hours, as the quote was picked up by various media outlets, engineers everywhere took up the challenge to hack the iPhone.

Less than a month later, Jobs admitted defeat and announced that in February Apple would release a software development kit (SDK) for the iPhone that would allow developers to write native applications for the touch-screen handset as well as the iPod Touch. It was clear from the measured announcement that Jobs was skeptical, and he predicted that only a couple of hundred applications would result.[9] His prediction was wildly off. The iPhone app store launched on July 10, 2008, with 552 apps and today has more than 1.2 million apps.[10] (Google's Android offers a similar number.)

That makes for a lot of things that can be done with all the non-talk time available on your smartphone—the ninth example of excess capacity. Globally, the average smartphone user has downloaded twenty-five apps.[11] Out of the more than 2 million apps now available, some make you more productive and some make you dramatically less productive; some are high value and some are low value. The compelling part of working with excess capacity is that full-cost economics no longer applies. Some of those apps are worth the cost of the device. For example, before navigation software systems became apps on your phone, they were sold with their own portable, wireless, single-purpose device that cost about as much as a smartphone. In fact, many people were happy to pay up to $600 to have in-vehicle navigation. The vast majority of apps are most definitely *not* worth the cost of the device that runs them, but an enormous number of them are now economically viable when you don't have to take the cost of the asset (the phone) into account.

A series of distorted letters. This is formally called a reCAPTCHA (tenth example), one of the most elegant examples of how excess capacity can be put to use in surprising ways. In the late 1990s, Luis von Ahn and his colleagues at Carnegie Mellon University had been pondering how to foil computer bots that pretend to be humans and cause all sorts of havoc in large computer systems. The solution that they popularized is one that we all know well: those annoying little boxes of warped and scrambled numbers and letters that appear on our computer screen, requiring us to transcribe them before we can do certain things—send an email, make a comment, or sign up for something. That little test is one way of proving your humanness. In 2000, von Ahn's team coined the term *CAPTCHA* (for "completely automated public Turing test to tell computers and humans apart") for this tool, and soon the tool was being widely used.

Von Ahn would tell you that by 2005, "approximately 200 million CAPTCHAs [were] typed every day around the world." He could have rested on his laurels with that remarkable adoption of his innovation. But, being an engineer, von Ahn made some additional calculations. "It takes about 10 seconds to type a CAPTCHA," von Ahn said. "Humanity as a whole is wasting about 500,000 hours every day typing these annoying CAPTCHAs." So he wondered: "Is there any way in which we can use this effort for something that is good for humanity?"[12] And so reCAPTCHA was born in 2007.

reCAPTCHA takes the effort of typing the characters in a CAPTCHA and repurposes it to solve an entirely different problem. In order to make old newspapers or books useful online, they have to be scanned and the resulting images turned into machine-readable text to be usefully searchable. Sometimes the scanned or photographed image results in words that can't be decoded using optical character recognition (OCR). This is a problem. When the CAPTCHAs are constructed using words tagged by OCR programs as unreadable, we smart humans do what computers can't: We easily decode them! Tests have shown that reCAPTCHA text images are deciphered and transcribed with 99.1 percent accuracy, a rate comparable to the best human professional transcription services.

Today, 100 million reCAPTCHAs are seen by computer users every day. The *New York Times'* entire archive, dating from 1851, has been digitized by pairing OCR technology with the work of individuals whose screen logins are diverted to turning messy, all-but-illegible reCAPTCHAs into legible words and numbers. Having completed that task, reCAPTCHA today is hard at work deciphering street numbers photographed by Google Street View for use in Google Maps.

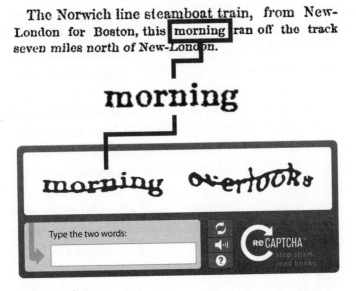

The Norwich line steamboat train, from New-London for Boston, this morning ran off the track seven miles north of New-London.

morning

morning overlooks

Type the two words:

ReCAPTCHA
stop spam,
read books.

Credit: recaptcha.com

Map applications are another use of excess capacity. Google created Google Maps for its own use, to make maps available to people Googling directions or locations. It opened up the use of those maps, at first for a fee, to developers who wanted to make use of them. At Zipcar, we used Google Maps to show our members precisely where individual cars were located. Eventually, under pressure from the hacker community, Google broadened the access to its map data. In June 2005, the company released the Google Maps application programming interface (API) (the eleventh example) to any user, for free. This meant that all of Google's years of skilled labor to create great searchable maps on the Internet could now be used by many more people and for many more tasks. Any moderately skilled user now can create a quick "mash-up"—an application that combines content from multiple sources to create a new service—in just minutes.

Just how many map-related mash-ups have been created? A good museum of projects exists on the blog GoogleMapsMania, which put up its first post in December 2005 and is still going strong almost a decade later. The blog showcases thousands of posts that run the gamut from a tally of the deaths of European migrants since 2000 to statistics on air pollution across the United Kingdom to the online game Mobbles. Access to low-cost excess capacity of maps has unleashed entrepreneurial, research, and creative juices in unexpected and unpredictable ways.

Old suits used to make rag rugs. All kinds of recycling or upcycling can be counted as the twelfth example of leveraging excess capacity. The rag rugs that my grandmother made were typically woven from old clothing that was beyond use because it was moth-eaten, worn, or no longer in style.

Reserve a Zipcar. We've already talked about how Zipcar (the thirteenth example) wrings the idleness out of the way cars used to be used. I'm no longer privy to the metrics, but it used to be that some Zipcars in mature markets would be in use as much as 60 percent of the time, as compared to personal cars, which are used about 5 percent of the time.[13]

Take a walk around Walden Pond while we are out there. In transportation policy lingo, this is known as "trip chaining" (fourteenth example): linking all of your errands together in one go. A round trip to the wool lady's house is twenty-eight miles. A round trip to Walden Pond is twenty-nine miles by a slightly different route. By combining the two trips into one, we will be traveling about thirty-two miles in total and saving time, miles, CO_2, and Zipcar rental time.

Roy pulls out his smartphone and enters the Concord address using Waze. Starting with the excess capacity found in smartphones, apps, and Google Maps, Waze goes even further. Think for a moment of all the years and the millions of trips that people have been driving with the assistance of turn-by-turn navigation. Meanwhile, two extremely valuable pieces of information were being generated every single time a navigational system was used: your route choice (fifteenth example) and your actual speed at each location at a specific time on a specific day of the week (sixteenth example). It was a gold mine of data that was overlooked and thrown away for years. It took Waze, pairing navigation with the smartphone, to realize the incredible value potential of that data. As Waze explains, "Imagine millions of drivers out on the roads, working together towards a common goal: to outsmart traffic and get everyone the best route to work and back, every day."

Whenever you hear companies and consultants hype the possibilities behind big data (which, by the way, is excess capacity because it's data scraped from something that has already happened and been recorded), what they are salivating for is an application as beautiful and compelling, as useful and valuable, as Waze.

The Sunday farmers market held in the tiny elementary school parking lot. The parking lot was built to provide parking for teachers and staff, so on weekends it is always empty (seventeenth example). Excess capacity is often found only at certain times. The most remarkable double-use I heard about was a Waldorf school in Seattle that let homeless people sleep in the gym at night as long as they left by seven o'clock each morning.

Memorial Drive is closed to vehicular traffic. I don't know what you do Sunday mornings, but all of us have noticed that between, say, seven in the morning and two in the afternoon there are very few cars on the road. Maybe people are at places of worship; maybe they're lazing away in bed or on the couch; maybe they're doing push-ups in their garage. But, for the most part, they aren't in their cars. So in Cambridge a 1.4-mile stretch of Memorial Drive, running alongside the Charles River, is closed to vehicles and open to bikes and pedestrians. Hundreds of people go there to walk, run, bike, chat, and generally revel in the reclaiming of this beautiful riverside park, usually a four-lane highway. What does it take to elicit such happiness? A dozen wooden barricades pulled across a few intersections, a vision, and political will.

The first such pop-up park, Ciclovía in Bogotá, Colombia, is also one of the largest and definitely among the most admired. Meaning "bicycle way," Ciclovía was started in 1976, and for its first five years consisted of twenty-five miles of highway that were closed on Sundays and public holidays between 7:00 a.m. and 2:00 p.m. In the mid-1990s it expanded beyond its cyclist-centric beginnings by adding games

Credit: Gil Penalosa

and lessons, and soon it became the most important recreational space in the country. In 1998, the city managed to break a Guinness World Record when 37,731 people got together to do aerobics around a stage set up in the downtown area. Today, the city coordinates aerobics, yoga, and dance classes, as well as musicians and street vendors. There are currently seventy-five miles of roads where people can walk, run, cycle, and skate. Two million people participate each week—that's 30 percent of Bogotá's metro-area population! The cost of this health, happiness, community building, and source of civic pride? Sixteen cents per person per week.[14]

I've included many short examples of excess capacity because I want you to feel the breadth and expansiveness of the opportunity it offers. Excess capacity is everywhere. It could be your own; it could belong to someone else. It might be physical, temporal, virtual (think about open data), process-related, network-related, or experiential. It surrounds us. Its richness and potential are boundless. Excess capacity has been the basis for ideas big and small, scalable and one-off, world-shattering and community-enhancing, disruptive and ho-hum. All of these examples were built upon a foundation of untapped abundance, coaxing value out of something that was once unseen until it blossomed, generating a better return on investment for producers and consumers

REVEALING ABUNDANCE

The fact of abundance contrasts sharply with the shadow of perceived scarcity as I sit reading the news in my own house filled with the toys, papers, projects, and detritus of twenty years of family life, surrounded by hundreds of thousands of people living in their own equally stuff-filled abodes in an area that is riddled with highways congested with mostly empty cars and near an airport where planes take off and land constantly throughout the day. When I consider all this, I feel overcome. Americans are 5 percent of the global population yet consume almost 30 percent of the world's goods.[15] In the last three years, China has produced more cement than the United States did in the last one hundred years.[16] Dan Sperling, in his book *Two Billion Cars*, writes that today there are 1 billion cars and we are trending toward 2 billion in the next twenty years.[17]

There is more than enough physical stuff already; we just need to think about and organize it differently. We can share the assets we have already (cars, beds, phones). We can leverage the networks that we didn't even know existed (social media). We can share virtual goods that had been hidden (open data, open source software, open APIs). We can share talents, expertise, creativity, and insights that were previously unvalued.

In itself, excess capacity is just latent value. Actual value comes from making use of it. When I picked up my own children from school, I would also sometimes pick up a neighbor's child as well. I was getting more value out of my trip, doing what neighbors should do, and providing my own children with more compelling companionship than me alone. Making use of excess capacity in small local ways is fulfilling and useful, but it's not what this book is about. I'm interested in scaling this idea by making more efficient use of what we have around us and by uncovering totally new value there as well. Therein lies the path to abundance. Etsy, an online marketplace for makers, is not like a really big craft fair. eBay is different from both classifieds and yard sales. Airbnb is much more than a listing of 1 million bed-and-breakfasts. What distinguishes and transforms these activities is that platforms connect, organize, aggregate, and empower the participating peers. Without the platform—without Airbnb, Etsy, Lyft, TopCoder, or OpenStreetMaps, to name a few—the peer co-creators would not engage, the leveraged excess capacity would be limited, and the consumers of these products and services would not return again and again.

Excess capacity turns out to be a key input into a Peers Inc product or service. The cost of experimentation is lowered as new value is extracted out of something that already exists and is already substantially (or entirely) paid for. This is why excess capacity is so appealing, especially for entrepreneurs, whose biggest problem is almost always a lack of capital. This is why businesspeople and government officials who want to get higher returns on their investments should constantly be on the lookout for ways to repurpose those investments by opening them up. In all cases, leveraging excess capacity comes at a far lower cost than buying raw material. And execution can happen in a fraction of the time, since we don't have to find, source, build, or finance inputs.

So once you identify the excess capacity, how do you turn it into something that's attractive to enough people that making it accessible is worth the effort? The next chapter is all about the hard work and creativity it takes to transform a prime low-cost resource into something compelling and scalable.

THREE

Platforms for Participation

Simplify, Organize, Empower

EXCESS CAPACITY is the low-cost fuel that makes the effort of platform building worthwhile. Platforms organize, standardize, and simplify participation. While a platform brings excess capacity to life, making it all work requires a serious investment of time, skill, and money—key assets and attributes of large organized entities, the companies, universities, institutions, and governments that constitute the Inc. In his chapter I will explore the power of platforms for participation, and the unique role of the Inc in building them.

My friend Nick Grossman lives in New York City and has spent a decade leveraging technology to make cities more livable. Nick and his wife, Francesca, have a car, but like most dedicated urbanites, they don't need or use it most of the time. In spite of his technical skills and interest in using his car's excess capacity and turning it into a cooperative, neither he nor Francesca could rally together a sufficient number of friends to make it work. The fact that Nick's car is sitting idle for days and sometimes even weeks in its Brooklyn parking space offends his urban environmentalist sensibilities, but all his know-how and desire could not manage to make this a viable project. He lacked the expertise and the resources necessary to make his car accessible to others. And potential renters clearly found that the hassle and uncertainty of dealing directly with Nick outweighed the benefits (nothing personal, Nick).

What Nick and others couldn't do, platform-based companies like Zipcar could. It takes a company, like Zipcar, to build robust platforms that make it simple for peers to participate and to exploit the excess capacity identified. Think about what it takes to forge a resilient, frictionless platform for peer-to-peer car sharing. Acquiring the appropriate group insurance is at best a year-long effort (and at worst five years and counting in the United States) that no individual or insurance company would ever undertake for just one person's policy. Nor could an individual get the benefits of a bulk discount. Few individuals have the skill and the capital to build the Apple iOS and Google Android apps that enable people to find and rent a car quickly, or to create the hardware that unlocks the car doors and enables the ignition. And then there's the back-office billing. Institutions, of course, do all of this and more. They bring together a diverse array of skilled people who (if all goes right) turn complex challenges into simple, elegant solutions for end users.

A company with a platform, like Zipcar, makes it easy and safe for friends (and even strangers) to use someone else's cars. It establishes and enforces standards and contracts. It routinizes procedures for picking up cars, refueling them, and dropping them off. And it sets penalties for bad behavior and the means for recourse. Almost 1 million Zipcar members can share 15,000 Zipcars because the platform makes it easy. Of course, people always *could* share cars in cities, but they didn't in any significant numbers because of the transactional effort and the unwillingness to share with strangers. These platforms took an idle asset—the privately owned urban car—and made it simple to share.

Peers choose to participate on a platform because a bigger entity (the Inc) has spent lots of time and money turning something complex and expensive into something simple and inexpensive. It is the Inc that has the ability to make long-term and large investments, marshal teams with many kinds of expertise, extract economies of scale, and apply standard forms of interaction and quality. The unique role of the Inc is to do what peers can't—to create platforms for participation and put the assets of the large company, institution, or government (such as billing or satellite maps) into the hands of the smaller, autonomous peers who participate.

Alibaba, an online platform that aggregates the wares of hundreds of thousands of smaller vendors, went public in September 2014. It was the largest initial public offering in history, raising $25 billion.[1] In a letter to prospective investors shortly before the IPO, Jack Ma, Alibaba's chairman and co-founder, wrote, "Our proposition is simple: We want to help small businesses grow by solving their problems through Internet technology."[2] The largest IPO in history was the Inc of a Peers Inc paradigm: Alibaba does what a large entity does best and gives this power to the smaller vendors who do the rest.

THE THREE WAYS PLATFORMS USE EXCESS CAPACITY

There are three ways that platforms make excess capacity accessible to others. They can slice it or aggregate it, in each case letting co-creators use excess capacity more efficiently. Or they can open it, enabling co-creators to generate entirely new ideas, processes, products, and services.

Slicing and Aggregating: Right-Sizing Supply

Zipcar slices. It takes big, lumpy options (owning a car or renting one in twenty-four-hour increments) and slices them into half-hour increments so that people can consume just the amount of driving time they want and can pay only for what they actually use.

Zipcar's success has led to scores of companies that describe themselves as "We're like Zipcar for . . ." Each business has found a way to slice a previously existing asset into smaller pieces, to match the way we actually want to consume that asset. Bixi, B-cycle, CitiBike, DecoBike, Hubway, Social Bikes, and Velib are "like Zipcar for bikes."[3] Hello Health is "like Zipcar for online concierge medicine."[4] Ziplens is "like Zipcar for photographers."[5] SnapGoods is "like Zipcar for Gadgets."[6] And Cohealo is "the Zipcar for hospital gear."[7]

Other platforms aggregate the excess capacity of assets that were individually too small to bother with and make them into something reliable and consistent, thus creating enough value to make tapping into those resources worthwhile. Airbnb, which allows people to rent out all or a portion of their own homes, is definitely the company of reference here, and in recent years there have been many start-ups that describe their business as "like Airbnb for *x*." GetMyBoat is "like Airbnb for boats."[8] HovelStay is "like Airbnb for adrenaline junkies on a budget."[9] And Rover.com is "like Airbnb for your dog."[10]

Both Zipcar and Airbnb are examples of access platforms that, through slicing or aggregation of excess capacity, enable users to get more value out of an asset by using it more conveniently and cheaply than they could before.

All this slicing and aggregating is a good thing—particularly for physical assets. With a world population of 7 billion and climbing, we need to get the most out of every finite resource we extract.

Opening Up: Inviting New Value Creation

Now let's turn to the most amazing kind of platform, one that opens up excess capacity, the way Google Maps did. Not only does it deliver the efficiency of access platforms, but an open platform enables the creation of new value, and lots of it. Open platforms are generative—better than spinning gold out of straw, because you can put that same piece of straw through the spinning wheel again and again to create as much gold as human ingenuity will allow. The open data movement is a prime example.

In September 2008, Vivek Kundra, the young new chief technology officer (CTO) for the city of Washington, DC, thought he'd like to engage with the grassroots technical community in his city. He had heard about an engineer named Peter Corbett who was the CEO of a start-up that had three employees and who was one of the organizers of the local tech community. At their first meeting in Vivek's municipal office, he showed Peter the city's data catalogue. "If you were CTO of the city, what would you do with these?" he asked.[11]

What Peter saw on the screen was the largest amount of open city data in the world at that time. Several hundred databases covered everything from public school test scores to potholes, from broken parking meters to real-time crime reports—all the data one would expect to find in an organization that needs to educate, operate, build, and maintain a city. Here it was: excess capacity (the data had already been collected and paid for by the city for various purposes) on a beautiful platform for participation (the data resided in standard formats, making them easily accessible for engineers to grab and manipulate).

"It was like honey to a hacker," recounted Peter, "and real-time open data is like a drug." He told Vivek that he'd love to share it with his hacker community. "Why not hold a contest and give some cash prizes as incentives? We could call it 'Hack the District.'"

"I love the idea," said Vivek, but he knew the name wouldn't work. "Let's call it Apps for Democracy," he suggested.[12]

It is common for platforms to be nested within platforms, since they are nothing more than the simple(st) way to engage. So it was here. Apps for Democracy was created as a contest platform to draw attention to the availability of the city data via common API platforms.

Over the next weeks, Vivek and Peter's teams created a first-of-its-kind contest and website, built with $50,000 from the CTO's budget. They dedicated $25,000 to prize money and $25,000 to market and support the hackathons. Within thirty days, forty-seven apps had been submitted to the contest.[13] There were Google mash-ups that mapped marinas, libraries, post offices, gas stations, banks, hotels, construction projects, embassies, places of worship, vacant properties, recent building permits applied for, and housing code violations, all searchable by location.

Vivek's office calculated that it would have cost $2.2 million had the city contracted for these applications. This gave them a return of more than 4,000 percent on the initial $50,000 investment. As an added bonus, no procurement officers had to research and write requests for proposals, nor vet the responses. The entire contest had taken four weeks from ideation to award.

Open platforms keep on giving. The first round had produced those forty-seven apps, worldwide press, and accolades for the creative idea behind the Apps for Democracy contest. But that was just the first order of innovation. Peter was inundated with requests. He decided to write a guide, "How to Run Your Own Apps for Democracy Innovation Contest," and he made it open-source. This guide is its own platform for participation, making Peter's structure for building a contest for apps and his earned experience available to the world at large (earned experience that isn't shared is excess capacity). So far the guide has inspired more than fifty Apps for X contests worldwide. Country-specific contests have been run in Finland, Denmark, Norway, Bulgaria, and Australia, as have sector-oriented contests such as Apps for Climate Action and Apps for Development (the latter with the World Bank, which developed its own very robust data catalogue). There have also been Apps for the Army, Apps for Inclusion, and Apps for Healthy Kids, among others.

Only two months after the first Apps for Democracy demonstrated the creativity unleashed by the District of Columbia's prize challenge, President Barack Obama asked Vivek, then only thirty-four years old, to join the White House as the nation's first chief information officer. Within just two months of Vivek's arrival, the White House launched data.gov, the new home for government datasets.[14] Enterprising students, civic-minded engineers, and companies can now mine these datasets—converted into accessible formats—to extract whatever useful value they might see in it. More than 100,000 datasets are searchable by formats, tags, dataset types, topics, contributing organizations, organization types, and publishers. Following the U.S. government's lead, more than forty other countries have created national open data pools, including the United Kingdom, Kenya, Brazil, and India, opening up more than 1 million data sets for use by the general public. States and cities have followed suit, as have many international organizations, including the UN and the World Bank.

Data.gov itself has thirty-five pages of alphabetically organized listings of ways in which the data have been used. The range of organizations extracting new value from this already-paid-for federal data is wide. Some names are familiar, others not.

On the for-profit side, you can find:

- Archimedes, which creates analytical tools for doctors and patients to predict how specific interventions will impact specific patients. It uses data from the National Health and Nutrition Examination Survey, the U.S. Centers for Disease Control and Prevention, trial datasets from the Framingham Heart Study, and Medicare datasets.
- Trulia, a website that provides a greatly enhanced look at the residential real estate market. It taps into congressional district data and wildlife refuge data.
- HelloWallet, an app that helps people understand and plan for their long-term financial needs. It makes use of a federal survey of income and retirement program participation.
- SaferCar, which helps people compare the safety of new and used cars based on an aggregation of data that includes a database of federal new car safety ratings.
- The Weather Channel, which has as its foundation federal weather and climate data.
- The Climate Corporation (recently acquired for $1 billion) combines the weather and climate data with historical soil and crop data to analyze, predict, and provide insurance against the likelihood of crop failure.

But use of this data extends far beyond commercial exploitation. Some examples:

- The 2012 Global Hunger Index, an interactive map.
- Aqueduct, a "global water risk mapping tool that helps companies, investors, governments, and other users understand where and how water risks and opportunities are emerging worldwide."[15]
- The BioEnergy Atlas.
- The California Appliance Efficiency Database.

- A child safety seat inspection station locator.
- A credit card agreement database.
- The Ethiopia Toto Agriculture Portal, a pilot demonstrating "a global data-sharing platform that brings worldwide agricultural public and/or private data together and aggregates agricultural information into a single repository."[16]

I was delighted when I saw the opening sentence of Data.gov's "Impact" tab, "Open data is fuel for innovators," as it echoes the opening sentence I had already written for this chapter, "Excess capacity is the low-cost fuel that makes the effort of platform building worthwhile."

Nick Sinai, while deputy CTO in the White House, told me, "No one can anticipate every use of federal open data. But our experience has been that open data is fueling growth in a variety of economic sectors. To foster this economic growth, the U.S. government needs to do three things. First, we need to make it easy for entrepreneurs to find and use any public government dataset. To the extent possible, we need to put our vast trove of government data online, in machine-readable and 'liquid' form, while continuing to protect privacy. Second, supplying data isn't enough—data doesn't do anything by itself. Data is only useful if you apply it. We need to engage external and internal users of our data, in person and online, to prioritize releasing the most useful data sets first."[17]

Nick's third point, about problem prioritization, is one I will develop later in Chapter 8, on evolving legacy institutions. As Nick points out, data alone aren't enough; we need a platform to bridge the gap between low-cost (sometimes free) excess capacity and innovators. When all these data were in government coffers in obtuse and one-off formats, they were useless. Platforms are required. And open platforms permit an unlimited—abundant—numbers of uses.

FOSS SLICES, AGGREGATES, *AND* OPENS EXCESS CAPACITY

The free and open-source software (FOSS) movement taps into excess capacity in all three ways. FOSS aggregates engineers and their work. Coders volunteer their efforts and work on thousands of projects around the world. Many of them do the work on their own time, leveraging the excess capacity of this worldwide workforce of programmers and engineers. Many projects have teams of coders, each contributing in their own way, aggregating their efforts to produce databases, programming tools and languages, web browsers, and just about every imaginable piece of software you can think of. While aggregating, FOSS also lets you slice the code you are interested in working on into very small pieces.

GitHub is a cloud-based service that utilizes Git, a tool popular among programmers and originally written by Linus Torvalds (Linux's first mover). Git helps coders manage changes to the code and, more importantly, share the code with others. It is a far-reaching platform for participation used by millions around the world to keep track of their original source code and collaborate with other coders. An open-source project on GitHub can be made visible to everyone, and there are hundreds of thousands of projects. Each is available for reuse, is open to improvement, and can be repurposed in other projects. GitHub is itself an example of a platform that extracted new value from an open asset: Git—something that started out as a basic tool—was reused and turned into a service, GitHub. The majority of open-source projects are built on top of earlier efforts. In the open-source world, plagiarism is the sincerest form of flattery.

Although the great economies of scale in the traditional closed software industry enabled giants such as Microsoft and Oracle, the thousandfold-larger numbers of FOSS engineers, together with "free" pricing make FOSS an innovation engine that's hard to beat. A recent example of this trend is the free open source MySQL database platform, which now powers much of the modern Web. MySQL has unassuming origins: It began life as a Scandinavian academic research project. However, a combination of fortuitous timing and MySQL's open-source model led it to become the dominant database platform used in many early stage start-ups and Web apps, including Facebook and Twitter. Ultimately MySQL was acquired by Sun Microsystems in 2008, and in 2009 Oracle acquired Sun. The

MySQL story is more compelling when one considers that it managed to use its free and open-source model to fend off competition from database juggernaut Oracle and its CEO, Larry Ellison, perhaps Silicon Valley's most aggressive software entrepreneur. Wildly successful Peers Inc FOSS examples abound, including the popular Mozilla Firefox browser and the web server Apache.

FOSS, because it is free, easily accessible, and useful, is fueling unprecedented rates of software/platform adoption and affordable innovation. Feisty start-ups can quickly morph into disruptive billion-dollar companies that are transforming both the software industry and traditional bricks-and-mortar sectors such as hotels, education, government, fashion, and retail.

PLATFORM STRUCTURE DICTATES POTENTIAL FOR INNOVATION

We now understand three ways that platforms make excess capacity available: slicing it, aggregating it, and opening it. The first two, which create a right-sized asset and give access to it, are predictive. The platform builders (the Inc) have a good idea about how they expect innovators (the peers) to use the excess-capacity resource: an hour of a car, a night in an apartment, et cetera. These platforms exercise a fair amount of control over what participants can do on the platform (become a host; rent or drive a car), and they typically make lots of requirements of the peers before they can get to use the asset (fill in a complete profile, undergo background driving or criminal checks).

The third, which involves opening up excess capacity, is the opposite. Open platforms are extremely spare and as minimalist as possible. Since the platform builders don't know how the asset might be used, they have to leave it as open-ended as possible. There needs to be just enough structure to organize the asset, and nothing more. TCP/IP (which guides the Internet), open APIs, SDKs, various protocols, standards, and meta-rules are effectively platforms for participation that all leave as much as possible up to the participant.

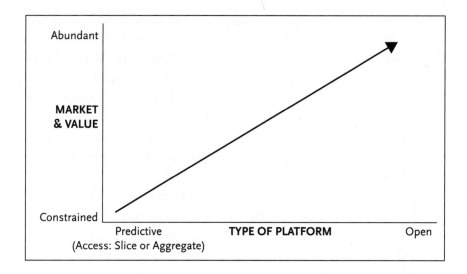

In general, there is an inverse correlation between platform complexity and its openness to innovation (and therefore to potential value). The less rigid and structured the platform, the more innovation. More structure produces less variation.

Platforms that are complex and controlled, such as Airbnb, don't leave much room for variation. Airbnb requires hosts to fill out lots of fields (home type, room type, number of people accommodated, city, availability, pricing, amenities, a description, photos, and contact information). Appropriately so, since this is what is needed at a minimum to rent your house to someone, and Airbnb isn't interested in facilitating other activities. Wide-open ones, such as GitHub and Google Docs (as well as the most open of all, the Internet), are delightfully simple, can be adapted to a large number of uses by co-creating peers, and uncover large amounts of value. Twitter, for example, requires just a username and email address. Based on that, you are allowed to fill out Twitter's 140-character string any way you want.

Structure matters, and infrastructure is destiny. The structure of the platform defines its possibility and its success. But even so, open platforms evolve and become the basis for a whole host of unpredictable uses.

WHY PLATFORMS?

Platforms have impressive properties based on their raison d'être: simplifying, standardizing, and easing participation. This means that once you've got the elements of the platform exactly right and people are interested in the excess capacity you are offering up, it will grow very quickly. The good platform has reduced the cost and effort of participating to its absolute minimum, making the barriers to entry as low as possible.

With growth come all the benefits of economies of scale. Platforms can be expensive to build, but the standardization of service provided, inherent in the platform model, means that each additional peer costs very little to add. At a certain point, the benefits are almost all to the upside. With a good idea, a great user experience, and a large market, platforms offer the biggest possible punch per investment dollar. In early 2014, WhatsApp was a three-year-old instant-messaging service that employed fewer than fifty people, sending more than 10 billion messages a day for their 450 million members.[18] That's right—a shockingly small staff was supporting the one out of seven Internet users who rely on WhatsApp, whereas telecoms employ tens of thousands of people to provide for a roughly equivalent number of customers. WhatsApp doesn't have to build any infrastructure (each one of us has already paid for our smartphones) and doesn't have to charge a monthly fee (we've already paid for monthly data plans).

One giant downside to platforms results directly from their ability to scale very fast and have similarly dizzying reductions in their costs per participant: They tend to become monopolies. If you are the platform builder, this seems like a pretty good thing, and it is one of the reasons we have seen so much venture capital money pour into Peers Inc companies. The funders hope that first-movers will get the whole market. But from the standpoint of a government, an individual, and market competition, this tendency is a problem. We will delve deeply into these issues in Chapters 7, 8, and 9.

At the end of the day, the point of a platform is to liberate the value hidden in excess capacity by engaging others: their assets, time, expertise, and creativity. Making use of excess capacity is fundamentally a collaborative act. It is sharing. The platform is the extended hand. It is half the handshake.

Now we move on to the other half, the peers. Platforms are made for peer participation; peers give them life.

FOUR

Peer Power

Localize, Customize, Specialize

IF THERE IS ONE THING we know about people, it is that we are all different. We live in different places and have different habits, interests, talents, life experiences, social networks, politics, communities, commutes . . . the list goes on. But companies, governments, and most big sprawling organizations all hate variation. Industrialization and globalization were all about standardization and sameness until the Internet made it simple and effortless to find, organize, rate, connect, and pay for small individual things. Platforms take the individuality of peers and, through organizing and resourcing, ultimately turn it into society's greatest asset. With platforms, diversity rocks.

When my three children were all under ten, the incessant squabbling in the backseat of the car was maddening. One of my tricks was to hold up my arm with its wristwatch and challenge them: "Let's see who can stay quiet the longest." This game worked every time. It was so crazily transparent to me as an adult, yet the three of them fell for it every time. At home, this game was adapted to "How fast can you run upstairs, find your shoes, and bring them back here?"

One day I found myself searching for "dumbest smartphone apps." Lo and behold, there it was: Hold the Button. How long can you hold the button on your screen? Can you beat your own record? Can you beat the app record? I know nothing about the person who invented this, but I would not be surprised if it was a parent being driven crazy by his or her children and desperately in need of a way to distract, focus, and calm them.

Of course, no one would buy a $600 device to play Hold the Button. But most of us *have* bought a smartphone for one or two features. For me, it is worth $600 to be able to send and receive email on a tiny, lightweight device that I have with me at all times. Yet I probably don't spend more than an hour a day actually reading or sending email on my phone. I also read books and articles on my phone when I'm on the subway, take and share photos, tweet, get directions, check in for flights, check the weather, download and listen to music and podcasts, check on website analytics, adjust the temperature of my house, and use the calendar, phone, timer, and calculator. And occasionally I download random apps like Hold the Button just to see what they are. The twenty-three hours of each day when my phone might have sat idle are transformed. This miraculous device constantly evolves to bring me more tools, information, convenience, and, yes, entertainment.

Apple's iOS and Google's Android platforms opened up the excess capacity in smartphones by making it accessible with SDKs, common APIs, and standard protocols. This combination is a magnet for enterprising people. They can build something beautiful without having to be experts in embedded systems and network engineering. Because the smartphone has already been paid for and is now available to them for almost free, they can build something useful, something silly, something experimental, or something to distract their kids. The power of peer diversity can be felt and seen in the existence of the more than 2 million apps built in a few short years.

This chapter explores the benefits of peer power, first for the peers, then for institutions, and finally for those of us who enjoy the fruit of this new way of organizing assets (we were formerly known as consumers).

THE BENEFITS TO THE PEERS

Who are peers? It depends on the platform and the relative size of the Inc that developed it. Peers can be companies big and small—for example, think of all those that have exploited and innovated on GPS, or small distributed wind and solar power suppliers contributing to a region's electric grid, or devices connected up to make the Skype platform useful, or individuals who post their photos to Facebook or videos to YouTube. Here I'm going to focus on the peers who are individuals since the shift in power is more meaningful to people than to devices. What is the impact on them? How does it feel to be a peer?

Carsten lives in Copenhagen. He'd been an accountant for close to two decades. Then one day, still gainfully employed at his chosen profession, Carsten heard about Airbnb. He decided to see if he could make a little extra money renting out the spare bedroom in his apartment to tourists. He could, and he was successful—so successful that within seven months Carsten had quit his accounting job and bought a five-bedroom apartment to rent out. Two years later, when I met him, Carsten had two apartments in the same building, twelve rooms to rent, and one full-time employee. He had found a new way of earning an income that he much preferred over the old—a transition that was seemingly by chance and completely under his own control. The other apartment dwellers in this building were delighted because he had turned what had been two rowdy, poorly maintained student apartments into quiet, clean, constantly supervised, and neighbor-friendly ones.

Mohammed is in New York City. He was working as an Uber driver when we met. Prior to that, Mohammed had supported his family and three employees for years as a garment wholesaler, importing clothes from China and selling them to American discount chains. But over the last few years, the rise of megastores, which made megapurchases of tens of thousands of the same T-shirt, meant that his purchases in the thousands no longer elicited the lowest prices. His business was down to one employee: himself. He had scheduled a buying trip to China in a few months. The previous fall, he'd driven four months as a full-time employee for a limo service to tide him over financially, but he hadn't liked it. Now, because of Uber, he had purchased a new roomy sedan outfitted with commercial plates and the appropriate livery insurance. As an independent driver with Uber, he could control the amount of money he'd earn in a week. If he needed $400 to cover rent, then he'd work the necessary hours to earn it. Mohammed could also rely on Uber to send him potential fares based on his proximity to the customer, rather than on seniority or a special relationship with the dispatcher. Mohammed told me if you were smart and hardworking, working for yourself was the only way to go.

Gretchen grew up in Lille, France. She had always wanted to be an artist, but her parents wouldn't let her go to art school. Instead, she graduated with degrees in political science and French. Her first jobs were corporate. With the birth of her first daughter, she sought more flexibility and control in her work. Although she started selling work in person at craft shows, Etsy made it easy to scale these first tentative efforts at commercial art to the online market, and from there engage with other sites as well. More recently, she trained as a therapist and sees clients during the school day while her children are away. Gretchen emailed me, "I cannot imagine working for someone else. Being my own boss affords me the independence and flexibility I need to express my creative processes, be they typically artistic or intellectually creative. I am not tied down to other people's wants and expectations and can choose the paths I want or need to focus on at any particular stage in my life."

In Providence, Rhode Island, David told me about his son, Ethan, who started playing Minecraft about two years ago. His father described him as a fairly normal twelve-year-old enjoying a group-building experience with kids his age from around the globe. Ethan turned out to be quite adept at building these virtual kingdoms in the sky and below the earth. He soon got a little more serious about studying architecture, and he built his own computer for gaming from components. When Ethan realized that there was a group of highly skilled builders online who were actually being hired by other kids to build custom games, he started doing some virtual building himself. It was fun, like "Legos on steroids"—and he charged a small fee of around $50, payable through PayPal.

Ethan is now extremely busy as a whiz-kid builder, creating monster customer games for which he can charge $500 to $1,000, and earning thousands of dollars each month. In the process, he has made mistakes common to a lot of young entrepreneurs: underestimating the time required to complete a project, going too far beyond his actual skill set, taking on more work than he could actually do in a given time period, and getting into ill-conceived partnerships. He has also learned a lot: how to build solid, trusting relationships based on an unspoken code of ethics and honor, and how to invest in his small business. To spur his productivity, Ethan recently partnered up with another teenager to purchase a turnkey network Minecraft business with a ready-made client base, compiled code, and website. He stands to start making a lot more money. His father emailed me that "no one seems to care if he is fourteen. He can deliver the goods."

I met Miriam, a newly minted lawyer in her twenties, in Boston. She works long hours and is at the office more than sixty hours a week. She's single and uses online dating sites to meet people. Her picks? Tinder and OKCupid (the latter perhaps one of the most popular). She likes dating this way. Like every other platform, the sites organize the content so that Miriam can quickly search and sort for people who have the gender, geography, and interests she's looking for. And because this is all online, no one is judging her choices. Communication is conveniently non-simultaneous if she chooses, although communications can reach her immediately on her phone if she wants. Because the sites meant for dating found that ratings and comments were off-putting, other sites have been created to do this. Most famously, LuLu, an app where women rate men, is used by one in four college students (according to the founder, Alexandra Chong).[1]

Vanessa and Ana are sex workers who have embraced websites to find clients. Estimates are that just 20 percent of sex workers in America find work walking the streets.[2] Instead, platforms such as AdultWork, Roomservice2000, and Peppr allow women to create profiles about their physical characteristics (height, weight, measurements, hair color, ethnicity), list their services and rates, and receive customer reviews. Buyers too can have profiles with health and background checks. In the United States, sex workers can report abusive clients to the National Blacklist, a searchable online registry. And online discussion forums sharing advice among workers is common. As with other marketplaces, these websites have made it easier for both buyers and sellers to find what they want, with better protections for both, and have removed middlemen. Vanessa and Ana said that they enjoyed the flexibility of scheduling their own bookings, felt safer, and were better able to protect their anonymity. An in-depth review of industry implications in the *Economist* concludes: "Sex arranged online and sold from an apartment or hotel room is less bothersome for third parties than are brothels or red-light districts. Above all, the web will do more to make prostitution safer than any law has ever done. Pimps are less likely to be abusive if prostitutes have an alternative route to market. Specialist sites will enable buyers and sellers to assess risks more accurately. Apps and sites are springing up that will let them confirm each other's identities and swap verified results from sexual-health tests."[3]

Chris Anderson, former editor of *Wired* and author of *The Long Tail* and *Makers*, tells the story of Jordi Muñoz, who with him co-founded 3D Robotics. Chris writes, "He was a 19-year-old high school graduate in Tijuana, Mexico when I met him online." In the community of unmanned aerial vehicle (UAV or drone) enthusiasts, Jordi was a standout. Jordi had been interested in remote-control planes since he was a young schoolboy in Tijuana. He found himself in San Diego with a pregnant American wife, unemployed and bored. "It was a nightmare; I was disconnected from my family in Tijuana, I couldn't work because I didn't have a green card, or go to college," said Muñoz. "I started using my computer like a drug. I felt desperate and stupid. But I realized microcomputers had great potential for phones, cars, and planes."[4] His mom sent him a Nintendo Wii and a radio-controlled toy helicopter to help pass the time. (Go, moms!) Muñoz hacked the sensors from the Wii, wrote some software, and attached them to the helicopter. The result was the first-ever autopiloted drone. Chris Anderson saw the video recording Jordi had posted on DIYdrones.com, a platform for participation created by Chris himself. For two years the two communicated entirely online, with Jordi improving his skills and getting deeper into the community, and Chris increasingly impressed by him. In 2009, without ever having met in person, Chris asked Jordi if he'd like to co-found 3D Robotics. By 2014, 3D Robotics was the largest U.S. personal drone maker, with $21.6 million in revenue and two hundred employees. Jordi, now twenty-eight, is its chief technology officer.

Sites such as YouTube, Facebook, Twitter, eBay, and Airbnb could not exist without co-creators, people who reach out to friends, strangers, and colleagues across the Internet. These platforms need peers. And the advantages of engaging as a peer in this new organizational paradigm are plentiful, seen in story after story. What's deemed important is different from individual to individual. Some characteristics unite them: People opt in; no employer chooses them, no certificate or degree sanctions them, their right to participate does not depend on experience. Fourteen-year-old Ethan can earn thousands of dollars a month, and an accountant can become a hotelier. Chris Anderson couldn't determine Jordi's age from their online exchange, nor gauge his accent or assess his social background or lack of academic pedigree. Chris placed his experience with Jordi in a broader context, telling me, "In the 21st century, it matters less and less where you live, how old you are, what school you went to (or didn't), or where you've worked. All that matters is what you can do; online innovation communities are the ultimate 'do-ocracies.'"

How we uncover our personal strengths is transformed. Gretchen's parents weighed in on her early career options. Many people don't feel like they have many options; others may make a choice but change their minds later in light of new life circumstances. Others might be like me. When I was just starting to work, it took me years to figure out what I liked to do and what I was good at. I hated my first job, and my second as well. But my mother wouldn't let me quit right away. "You have to stick at it at least a year, otherwise you'll look unreliable on your resumé," she said. But the world has changed since then. My resumé in the Peers Inc world becomes irrelevant, and I can try my hand at many things at once and more quickly figure out what I want to do more of. This world is now a reflection of the famous *New Yorker* cartoon where one dog seated at a computer turns to another dog on the floor and says, "On the Internet, nobody knows you're a dog."[5] With the rise of social networks and recent revelations about spying by the U.S. National Security Agency, the updated caption might be "On the Internet, everyone knows you're a dog." In the Peers Inc economy, a more apt caption is "Everyone knows you are a dog, and nobody cares." It's your work product and your reputation that matter.

The implications can be seen in a *New York Times* article about the Peers Inc start-up Instacart: "Instacart's success suggests that rather than simply automate workers out of their jobs, technology might create new labor opportunities for people who haven't acquired formal credentials or skills in an economy where low- and medium-skilled workers face a bleak outlook. Like the ride-sharing service Uber, Instacart creates work by connecting affluent customers who have more money than time with part-time workers who have the opposite problem—lots of time, not enough money."[6]

At first blush, this way of working seems very democratic. Anyone can participate! But in many platforms, however, participation quickly becomes a meritocracy, and poor performers are rapidly winnowed out through negative comments and poor ratings. The bad or unreliable drivers on Uber, the hosts with dirty apartments, and the errand runners on TaskRabbit who never seem to be on time won't do much business. Neither will freelancers on Guru, eLance, and oDesk, medical practitioners on ZocDoc, entrepreneurs on Kiva, and food preparers on Feastly if they have bad reviews. High-quality peers are valuable co-creators. A small subset of individuals will have work that stands out because it is so much better than the others'. Jordi Muñoz is clearly one such example.

Sophia Amoruso is another. "I'm really grateful to eBay for giving me a platform to launch my business," Amoruso said.[7] At twenty-two years old and with just one year of community college under her belt, her job prospects were bleak. She got a job she hated as a security guard, checking IDs for art students. Today, eight years after quitting that job to start selling vintage clothing on eBay, she is founder and CEO of NastyGal, a $100 million business with more than 350 employees selling both new and vintage clothing to millions of women around the world. Amoruso has also proved to be a master at leveraging social media platforms: Starting from her 2006 base on MySpace, she has grown NastyGal's presence to 1.3 million followers on Instagram and 300,000 on Twitter. Listening to her talk about her first year selling her unique vintage clothing, it is clear that Amoruso is not the feckless youth prospective employers might have judged her to be. She read *Starting an eBay Business for Dummies*. She wrote clothing descriptions and styled the clothes for high-quality photo shoots using art school students as models. She also paid close attention to customer questions and figured out who her customers were (women in their twenties who confidently wore quirky clothing). "It was really natural. It emerged out of who I am"—a tenacious, thoughtful, hardworking, enterprising young woman that employers overlooked.

If Peers Inc rewards the exceptional, what about the mediocre? Is there room for them? Merit is sometimes based wholly on impersonal attributes, such as the precise location of your 3-D printer (for local manufacturing) or home Wi-Fi router (so someone can connect), how much processing capability you have on your server (for use by an organization such as SETI in its search for extraterrestrial intelligence), or whether you are available to work at an awkward time (for taxi, delivery, or emergency service). Indeed, there is a whole range of Peers Inc collaborations where location or timing is the attribute of greatest importance, and still others where no money is transacted or where the "peer" is a device.

The autonomy that a Peers Inc environment offers comes with many benefits. Flexibility to choose your own time and location for participation is important to making a successful Peers Inc organization. A robust 2014 survey by the Freelancers Union and eLance-oDesk (a newly merged company that boasts 2 million businesses seeking the services of 8 million freelancers from 180 countries) found that the two most common reasons for going freelance were "to earn extra money" (68 percent) and "to have flexibility in my schedule" (42 percent).[8] Etsy's 2013 survey of 5,500 of its sellers found that for most of them, "growth isn't just about making money, but is balanced with business independence, flexibility, and personal well-being."[9] Jennifer, a physician who decided to quit her job as a medical examiner to become a full-time dog-sitter, becoming one of tens of thousands of individuals who have chosen to board dogs in their homes and participate in Rover.com, said in an interview on GeekWire, "I'm definitely more motivated because I'm running the show. I like the flexibility a lot more."[10] Renting out an apartment attached to her house in a small town in Long Island, Celina expresses the same sentiments: "Airbnb has made it possible for me to stay home with my 3 small children full-time. Having a 6-month-old, 3-year-old and 5-year-old, staying home with them has been so important to us—but we have struggled to make it work financially. Airbnb gives me the opportunity to never miss a moment of my children's lives."[11] I heard a story of a San Francisco Lyft driver who had picked up some jobs in San Diego during the four days he was there attending a wedding, and another from an UberX driver in San Francisco who was thinking of driving cross-country as part of the process of relocating to New York and of continuing to earn income as a driver while doing so. Working on a Peers Inc platform can offer flexibility that is rare in most service jobs.

Autonomy can result in many kinds of benefits. A recent Gallup poll of corporate workers worldwide found that 87 percent of them "are emotionally disconnected from their workplaces and less likely to be productive."[12] In a Peers Inc world, where workers have more control over the time, location, amount, and type of work, one would hope for much greater satisfaction and connection to the jobs they choose to do. Another benefit of autonomy appears to be better personal health. Several studies over the last two decades, in both North America and Europe, have found a correlation between job control and health outcomes. A 2005 study published in the *British Medical Journal* concludes: "A substantial part of the relation between social class and health could be attributed to job control."[13] Personal stories confirm this as well. A single parent working for Starbucks in San Diego reported that store managers would schedule her work hours for different times every week, leaving her constantly scrambling to find babysitters for her son and making it difficult and stressful to hold down the job.[14] New work-shift-scheduling companies are giving hourly workers the ability to choose shift times that work for them—just as Zipcar did when it put the cars' calendars in front of the members, letting them, instead of the company, do the optimizing. Depending on how much real autonomy and choice these programs provide, they could result in much greater control and happiness on the part of hourly workers.

It is curious that we encourage companies, NGOs, states, and governments to make sure they have diversified sources of revenue. Yet when we come down to the smallest and most vulnerable economic unit, the individual, we favor the notion that people should work one job at a time and have only one source of income. When they lose that one job, they are suddenly unemployed and have no income. But when people are doing several small jobs at the same time, losing one doesn't leave them so vulnerable. The underlying gift of economic agency is the primary advantage of being a peer. You are in charge of when, where, and how much you will earn. You don't have to sit passively waiting for an employer to choose you. You now have multiple ways of making a living. Maybe this is the modern technology-enabled equivalent of a hunter-gatherer economy. I stumbled across a tweet that describes just a subset of the new economy: "Thinking of renting house out on #Airbnb and then putting on my #Uber hat & chauffeuring guests around using #Zipcar."[15] Gretchen, the artist-therapist-mom, sums it up: "Etsy allows people to try out something new with minimal expense. Other new options (Airbnb, for example) allow people to have a little added income while experimenting as well. There is a shift away from the traditional work environments, and people are looking for more freedom and flexibility. So many of these new ways of making money allow such freedom."

I asked Joe Gebbia, one of Airbnb's co-founders, to describe a surprising or unanticipated aspect of his journey from humble start-up to a globe-spanning enterprise with a multibillion-dollar valuation. His reply was beautiful, and totally unexpected (to me): "The freedom and joy people feel in their economic empowerment, which they never knew they had." Airbnb has tapped into the enthusiasm felt by people doing what they *want* to do, on their own terms, rather than what they're *assigned* to do. Using the Airbnb platform, thousands of enterprising individuals have been able to create their own opportunities, without some corporate boss deciding whether they were right for the job. Reid Hoffman, co-founder and former CEO of LinkedIn, said, "I actually think every individual is now an entrepreneur, whether they recognize it or not."[16]

But what about the downside? I know that some readers have been squirming at my listing of all the positives, wanting to put a halt to this one-sided telling and bring me to my senses. Isn't this just a path to exploitation? Won't wages fall to the lowest possible levels? Doesn't this enable companies to simply wash their hands of any responsibility to the workforce? These complex issues will be addressed in depth in Chapters 7 and 11. I will note, however, that many people—as many as 40 percent of the total working population in rich countries such as the United States and a significantly larger fraction in some emerging economies—are already working as autonomous agents, hustling several jobs in order to make a living. The Peers Inc difference is the empowerment delivered by the platform. Individuals are given the powers of the corporation, and in many cases they are valued for their unique contribution. With industrialization, we have been taught to value a steady job and benefits and to ignore boredom, underemployment, and a tenuous reliance on a single source of income. The collaborative paradigm values economic agency, resilience, passion, learning, autonomy, and unique contributions. Likewise, the collaborative economy downplays the need to hustle as well as the lack of benefits and workplace protections, addressable issues that I will discuss in Chapter 7.

The rules and systems we have in place today to protect workers are a direct result of and response to the last hundred years of an increasingly industrialized economy. If peer collaborators and freelancers (in the United States) are increasingly required to pay for their own health care and retirement funds, the pressure will mount to untie those benefits from full-time employment. (This already is true for most European countries.) The current situation is certainly untenable either way, since many large corporations already exploit workers by keeping their hours to just below the number required to provide benefits, and even many Americans who are working full-time struggle to earn a living wage.[17]

There are many ways to be paid: by the hour, month, or year; by output; and through non-monetary exchange (school credits, reputation, barter, etc.). The Peers Inc collaborative economy will be no different. It will eventually lead to rethinking taxation, social supports, and regulations. We've spent decades trying to figure out the right mix of worker protections, taxes, and benefits in the post–World War II economy, and now we have to start anew. We need to determine the right approach for a workforce that is much more entrepreneurial and isn't dominated by full-time factory, service, or office work.

The lack of delineation between work time and leisure time is now, sad to say, completely lost (thank you, smartphones). Gone is whatever clarity that may have existed between personal and commercial use; between public, private, and personal property; between zoning for commercial, light industry, or residential use; between work and hobby and passion. This transformation can be felt every time we answer a work email after hours, every time a person works from home, every time we sell something of real value on eBay, every time we rent out our private car or spare bedroom, every time we pick up some extra money from tutoring, cooking, consulting, driving, moving, or designing in our "free" time.

The current capitalist economy is showing signs of weakness. Job creation is inadequate to meet demand: Youth around the world are having trouble acquiring first jobs. Recovery from economic downturns is slower. Very low interest rates limit the usefulness of one of government's most relied-upon financial tools. The economic benefit of expansion that does happen is collected by the top 1 percent.[18] The structure of the Peers Inc economy is increasing the pressure on the status quo as companies choose to let peers, rather than employees, do the work. We need new rules to enable and protect the workers; these will be discussed in Chapters 7, 8, and 9.

THE BENEFITS TO INSTITUTIONS OF ENABLING
PEER COLLABORATION

There are always more smart people outside your organization than inside.[19] And this is precisely why Peers Inc is the structure of choice if we want to speed the pace of innovation. In the case of the smartphone, it was the addition of apps by students, engineers, entrepreneurs, designers, game makers, hobbyists, dabblers, and companies big and small that turned a phone into a device, a tool we don't just use for an hour a day, but are constantly engaged with during all waking hours. By the end of 2013, barely six years since the iPhone was launched, peers had created more than 2 million apps. I'd say with some confidence that those six years have to represent one of the most innovative periods in human history. Give dozens, hundreds, even thousands of people the ability to iterate on a common platform and the results will deliver spectacularly creative innovation. Venture capitalists will tell you that innovation is a numbers game—it takes hundreds of ideas to ultimately yield the big breakthrough. When the right platform delivers the opportunity to innovate to countless peers, when an alluring opportunity is made accessible to the masses, we can count on a wealth of ideas being put forward, being refined, and ultimately succeeding.

Peter Corbett, in a talk he gave encouraging other city officials to replicate his Apps for Democracy success, emphasized the same idea: "The most important thing you are going to do is to build a body of hundreds if not thousands of tech developers who really want to use their skills to ameliorate the world's hardest problems. . . . Don't get blinded by the shiny little iPhone app. That's not the story, that's not the game. It's having a body of people, a community of people who are really passionate about your data, your problems and their solutions, for the constituents you serve."[20]

YouTube might be the classic example of the power of diversity on a platform for participation. Look at the creativity possible when millions of people with a wide range of interests work in the same media. Everyone knows that a snippet of kittens playing is adorable.

But imagining a philosophical Spanish-accented French-speaking English-subtitled voiceover narration by a depressed housecat— Henri—filmed in black-and-white and accompanied by the slow melancholic classical piano music of Erik Satie is genius.[21] No matter how much deep thinking I put into it, I would never have come up with the wonderful mystery of "Wind and Mr. Ug," a tale of two friends who live on a Mobius Strip, conceived and animated by Vi Hart.[22] Nor would I have ever imagined the phenomenal fascination of toddlers with the unwrapping and opening of plastic Easter eggs to reveal the toy surprises inside, viewed 140 million times.[23]

The incredible creativity that arises from diversity is also on display in SoundCloud, which does for audio what YouTube did for video. David Noel, an early employee who is now community manager for the company, explained, "When we started, this was about friends sharing music with friends, or a business using us to share clips, like a diving company owner in Florida who would share clips of whale songs to promote his business. . . . What was just a workflow tool turned into something unanticipated, which was communities of artists interconnecting and creating new music."[24] Founded in 2007, SoundCloud now has more than 250 million users. Eric Wahlforss, SoundCloud founder and chief technology officer, expressed his surprise in how the service evolved: "We saw people using it in novel ways."[25] Today, you can listen to both aspiring and accomplished musicians, audiobooks, podcasts, and clips, while also viewing comments from other audience members, which pop up along the audio timeline.

Founded in 2009, Quirky is on a quest to uncover the best in peer innovation of consumer products. Some of Quirky's self-selected members are people with inventive ideas. Other members— "influencers"—weigh in on whether product ideas are viable and merit consideration for production. Quirky staff, with expertise in product design and manufacturing, hone well-rated ideas, edging them closer to actual production. Influencers continue to vote on marketing decisions such as naming, taglines, color, and price.

Quirky understands that the power to innovate and be creative lies with individuals, while the company is better at guiding and ultimately producing consumer goods—taking over all the complex steps that lie between the idea and a mass-market product. Quirky does everything it can to support close collaboration. When Josh Dean profiled the company in *Inc.* magazine, he made a compelling case for what a good platform for participation does:

> If all Quirky did was tap a motivated hive mind for latent ideas that fill small and important market gaps, it would be a clever company. But it does something far bigger and more complicated. Those ideas need to become things, and that's where Quirky really brings the muscle.
>
> Immediately after a product has been selected [during evaluation], it moves on to design and conception, where Quirky's industrial designers and engineers use several million dollars' worth of prototyping equipment to realize and refine what most likely arrived on their desks as a thinly sketched idea. Lawyers and IP experts register patents and address regulatory and compliance issues, while the production department sources materials and decides which of the 21 core suppliers and factories (nearly all of them in Asia) will make the product. A quality assurance team tests that product. Packaging for the product is designed in New York and sent to the factories. Packaged products are shipped off to five global warehouses and distribution centers, which in turn send those boxes on to 35,000 retail locations.[26]

As the company has grown, Quirky has been able to partner with both physical and online retailers to sell its products. A $69 million financing in November 2013, including $30 million from GE, allowed Quirky to spin off Wink, a wholly owned subsidiary.[27] Wink provides a technology ecosystem (a platform) that makes it simple to bring together connected-home devices with smartphones, giving GE a way to participate in both the Internet of Things and crowd-sourced innovation. (Chapter 8 will delve into the ways in which large mainstream companies are adapting to the new organizational paradigm.) The first GE + Quirky–branded product was the Aros air conditioner, which lets you change the room temperature setting from a distance when you are away, and which automatically instructs your Aros to begin cooling the room to a predetermined temperature when your smartphone is within a certain proximity of home. Linda Boff, executive director of global brand marketing at GE, shares the same awe as Peter Corbett at the power of Peers Inc collaboration: "[Quirky gets] this amazing community to help think about the everyday problems that all of us have."[28]

Quirky boasts a membership of more than half a million peers. At a time when product life cycles are shrinking and competitive advantage is eroding faster than ever, the boundless creativity of thousands of peers keeps this Peers Inc organization on the upside of the change curve. Quirky's members submit 2,000 ideas each week, although to date just over one hundred products have made it to market. The winnowing process is fierce. When an idea makes it all the way through the many levels of review and results in something that can be bought and sold, all of the participating members—the inventors and the influencers—earn weighted royalties based on their participation in the creation of a successful product.

One peer was Jake Zien, an eighteen-year-old with a winning idea for a power cord that could accommodate many large plugs simultaneously. Jake's idea was for a joined set of outlets that could flex, offsetting the plugs from one another. But how could he get this idea to market? He was just a kid with a good idea—no money, no connections to product designers and manufacturers, no patents. Jake uploaded his idea to Quirky in April 2010. Four years later, according to his Quirky profile page, he had earned $660,000 in royalties, likely making him Quirky's highest earner. Garthen Leslie, whose idea for the app-controlled Aros air conditioner was commercialized in 2014, has earned $62,000. Sixty-five percent of his earnings stem from that idea; the remainder of his earnings is gleaned from his efforts as an influencer.[29] Most participants con-

Credit: Quirky.com

tribute very small amounts of time and earn little. This is a pattern of peer production we will explore in greater depth in Chapter 6.

The foundation of Quirky is firmly rooted in the Peers Inc triad:

Excess capacity: aggregating routine insights by consumers into product opportunities, failings, prices, packaging, and names

+ *Platform:* deep technical expertise, distribution channels, branding—the things an Inc does best

+ *Peers:* doing what they do best: innovation, customization, specialization

Peers Inc gives the individual the power of the corporation and lets individuals focus on what they do best. Generally speaking, people are talented in specific, discrete areas. Quirky channels individual contributions into eight categories: idea, research, design, style, name, tagline, price, and sales. Most participants choose to work in just a few of these. But working with a group of people, Quirky is able to draw together all of their strengths with the goal of bringing a product to market.

Innovation stems not just from lots of minds iterating on a platform but from lots of *diverse* minds. NASA recognized this and posted challenges to InnoCentive and TopCoder—challenge-and-prize platforms that attract professionals with advanced degrees and engineers. Reading the challenges, it's easy to imagine how exciting it would be to work on them, how they must have provided hours and hours of intellectual joy for hundreds of people in many different professions who have wanted to be involved in space exploration since childhood but whom reality forced down other paths—after all, how many astronauts does the world need?

The challenges included tracking asteroids given a specific set of NASA data; delivering email and calendar updates between Earth and the International Space Station (44,000 miles distant) reliably, safely, and securely; tracking food intake for space travelers; and using algorithms to crunch seventeen years' worth of data from the Saturn-orbiting Cassini rocket and uncover interesting patterns in ring phenomena and structure, or detect new moons.

The TopCoder community, consisting of 630,000 data scientists, developers, and designers were offered up these and other challenges in 2013 and 2014.[30] So far, NASA has received thousands of different submissions from more than twenty countries. By mid-2014, the contest winners had taken home over $1.5 million. Jason Crusan, director of the Advanced Exploration Systems Division, said that "tapping into a diverse pool of the world's top technical talent has not only resulted in new and innovative ways to advance technologies to further space exploration, but has also led to a whole new way of thinking for NASA, and other government agencies, providing us with an additional set of on-demand tools to tackle complex projects."[31]

Karim Lakhani, who has extensively investigated the way communities and contests can be used for innovation and has run large-scale experiments for both Harvard Medical School and NASA, told me that his analysis of more than 150 scientific contests revealed that "the best solutions came from solvers who had expertise that was quite far from the problem domain. In fact, the farther the problem was from their own specialized knowledge domain, the more likely they developed a winning solution."[32] I love this stunning observation, since it captures how the diversity of peers delivers innovation.

Diversity allows Peers Inc companies to engage in customization, localization, and specialization at a much lower cost than would be possible for a company trying to do it without the peers. The skills, knowledge, and precise expertise found among peers give big companies immediate access to local partners, because the peers are the already established partners in these collaborations.

Take Lyft, a website and mobile app that lets car owners turn their personal cars into taxis. Lyft's platform aggregates the excess capacity available in both the owners' free time and their idle cars to create a service that offers rides seven days a week, twenty-four hours a day. Lyft does what companies can do best: It performs criminal and driving background checks on the drivers, provides insurance, negotiates with regulators, markets the service to customers, and ensures quality and consistency. Lyft also built the easy-to-use app and collects the payments. Taken together, what Lyft does is beyond the talents, time, or budget of any single individual.

Likewise, the peers—in this case, individual car owners and drivers acting as free agents—do what is expensive and difficult for the company. Just one year after the platform's launch in 2012, its drivers were transporting more than 30,000 people a week, and doing so on their own schedules. The peers were providing cars and drivers at a wildly rapid pace that matched demand in different markets. Two years after the company's founding, Lyft had completed more than 10 million rides in more than sixty-five cities across America.[33]

It is the very local, small scale of each individual trip that made this an exactly right effort for the peers to undertake, rather than the Inc. And it is because excess capacity was being tapped into—both car and free time—that car owners were willing to try it. Those first drivers who signed up didn't have to buy a car or make space in their schedule in order to try out this new means of income generation. If they got a fare, that was great. If they didn't, not much was lost.

Imagine the cost and time required to create a new, nationwide taxi or limo business the old-fashioned way. In addition to handling billing, insurance, branding, and customer service, the company would have to lease and maintain vehicles and hire drivers. Lyft, on the other hand, by relying on the distribution and idle capacity of existing cars and drivers, gets system resilience as a bonus by collaborating with lots of peers. Even if cost were no object, it would have been close to impossible to deliver that number of rides and city expansion in just two years any other way. The logic and potential behind this accelerated speed is explored in Chapter 5, where I look at what happens when you purposefully put the three building blocks—excess capacity + platforms + peers—together.

THE BENEFITS TO CONSUMERS OF PEER POWER

Thus far I've focused on the benefits of collaborating from the perspectives of the Peers and the Inc. But when we look at it as consumers, peer diversity and localization offer me another win: a truly flexible offering. With peer-to-peer car rental, provided by companies such as Drivy, Getaround, and RelayRides, the extreme diversity of offerings means that these services can offer cars at a wide variety of prices, provide very specific amenities (such as car seats, bike racks, tow hitches), accommodate special requirements, and make exceptions as needed. Consumers are able to choose the price/value combination that best fits their own unique needs.

I travel a lot, staying with friends when I can and in rented rooms when I can't. For very short business visits, a hotel is usually most convenient. There, for my client's $200–$400 a night, most hotels have decided that I value six or more pillows on my bed and a large flat-screen TV, but access to the Internet comes with an extra charge. The industrial hotel's price/value calculation might not jibe with our own, yet under industrialization, consistency of product was the most important attribute: every hotel room the same, every french fry identical. I think we need to look again. In a Peers Inc structure, we can get the consistency and quality that we demand, while also enjoying a very special and unique product.

Thus, when I am staying someplace for more than a few days, I choose to stay in a rental hosted by an individual, such as those found on Airbnb or VRBO. In this way, I get to choose what I value most for my money: free Wi-Fi access, proximity to public transit, and, if possible, a good view and some sun. Every person can choose for him- or herself what matters most, because there is such a diversity of offerings. When my husband attended an SXSW conference, his personal requirements included free Wi-Fi and a free bike so that he could ride to the conference every day and do some easy exploring of Austin.

Delight comes from the out-of-the-ordinary transaction—the extraordinary, the delight of beautiful uniqueness. That is not to say consistency is bad. It is actually great a lot of the time. But there is a time and place for everything. I like my smartphone—the machine itself—to be manufactured using the industrial model, because the guaranteed ability to work exactly like millions of other smartphones is critical to me. However, for the app side of the equation, uniqueness, customization, and localness are important to me. The world no longer needs to choose between the two stereotypes of commoditized industrial efforts (consistent, low-cost, yet faceless) and the unique vitality of local small-scale production (highly variable and unreliable). In the Peers Inc world, which leverages the diversity of peers to provide a diversity of experience, we are all like Dorothy stepping out of her black-and-white Kansas home into Oz, the world of color.

A peer-to-peer car sharing member told me of an experience she had picking up the keys for a car she was taking to the Île de Ré, an island off the west coast of France. The owner told her, "Oh, I love Île de Ré. This side is where all the cliffs are. That side has the beaches. Here is my favorite beach, and here is my favorite fish restaurant." Neither Zipcar, Hertz, Avis, nor Enterprise is going to give you that kind of local knowledge. Yelp, Trip Advisor, and many similar travel sites are based on the same principle. While the Michelin Guide hires staff and pays for the meals and hotels to ultimately review thousands of places, TripAdvisor engages the free enthusiasm of individuals to write 190 million reviews of 4.4 million places.[34] We consumers now have all types of establishments rated and commented on, not just the few deemed comment-worthy.

In many of the examples I've used so far, the peers have been individuals or small companies motivated in part by money. But that is not always the case. Waze, the app Roy and I used on our trip to Concord (mentioned in Chapter 2), is a Peers Inc company where the peers are both millions of smartphones tracking their owners' travel routes and speeds and the owners themselves adding additional personal observations about road conditions. It is the Peers Inc version of a GPS-based navigation system app, incorporating the historical and real-time travel speeds and route choices of "Wazers" to determine the best way to drive from one point to another at any given moment. Founded in 2008, the service has more than 50 million active users, concentrated in thirteen countries.

No money changes hands between the Wazers and Waze. The app is free. The terms of use are clear: By using the app, your location and speed will be used to help figure out traffic speeds and best routes for the whole community. Waze has also introduced a game structure. By entering additional information about their trips—marking the location of breakdowns, police, closed roads, and other temporary hazards—users can win points and gain status. Waze succeeds, and beat out its navigation system competitors, by dint of the millions of real-time, very local, very specific contributions of the drivers in the Waze community.

GPS is itself a platform for participation (enabled by the Standard Positioning Service and other protocols) that makes available the excess capacity of the U.S. government-owned and -operated navigation system. With GPS, the peers might be individuals, small local companies, or big multinationals—any of millions of different entities worldwide who have thought up the myriad of ways GPS might be useful. Waze is one of them. We can be sure that when the government researchers and scientists first envisioned and built the GPS system, none of them were imagining it would enable individual drivers to communicate their speeds and locations to the benefit of all. The peers who innovate on the GPS platform range from individuals programming an adhesive chip so that they can locate their lost keys to giant farming conglomerates tracking cattle and pharmaceutical companies verifying distribution of their drugs.

We've covered the basics of unlocking excess capacity, building platforms for participation, and engaging the power of peers. In the next chapter I want to delve deeper and look into what happens when we combine the economics of excess capacity with the discipline of the platforms and the diversity of large numbers of peers. The Peers Inc collaboration points to a viable, scalable, humane way forward in a world overshadowed by anxiety about the future of employment, the scarcity of resources, the rapid pace of change, and the future of capitalism on a finite planet. It offers up discrete and unique roles for governments, companies, institutions, entrepreneurs, and individuals. When this is done well, seemingly magical and unexpected powers result. We stand at the edge of a waterfall, with the momentum of 7 billion lives, two hundred governments, and hundreds of thousands of institutions pressing us forward. Chapter 5 will explain the reasons for my optimism: We have within our reach tools for meeting this out-of-control, terrifying, and unprecedented change with directed, thoughtful, and empowering transformations, just when we need them most.

FIVE

Bringing It Together

The Three Miracles

SO FAR I'VE DISCUSSED the three components of the Peers Inc transformation: excess capacity, platforms, and peers. Now I'm going to reveal what's possible when we join the three together—business models (and life models) that will enable the breakthroughs we need to get us through the twenty-first century, and beyond.

This sounds like a big job, but the signs of this transformation are all around us, in a patchwork fashion. It's just a case of naming the phenomena and providing an analytical framework that enables all of us to take part. I want to show you the whole thing: the Peers Inc quilt.

People pondering the big picture on planet Earth right now are often worried; some slip into despondency. But transformation at the scale required to meet our growth challenges is ongoing. We can do this, together, and Peers Inc gives us an organizational framework that can help us meet many of our environmental goals profitably, and with a higher quality of life than before. If this sounds bold, it is; that's why I've subtitled this chapter "The Three Miracles."

"You can't solve exponential problems with linear solutions," says Banny Banerjee, director of Stanford's Change Labs and a professor of mechanical engineering. But we know that we can find abundance in excess capacity; that platforms can organize, simplify, and provide peers with resources; that in the process, they radically accelerate learning and propagate new discoveries; and that by engaging with peers as co-creators, we bring passion, ingenuity, and local and customized applications together into resilient and redundant systems. Everything gets better because the parts together form a new whole. The Peers Inc organization can produce previously impossible growth, unprecedented acceleration of learning and innovation, and the powerful joining of human experience, adaptability, and pattern recognition with supercomputing. The three miracles potentially provide us a way forward through climate change, resource scarcity, and explosive population growth. They also produce some rewarding business opportunities along the way.

We can, in fact, make megacities livable and address the needs of the more than seven billion people now on the planet (a figure expected to grow to eleven billion by 2050) through more efficient use of our resources. We can enable people to build satisfying lives in which their individuality is valued. We can quickly build resilient cities with the localized responses required to deflect the worst effects of global warming. We can perform seemingly superhuman feats together, things that would have been impossible in earlier times.

MIRACLE #1: EXCESS CAPACITY LETS US DEFY THE LAWS OF PHYSICS

In 2000, the largest hotel chain in the world, the Intercontinental Hotel Group, had 645,000 rooms in 4,400 hotels—the Intercontinental, Crowne Plaza, Holiday Inn, and Candlewood Suites brands. They were in more than one hundred countries, an empire that took sixty-five years to build. It would be crazy to imagine beating them out in just a couple of years. For one thing, it'd be physically impossible: In each of those one hundred countries you'd have to find the sites, buy the land, get the architects, review the plans, finance the deals, hire and manage contractors, build the hotels, decorate and furnish them, find and train staff, advertise and market, and hope to hell that you had chosen the right locations to support the demand you'd need to pay back all those financing costs. You'd also have to pray that there'd be no unexpected hurricanes, flooding, wildfires, or droughts. Just pushing the paperwork would be a superhuman effort, never mind actually making the business case for people to lend you the money: What if there was an economic downturn? There is simply no way for a business to build that kind of scale starting from scratch.

Consider that Hilton Hotels has been in the business for more than ninety-five years and has amassed only 610,000 rooms in 3,800 hotels in eighty-eight countries.[1] And the French chain Accor, in third place, took forty-four years to produce its 610,000 rooms in 4,452 hotels in ninety-two countries.[2] By all the existing rules of the game, attempting to rival these companies' market shares within just a few years would be totally impossible.

Yet Airbnb did it in just four years. By business standards—by any standards—this is a miracle. It is a completely new game. Nothing on earth could be further from business as usual. And this is not the virtual-assets, Snapchat type of growth. These are hard physical assets, with beds, bath towels, and soap.

The figure below shows how the old-fashioned, physics-constrained, business-as-usual trajectory compares.

What happened? The magic of the Peers Inc model. Airbnb's platform unlocked excess capacity, built a compelling platform for participation, and the peers collaborated to provide the service in almost every place where people live. This pace of growth could not have happened any other way. The rooms existed, already built and paid for in cities and countries around the world, albeit owned by hundreds of thousands of different people. Airbnb made it simple and financially compelling for people to become micro-hoteliers. The company sent skilled interior photographers into major markets to capture interiors in an alluring way, facilitated communications between host and guest, provided insurance and guarantees, and did the lion's share of the marketing. The platform unlocked the value of those spare bedrooms and apartments by organizing and aggregating it in a way that was useful to consumers.

And Airbnb is not an outlier. BlaBlaCar lets people driving between cities sell the empty seats in their cars to others going the same way. In 2014, only ten years old, the company transported

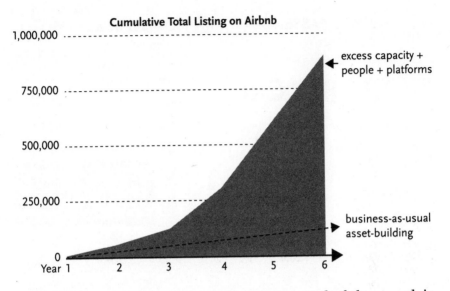

Cumulative Total Listing on Airbnb

excess capacity + people + platforms

business-as-usual asset-building

Impressively, the growth in paying guests matched the growth in rooms.

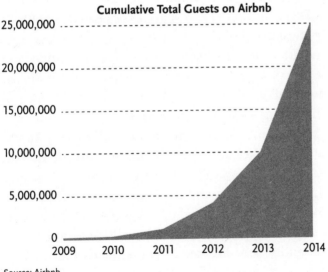

Cumulative Total Guests on Airbnb

Source: Airbnb

2 million people a month.[3] Moving the same number of people would require 5,000 full high-speed-rail trains or 5,000 cramped 747s. BlaBlaCar accomplished this without laying any track or buying any trains or planes. Go, excess capacity!

PASSENGERS TRANSPORTED

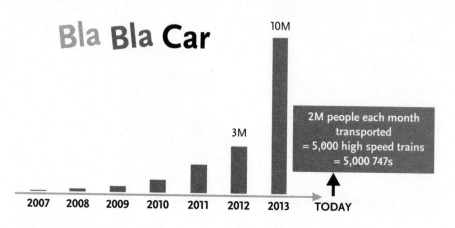

Because platforms allow a multitude of peers to quickly transform existing untapped resources into compelling accessible products and services, the Peers Inc model can spark exponential growth. It does not have to physically build many assets to grow—it leverages what is at hand, repatterning existing assets into vast new utility and value. This is the gift of a peer partnership. Airbnb and BlaBlaCar could not have done this on their own. The peers have been integral in building and financing these infrastructures.

WhatsApp is another mind-blowing example. Like every smart-phone app, WhatsApp makes use of the device you already bought and the Internet connection you already paid for. WhatsApp also uses your existing phone number and the numbers in your contacts to provide its service, unlike Skype, which requires each person using it to acquire a new, Skype-specific number. WhatsApp lets you send text, photos, and videos for free to your friends—turning all that content into data and avoiding the extortionate fees charged by telecom providers to send messages via SMS. Four years after it launched, 450 million people were active users of the app, with a million more joining each day.[4] And unlike any of the other most popular apps (Google Maps, Facebook, YouTube, Twitter, Skype),

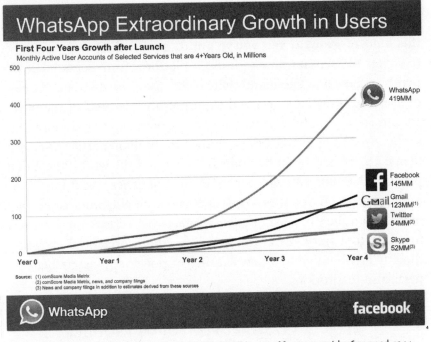

Credit: http://files.shareholder.com/downloads/AMDA-NJ5DZ/2971143669x0x727110/3b516115-909d-4044
-b758-d1742a46a135/Facebook_02_19_14.pdf

WhatsApp is the only one that isn't free, charging $1 per year start-
ing with the second year. WhatsApp sends an average of nineteen
billion messages a day, approaching the entire global SMS telecom
volume.[5] Skype, Twitter, Gmail, and Facebook—Peers Inc structures
all—showed phenomenal growth in their early years, yet Whats-
App's pace of growth eclipsed them.

Closed internal efforts, without access to peers' assets and labor
inputs, can never approach these growth rates. Consider that for an
individual to list her apartment on Airbnb, she needs to clean it,
photograph it, write a description, and then market it to her social
networks, all before earning a rental. Now think about how many
peers are doing this same work for free. Suddenly we see that the
combined peer investment into these platform companies can be quite
substantial. This is cooperative capitalism—and, of course, Peers Inc.

These growth rates are seen over and over when the Peers Inc paradigm is in place. Of course, not every opportunity will deliver this kind of growth, and you've got to get all the parts just right. (Chapter 6 discusses how to build a platform from scratch.) It depends on how much demand there is for what's on offer, on the ease of use, and on what assets and expertise are required of the peers. Within twenty months of its founding, Coursera offered more than six hundred unique, free online courses to 6 million participating students. Organized by individuals from around the world, the TEDx platform has hosted 8,000 events in 130 countries, resulting in 200 million views on YouTube. YouTube has more video uploaded each month than the three major television networks created in total during their first sixty years. In every case, the exponential growth is directly attributable to a new sharing of power and assets between peers and institutions.

MIRACLE #2: SMART PLATFORMS PRODUCE EXPONENTIAL LEARNING

Luis von Ahn, who coined the term *CAPTCHA* and was the founder of reCAPTCHA (see Chapter 2) way back in 2007, when he was just twenty-seven, has moved on to newer things. He co-founded a company that within two short years was already teaching a new language to more people than the entire U.S. public school system did. By the end of its third year (2014), Duolingo had 50 million active users improving their language skills in one of fifteen languages *for free*![6] How can Duolingo possibly afford to do this? By multipurposing the efforts of those learning, using them to translate some of the Web for a fee. Right now Duolingo learners are translating CNN and Buzzfeed from English into French and Spanish. CNN and Buzzfeed are paying Duolingo for these translation services at a fraction of the per-word fee professional translators charge. The translations happen quickly as well: Duolingo's algorithms turn the real-time efforts of those thousands of students into translations as accurate as those of skilled professionals in a matter of hours.

But the real beauty of Duolingo is the spectacular iterative learning, the kind that can only take place with a Peers Inc company. To understand how, let's first look at the standard unit for language acquisition—one semester of college-level instruction, or about 130 hours of instruction. Now put yourself into the shoes of a professor. During your first semester of teaching, you have perhaps thirty students. By the end of the semester, you'll have learned what you are bad at, how you might improve your teaching techniques, and what works (or doesn't) among those thirty students. You get to try out your improvements the next semester. So every year you get two cracks at it. Teach for thirty years and you'll have had sixty cycles and eighteen hundred students on whom to improve your teaching techniques.

Now let's move on to Rosetta Stone, a twenty-year-old company that uses audio and print to teach language. Rosetta Stone is a premium product, bought by businesspeople and diplomats, sold in airports around the world. Why buy it? Because the company promises that you'll learn a semester's worth of language in just fifty-five to sixty hours, a huge improvement over the 130 hours you'd spend sitting in a classroom.

At Duolingo, Luis has so many learners that he can conduct a hundred experiments simultaneously, each one tried by 150,000 people, and in forty-eight hours he can know categorically which is the best way to teach a language. Within just twenty months of launch, Duolingo had reduced the time it takes to learn a semester's worth of language to an average of thirty-four hours.[7] Not 130, not 55, but 34. These numbers were verified by outside researchers at Queens College and the University of South Carolina, and Duolingo always has a sampling of students taking standardized language tests for ongoing benchmarking.[8]

This pace of learning is possible because of the collaboration between peers and platform. It requires knowledge inputs from both parties. While the Inc sees almost all of the activity happening on the platform, the peers are generating the critical variation and innovation. A platform can accelerate the learning process by improving its own processes, as Duolingo does when it sees where and when people get stuck, become lost, or drop out of the system. It can also identify peers' best and worst practices and make these improvements knowable to all, as eBay, Etsy, and YouTube do when they offer online tips, training videos, and conferences.

There's a Thomas Edison quote that fits beautifully here: "The real measure of success is the number of experiments that can be crowded into twenty-four hours." Patrick Whitney, dean of the Institute of Design at the Illinois Institute of Technology, told me that the number of use cycles is the critical element. His example was old farm implements, appreciated by designers for being simple, elegant, and well honed, the result of improvements over many generations and hundreds of years. With Peers Inc, we are no longer restricted to just a few iterations (as an individual), dozens of iterations (as a team), or hundreds of iterations (as a group of franchises). In a Peers Inc model, thousands and even millions of people are iterating on a single platform, generating unimagined variation that can almost infinitely collapse the time it takes to learn from our mistakes. The result can be rapid, successful iteration for popular and responsive platforms.

This sort of rapid prototyping and innovating is *exponential learning*. Creative ideas and approaches are a natural result of peer diversity. Finding those innovations and sharing them is the hallmark of a successful platform. Duolingo learns fast because it pays attention and is very data-driven. As Luis explained to me, Duolingo takes the unprecedented number of student use cycles and applies computing power to analyze and discover best practices quickly. As students struggle with questions, the system tracks their errors, aggregates the data, and learns from the patterns it observes in real time. The platform is also able to respond in real time to student progress and tailor individual lessons, so students are challenged in the most relevant ways.

We need to name this new law of accelerated learning, possible only in a Peers Inc world. Moore's law addressed the increasing power and decreasing cost of computers, and Reed's law concerns the value of a network scaling exponentially relative to its size. We now have enough experience with the power of platforms to put forth the law of Peers Inc: On attentive platforms, the pace of learning for the Inc accelerates with the number of participants on the platform.

MIRACLE #3: DIVERSE NETWORKED PEERS MEANS INSTANT ACCESS TO THE *RIGHT* MIND

The third miracle seems mundane: Networked peers let us quickly find help or advice in unique situations when we need a different perspective. We need to hear from somebody whose experience closely matches our problem and who can guide us one step at a time.

We've all searched for recipes that make enticing use of the four remaining ingredients found in our kitchen on a Thursday night— kale, onions, pasta, and lentils—while our forebears would have stood in their kitchens, scratching their heads.[9] We've run to Google for urgent answers to obscure questions such as "How do I get this squirrel to go back out through my bedroom window?" (I actually did this during a live-streamed lecture from my home to students in Beirut.) And we've relied on Waze to tell us that a car breakdown two miles up ahead has blocked traffic and we should quickly take this detour.

Being able to connect to another person's experience at just the right time can save us from unnecessary mistakes—think of the teenager who almost put a new cashmere sweater into the dryer. We marvel, perhaps say to ourselves, "Thank you, Internet!" and keep going. That little sensation of "How did we ever get by without this?" is our third miracle's quiet footsteps: We are all helping each other learn from experience now, without quite so much painful learning from our own mistakes. All these small things add up. But there are some big things, too—life-changing, lifesaving things.

Notes Dr. Peter Buxton, "In the mid-1990s, my team and I combined one of the first commercially available digital cameras with a newly available communication tool (email) to send back clinical images to specialists. On one occasion, and without any additional lenses, we aimed the camera down a microscope and were able to obtain images that allowed us to accurately diagnose malaria in a patient on the other side of the world."[10] Dr. Buxton's pioneering work in telemedicine took the cutting-edge tools of the day and assembled them into something completely new: Doctors helping other doctors help their patients at the speed of light (or at least the speed of 1990s email). What might once have been a hand-drawn pencil image of what was seen through the microscope, sent by regular mail and delivered in a couple of days (or overnight through FedEx or UPS) was now an email sent by modem and delivered in minutes. Today's telemedicine systems are even more remarkable: real-time collaborations between doctors all over the world, networked for patients' benefit, sometimes with smartphones alone. In twenty years the horizon of help will be even wider: We can only guess how robotics or virtual reality might extend the reach of doctors and allow them to touch their patients' lives. Imagine if we could access all the excess capacity of doctors and nurses all over the world in a global telemedicine volunteering platform. How many people could be reached?

Even more, this is not just about experts sharing expertise; it's also about having the knowledge and imagination to respond right on the spot. It's about the *right* person being there for us at exactly the *right* time.

HelpAround is a start-up dedicated to keeping diabetics out of tight corners, with community support. Diabetes care often requires sophisticated medical supplies, and if the pharmacy is unexpectedly closed or out of stock, it can create a window of risk for an avoidable crisis. However, because diabetics are peers and many have a little excess capacity (someone who has a box of supplies intended for a month can easily carry a friend in need through a weekend, until stores open again), with the right platform they can protect each other from supply chain glitches and other problems, large or small.

Annie Hemmesch describes her experience of using HelpAround to overcome unhelpful changes in her health insurance coverage: "I was desperate to find sensors. I could only get my hands on one or two at a time, and that was not enough to cover me for the duration of my entire pregnancy. . . . One woman, whose daughter had switched to a different brand, said she no longer needs them. Another woman, who was my age, said, 'I never use them, here you go.'"[11]

Because the HelpAround platform is so specific, it helps diabetic peers get exactly the support they need in a pinch. To at least one user, reaching out for this excess capacity in the network felt like a miracle.

InnoCentive is a modern version of the venerable practice of spurring innovation through the use of prizes. It's a latter-day version of the prize set up by the British Parliament in 1714 to source a simple and practical method for determining a ship's longitude while at sea. More recently, InnoCentive issued a challenge from a large multinational consumer products company looking for a polymer with specific characteristics. No one within the company's R&D labs had been able to crack the problem. Within weeks, winning solutions came in: from an aerospace physicist, a small agribusiness owner, a transdermal drug delivery specialist, and an industrial scientist.

TopCoder, a similar platform dedicated to software challenges, has also produced startling results. TopCoder ran a challenge from Harvard Medical School to develop new algorithms for genomic analysis applied to the immune system. Within two weeks, solvers from outside the university—none in the fields of computational biology or life sciences—had produced genomics algorithms a hundred times faster than the current solution.

The miracle of finding the right person at the right time is also transforming political activism. An activist and writer known by her Twitter handle, @FeministaJones, led an organizing movement for a national moment of silence (#nmos14) in response to the police killing of Michael Brown, a black teenager walking down the middle of a street at midday in Ferguson, Missouri, on August 9, 2014. Within just three days, Jones's digital organizing—mostly on Twitter, Facebook, and Google Docs—resulted in thousands of people in tens of cities nationwide coming together. And while the mainstream media reported on the case slowly and sporadically with a handful of reporters, it was people in the right place—protesters, bystanders, eyewitnesses—who live-tweeted up-to-date news, videos, and photographs of events unfolding in Ferguson.

Jones describes the power of social media platforms to organize swiftly and effectively in the wake of the 2012 murder of Florida teenager Trayvon Martin: "Protests and vigils [were] organized within 48 to 72 hours, using outlets like Twitter and Facebook. A Change .org petition from Martin's parents began circulating on Twitter and eventually received 2,278,988 signatures, which led to charges being filed against [George] Zimmerman, who had not been arrested or charged by Sanford, Fla., police."

In these examples, as in others, platforms enabled peers to organize, report, and raise funds, resulting in enormous physical gatherings, powerful petitions, and significant alternative public narratives, which is why we have seen the incredible emergence of social justice activists, particularly anti-racist feminist activists, blossom online. Jones writes, "Twitter has become one of the most important tools of modern sociopolitical activism, a powerful force in the Zimmerman trial aftermath and beyond."[12]

Increasingly, as we connect more people and their knowledge, this finding-the-right-expert is yielding ever more valuable results. Finding such people used to be hard—so difficult that there was a saying to describe it: "It's like finding a needle in a haystack." Today, thanks to big-data-analyzing, number-crunching, wireless-bit-sending platforms, we can open up our hand and that needle will fly into it, as if we had a big magnet. Everyday experts are adding important information in real time, and we are getting it out in real time.

The miracle of instant access to the right mind has two very important implications as we move into the future. First, it means that each one of us has access to the collective mind of the world. Wikipedia is but a first taste; imagine it expanded to all human knowledge and know-how. Second, given the size, scope, and location of problems in the world, it means that each person will, at different times, be the *right* person—if we've connected that person to others.

Imagine how very differently the Ebola epidemic could have played out if the people of Guinea, Liberia, and Sierra Leone had been fully connected. The first few cases would have been quickly put into the relevant country's health system. Those individuals' experiences were early sensors warning of what might come. We could have averted the thousands of horrific deaths, decimated families, countless hours of suffering and worrying, and billions of dollars in medical aid if we had listened to the right person at the right time. The U.S. Agency for International Development's Ebola Grand Challenge is the late-breaking but now deep-within-the-crisis Peers Inc approach, using the OpenIdeo platform to collect insight into the situation on the ground and integrate learning from hospitals and universities.[13]

Today, we connected peers have access to crowdsourced best practices plus supercomputing power plus the insight of people who are right there on the ground and just a step ahead of us. Institutions tasked with responsibilities as enormous as fighting diseases such as Ebola are catching up as fast as they can. Even the U.S. Department of Defense has a disaster relief expert coordination team, STAR-TIDES, striving to provide the deft touch, the fluid access to expertise required to assist teams in the field with a connection to the right people at the right time. And Occupy Sandy's smooth collaboration between the Federal Emergency Management Agency and volunteer networks (see Chapter 10) showcased the potential of mutual aid in a domestic crisis. The much-needed response platforms that will allow us to share our excess capacity in order to help each other in a crisis, learning and becoming wise from our collective experiences, are coming.

HUMANS *AND* MACHINES, NOT HUMANS *OR* MACHINES

Since the advent of the earliest computers, people have been telling stories of a dystopian future where computers (or robots, or Cylons) simply replace all of us, and people are made obsolete. In the Peers Inc paradigm, however, humans and their individuality are the key component, irreplaceable because of their humanness. This was foretold by an unsung pioneer of the digital age. "Human brains and computing machines will be coupled together very tightly, and the resulting partnership will think as no human brain has ever thought and process data in a way not approached by the information-handling machines we know today," wrote J. C. R. Licklider, an early American computer scientist, in 1960.[14] The combined talents of humans and computers, when working together in partnership and symbiosis, will definitely be more creative than any computer working alone.

In *Thinking, Fast and Slow*, Daniel Kahneman describes the two modes of thought that we all engage in. "Thinking fast" is what we usually do. He argues that humans are great at fast pattern recognition, recognizing subtle local cues and context, and adjusting immediately to take these into account. Conversely, computers are pretty terrible at these things. While we have to trick ourselves into "thinking slow," taking the time to make the mathematical and rational calculations, this type of analysis is easy for computers. The optimal Peers Inc platforms allow computers to do what they do best—complex and not-so-complex math—and deliver the results to people, allowing us to engage in what we do best: creativity, pattern recognition, and contextualizing.

In an interview on *The Colbert Report*, Vint Cerf, the Internet pioneer, remarked "[There are] about 3 billion people online right now. Every time they come up with new ways of using the Internet, we all gain something from that."[15] Over the last twenty years, as we've explored the powers the Internet can bring us, companies—the Inc—have figured out that individuals actually have a huge amount to offer. This is the takeaway from the last chapter: realizing, appreciating, and tapping into the power of peers. Every one of us walking around with a smartphone now has superpowers; with the right platforms to support us, we can grow exponentially, seeming to defy physics, learn exponentially, and connect with almost telepathic speed to the right mind we need to help us. This active interaction transforms what is possible. We are co-creators, not passive users, and each time we stumble upon innovation—whether we create it ourselves or see it in others—we can share it far and wide.

The first big breakthrough to bring the power of computers to the people was the personal computer; as Steve Jobs sold it, "a computer for the rest of us." And then came the smartphone, which made that power *even more* accessible. Now, with the $40 smartphone, the real democratization of computer power is here. Unlike water pumps, cars, guns, and other technologies, which simply augmented humans in a passive sort of way, platforms for participation are recursive. They both empower the individual and draw increased power back from them, making the whole product, service, or network stronger.

Sometime in 2015 the world saw its two-billionth smartphone in use. How will we leverage them to transform our world into one that can sustainably support our population? If we can find a way to make smartphones a platform for solving our greatest challenges—poverty, public health, climate change—as the number of phones climbs from two billion toward a time when almost every adult has a smartphone, the positive impacts can grow as fast as the phones themselves spread. The introduction of a new app on a smartphone requires no increase in system complexity or long latency lag to positive behavior changes. The three Peers Inc miracles demonstrate that with the right platform, change can be nearly instantaneous. This gives me deep hope.

MAGNETIC INEVITABILITY

Any institution unencumbered by legacy assets—factories, buildings, vehicles, workforce—will choose to take the Peers Inc path. Companies that are organized as Peers Inc will grow bigger, learn faster, and be smarter than their closed, we-do-it-all-ourselves counterparts. Let's go forward one generation—twenty years.

Manufacturing will be trending toward Peers Inc. The promise of 3-D printing will be a reality for many of the physical goods we consume. Very small-scale manufacturers will be producing and repairing based on the algorithms established by the brand platforms.

Transportation of both people and goods will be Peers Inc. The complex algorithms that move vehicles safely through space will be done by the Inc; the vehicles will be owned and maintained by smaller peers around the world.

Education will be Peers Inc. We already see the movement in higher education toward MOOCs—massive open online courses— where the best teachers in the world will provide instruction through videotaped lectures watched at home, while in-person class time is reserved for personal and intimate group instruction.

The energy sector will be mostly converted to Peers Inc. A smart grid will be supplied by millions of distributed small solar- and wind-powered plants—co-generation.

Communications will include a significant Peers Inc component. In addition to fiber, satellites, and cell towers, individuals' devices (cellphones, laptops, cars) will be receiving and forwarding wireless data, acting like mini cell towers—infrastructure built and owned not by big companies but by the peers themselves.

Personal fitness and health will be Peers Inc. People who are watching their weight, improving their sleep and exercise regimens, and following doctor's orders will contribute their personal data via sophisticated and user-friendly devices, as is already happening today. Some of that will be anonymized and become part of large population databases that will transform public health and the de-livery of health care.

Smart health, smart cities, and big data (together becoming the Internet of Things) are in fact all grounded in Peers Inc: repurposed data that is collected by all kinds of peers and organized and ana-lyzed by various Incs, empowering individuals and cities to make better decisions, learn faster, evolve more quickly, and have a different relationship with our environment.

We can see the transition happening today. Google is wholly a Peers Inc configuration. It is our searches, our clicks, and our links that inform the search engine, and millions of companies small and large that buy Google ads. Many Google-generated ads are located on webpages created by peers and viewed by people Google had no part in attracting. Amazon launched its merchant services fifteen years ago, repurposing the processes it had created for itself. At the end of 2013, 40 percent of unit sales at Amazon are for other companies' goods—products offered by 2 million Amazon Marketplace sellers.[16] Just ten months after Duolingo made it possible for anyone to use its platform to create lessons in new languages, 22 percent of its learning community, totaling 1 million people, are learning on these new user-generated language pairs (like teaching Portuguese to English-speakers). (I will delve into this more deeply in Chapter 7, when looking into how government needs to respond to these dramatic changes, and in Chapter 8, when I explore ways in which some legacy institutions are making the transition.)

WHERE WE NEED MIRACLES

A key attraction as I started uncovering the Peers Inc paradigm was its potential to address climate change with the innovation, speed, and scale that such a huge and serious problem requires. The problem is so close and so big that using the Peers Inc structure and reaping the benefits of the three miracles is the only way out that I can see. In the remainder of this chapter, I outline the magnitude of the problem, and then explore examples of solutions that are using Peers Inc to effect change at the necessary scale and speed.

I am not one of those people who understood the magnitude of climate change early on. I remember realizing in 2005, while I was a Loeb Fellow at Harvard, that this was a very big problem, maybe even the number one problem in the world. I remember an embarrassing and egotistical moment when I was sitting in a small classroom at Harvard discussing how we might put on a Loeb alumni conference focusing on climate action. I looked at the handful of people around the table and then at the dismal, gray, rainy, early twilight winter day outside, and I withered at the futility of it all. How could it be that the fate of humans around the world was riding on these pitiful efforts? Of course, there were thousands and probably hundreds of thousands of people around the world sharing my concerns at that moment. But I hadn't met them yet.

My Zipcar experience made me completely aware of the whole spectrum of problems brought on by cars in cities; CO_2 emissions are just one of many. I recognized that transportation was clearly the place where I could have an impact. Since then most of my talks, writing, consulting, and start-ups have focused on getting us closer to a more sustainable world.

My mind, though, was truly opened when I read the much talked-about World Bank report "Turn Down the Heat: Why a 4°C Warmer World Must Be Avoided." The World Bank is a very conservative financial institution, very capitalistic, very market-driven. Its report was compiled from the same source materials consulted by the Intergovernmental Panel on Climate Change (IPCC) for its November 2014 synthesis report and was reviewed by the same top scientists.[17] The top-line finding: Even if every country does everything it has promised to do in order to reduce CO_2 emissions, we are on track for a 4°C (7°F) increase in average global temperature by 2100.[18] Since I had no idea what such an increase actually implies, I decided to search historical climate temperatures to see what the world was like when it was 4°C cooler than it is now and get a sense of what changes such a shift had already brought about.

It turns out that the last time it was 4°C cooler than it is today was during the last Ice Age about 20,000 years ago. During that period, much of the northern part of the United States and Europe—maybe the spot where you are sitting right now—was under several kilometers of ice. That's the difference a rise in average global temperature of 4°C can make: Start with a couple kilometers of ice, add 4°C and 20,000 years, and presto! we have America's breadbasket. The temperature rise we're looking at right now is taking place over a matter of *decades* and getting hotter than today's average. The last time it was 4°C (7°F) warmer than it is right now was 15 to 25 million years ago. Humans didn't exist then.

I also learned that while we always talk about *average* global warming, temperatures over land, where we all live, are higher than over water. In the U.S. Midwest, average temperatures are predicted to be 6°C (11°F) higher in the summertime by 2100.[19] The World Bank report continued with worse news. Scientists forecast that if countries just keep going as they have (called business as usual) and don't make any adjustments, we will see land temperatures that are 6°C higher in places *by the 2060s.*

If it is going to be that much higher over land by 2060, then I can guess that it will start to be really unpleasant as early as 2040. I don't know about you, but I absolutely intend to be around in 2040. When you hear leaders talk about why we should address climate change, they are always saying things like "Do this for your children, and your children's children." My children's children? I'm planning to be around then too! My own young adult children are weighing whether to even have children. The question they are asking is whether they want to create humans that they love deeply who will come of age in the middle of the rapid, ugly demise of humankind. People are going to die from starvation, from hurricanes, from mudslides, from flooding, from disease, from resource-driven wars. And lest you think that you are protected because you live in one of the world's richest countries, remember that there will be hundreds of millions of climate refugees, desperate and angry.

Having read the report, I basically couldn't believe I'd understood it correctly. Had I misinterpreted the facts embedded in the careful scientific prose? I emailed two friends, one whose full-time job is focused on international climate policy and another who works on U.S. domestic climate policy, asking, "Are these the facts? Have I gotten this timeline right?" Both rapidly and soberly replied that yes, I'd gotten it right.

I try to imagine the implications behind the stern scientific synopsis highlighted for policy makers in the November 2014 IPCC report: "Continued emission of greenhouse gases will cause further warming and long-lasting changes in all components of the climate system, increasing the likelihood of severe, pervasive, and irreversible impacts for people and ecosystems. Limiting climate change would require substantial and sustained reductions in greenhouse gas emissions which, together with adaptation, can limit climate change risks."[20] By 2100, researchers say, one-third to one-half of all the earth's species could be wiped out.[21]

It is looking increasingly likely that no matter what we do, we won't be able to hold climate change to an increase of just 2°C (4°F), which was once felt to be the highest "safe" level of global warming but which many now believe is still too high. Worldwide CO_2 emissions have to peak by 2016 and then begin a rapid decline if we are to have even a chance of meeting that problematic goal. As I travel around the world (yes, by plane), I feel the immensity of the problem and the daily momentum of seven billion people living their lives. The size and scale of the climate problem seem daunting, as does the impossible pace at which we need to reduce greenhouse gases if we wish to avert the suffering and death of millions of people.

In college, I read a lot of philosophy. This was back in the day when you couldn't click on a vocabulary word you didn't understand and get its definition. I remember reading a lot about "existential crises." I thought it was when you went into a dark room and bleakly pondered, "Who am I?" I've only recently understood that the word *existential* means "relating to existence" and that an existential crisis is something that puts your very existence at risk. This is where we are today. Every one of us is facing an existential crisis.

Fully coming to grips with the enormousness of what is happening in our lifetimes comes in stages: denial, fear, anger, depression, and then action. I'm in the action phase. As a good friend said to me: No matter what, we can know that at each and every moment less carbon is better than more carbon. We must do what we can, as quickly as we can.

My optimism about the potential for a solution to our climate crisis is based on the pace of change we have seen with the Peers Inc model. Engineers are enthusiastic about the promise of new biofuels, and city planners and policy makers see the potential of building and rebuilding cities and suburbs around the world. These steps are important and will deliver CO_2 reductions in the long term. But remember the time frame. We've waited far too long to get started. We need significant emissions reductions today, right now, using the people and assets we have right now.

Changing behavior is admittedly really hard, but it *can* be done immediately, while changing physical infrastructure (such as building more subways and new cities) necessarily takes a long time. When, for example, the cities of London and Stockholm introduced stiff fees to enter the central districts of those cities by private car, traffic (and CO_2 emissions) declined by 25 percent almost overnight.[22]

Likewise, Americans could stop air-conditioning homes, offices, shopping malls, conference centers, and movie theaters to freezingly unpleasant temperatures overnight too. If every American set his or her thermostat one degree higher for air-conditioning and one degree lower for heating, the United States would cut its energy costs by $10 billion per year.[23] Nice ideas, and we should do them starting today, but alone they won't get us where we need to go in time. We need to focus on Peers Inc solutions that can scale rapidly. Many hands make light work.

About 22 percent of CO_2 emissions in the United States stem from use of personal cars. The potential to significantly reduce this lies in the boom of novel transportation start-ups using the Peers Inc model. Taken as a group (and used in conjunction with public transit), they are meeting the transportation needs of city dwellers better than the current one-adult-one-car model dominant in the wealthy countries. They make getting around using other people's shared vehicles and shared rides a faster, cheaper, and more convenient option than owning, parking, and maintaining your own car. The platforms—almost all relying on smartphones—deliver convenience and reliability, key to competing against car ownership. There are peer-driven black-car services; peer-owned and -driven taxis; one-way urban cars (rather like taxis you drive yourself); round-trip cars available by the hour or even by the minute; peer-to-peer car rentals; apps that facilitate the sharing of taxis and long-distance trip sharing; shared shuttles to work; municipal, hotel, and university bike sharing; and peer-to-peer bike rentals. Each one of these reduces the need to own your own car and encourages you to think about the cost of each trip and choose the mode that best matches your needs. Between 2001 and 2009, millennials (those between the ages of nineteen and thirty-four) reduced the miles they traveled by car each year by 23 percent.[24] The new transportation services have helped make this happen. I expect this trend and this new preference for non-personal-car travel to continue. As vehicles switch to clean energy, we will be almost home free in terms of city transportation emissions.

Freight too is seeing efficiency gains thanks to Peers Inc platforms exposing excess capacity and making it useful. A company called uShip (and Shipley, its smaller UK cousin) offers what is called "load-balancing," meaning that instead of trucks going to a destination full and returning empty, loads can be found for the return trips, thus making the weights transported more equal for all legs of the truck's journey. Worldwide, big trucks run empty about 30 percent of the time![25] Making this excess capacity visible and available means that people who are willing to accept more flexible delivery schedules can ship at reduced prices. Ten years in, uShip has brokered $500 million worth of shipping across nineteen countries and six continents.[26]

Thirty-five percent of U.S. emissions come from the electric power industry.[27] Moving from centralized, mostly fossil-fuel-driven power to renewables is a challenge, since we've spent the last one hundred years making access to electricity as easy and simple as possible. Like all basic infrastructure, our electric utilities are platforms. They've done all the hard work we as individuals couldn't do (sourcing coal and building power plants, delivering on economies of scale). Switching out this simple and convenient supply system to renewables is not trivial. The heavily regulated utilities make more money when they are the ones to make the investment in big fossil-fuel-burning plants; they don't get (nor do they deserve) a return on individuals' investments in solar power. Likewise, every time a household installs their own solar panels, it reduces demand from the existing power plants, reducing the utility's profits. So we can't look for help from the utilities unless or until we change the regulations that affect their profit making.

I know that it took my detail-oriented engineer husband seven months to research, source, figure out the relevant tax breaks for, and arrange for the installation of solar panels on the roof of our house. The pain of figuring out the most productive and cost-effective solar installation is equally acute for organizations much larger. Amy Hargroves, director of corporate responsibility and sustainability for Sprint, noted the same lack of time, relevant expertise, and frustration that affected my husband. "We don't have a full-time team to wade through all these options. We don't have someone to manage a power facility," she said. "How can we make this easier for smaller companies?"[28]

Enter SolarCity. The mission of SolarCity, founded in 2006, is to accelerate the mass adoption of clean energy. Their marketing copy pretty much sums up exactly what we've been describing as the purpose of a platform for participation: "Every aspect of your solar system—taken care of. SolarCity's team handles custom design of your system, engineering, financing, permits, applicable rebates, installation, on-going monitoring of your system performance and maintenance." SolarCity simplifies the process as much as possible and passes on the low costs that come from economies of scale. What are the excess capacities being leveraged? I see two. One is the rooftops. SolarCity isn't paying for that space, as it would if it was building solar without the collaboration of the customer. Two is the electric bills consumers are already paying. The economic payback period for installing residential solar photovoltaic systems ranges from five years in Brooklyn, New York, to fifteen years in Portland, Oregon. Many factors play into this payback, including local weather, the cost of electricity, various federal and state tax incentives, local utility provider rebates, regulations, and policies.[29] So, given a period of five to fifteen years, the cost of conversion from fossil fuel energy to solar energy is basically free. This means that we, citizens of the world, are also getting these reductions in CO_2 for free.

Which leads me to my favorite platform for reducing greenhouse gas emissions: a carbon tax. Each of our many billions of consumption decisions, trillions of dollars' worth, could be multipurposed to include investment in a low-carbon world. In a 2012 study, analysts determined that 60 percent of the urban areas we will need by 2030 have yet to be built.[30] If we build that infrastructure with the real cost of emissions taken into account, we address the problem of emissions in buildings and transport infrastructures for as long as they stand.

The three components—excess capacity, platforms for participation, and peer power—make us efficient with physical, financial, and human resources; enable us to innovate quickly and effectively; create resilient and redundant distributed networks; provide economic agency; and create the potential for passion in our working lives. When you put them together into a Peers Inc configuration and work astutely at execution, you can get hypergrowth beyond what was imaginable, learn and innovate at heretofore implausible speeds, and have the best of computing power combined with hyperlocal adaptation. Peers Inc results in a thriving global revolution: the unleashing of millions of hands and minds newly empowered; the ability for whole sectors of the economy to experiment, adapt, and evolve quickly; the exposing of vast, pristine markets and new ways of interacting—and all with breathtaking and sometimes unsettling speed.

The world is changing very rapidly. The problems at hand are enormous. Peers Inc is the framework for our times. Any business that doesn't adopt this way of thinking will drown as the tsunami of the new collaboration washes over them. When you have a crisis that you need to resolve now and fast, think Peers Inc. Peers Inc marks an evolutionary leap into the future, changing the way we compete, create, and aggregate human effort.

In Parts II and III of this book I explain how to actually get it done. In Chapter 6, I talk about building a Peers Inc company from scratch. In Chapter 7, I look at how government can optimize the economic potential for both business (the platforms) and people (the peers). Chapter 8 assesses how legacy institutions are responding, and Chapter 9 delves into platform financing and the democratization of power. Each of these chapters ends up with conclusions that, happily, surprised me.

PART II

Execution

SIX

From Scratch

Learning, Power Sharing, and Building a Peers Inc Organization

Wherever the old city is working successfully . . . it is a complex order. Its essence is intricacy of sidewalk use, bringing with it a constant succession of eyes. This order is all composed of movement and change, and although it is life, not art, we may fancifully call it the art form of the city and liken it to the dance—not to a simple-minded precision dance with everyone kicking up at the same time, twirling in unison and bowing off en masse, but to an intricate ballet in which the individual dancers and ensembles all have distinctive parts which miraculously reinforce each other and compose an orderly whole. The ballet of the good city sidewalk never repeats itself from place to place, and in any one place it is always replete with new improvisations.

—JANE JACOBS, *THE DEATH AND LIFE OF GREAT AMERICAN CITIES*

I LOVE THIS PASSAGE by urban planner Jane Jacobs. Her description of a city street that works—a place where infrastructure encourages the intricate ballet of life to flourish—is an analogy for what is required when building a Peers Inc platform. It took months of eighteen-hour days to ready Zipcar for launch. Grabbing an emerging opportunity and growing a market share requires the right people with the right strategy at the right moment (and what's right changes over time) because they all must come together to create a resilient and inviting infrastructure for peers.

Special attention needs to be paid to the ebb and flow of power between the platform creators and the peers. Getting the balance of power right in the earliest stages will determine whether a platform takes off. Getting it right in the later stages will define the ultimate longevity of the company. Getting it right across the sum of Peers

Phases Most Peers Inc Organizations Pass Through

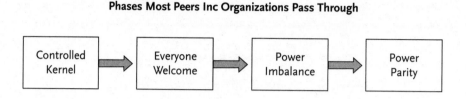

Inc organizations constructing the new collaborative economy as a whole will portend our ability to transition to an economy that provides people with more agency, more satisfaction, and more equality and that is ultimately more sustainable. The constantly shifting power dynamic between the Inc and the peers feels very different from the old economy, with its vertically integrated companies, in which hierarchy was the name of the game.

My hypothesis is that there are four phases that many (though not all) successful Peers Inc efforts travel through: the controlled kernel, the everyone-welcome stage, power imbalance, and power parity. An unsuccessful company may make it through the initial stages but not all the way down the path. In fact, I personally have built such a failed company, and I can't believe I'm about to tell you about it.

CONTROLLED KERNEL (PHASE 1)

Americans are so entrepreneurial that they aren't afraid to fail. Unlike other cultures, there is no stigma. Or so thinks the world when they admire American innovation. Small failures are more appropriately categorized as iterative learning, not failure at all, and are fundamental to earning success. But big failure is not fun; it's better to learn from other people's big failures. So here's my failure at building a successful platform for participation that didn't get past phase one.

I started raising money for GoLoco in 2006, and in April 2007 we launched it with a little over $1 million in investment capital thanks to angel investors who believed in me. GoLoco was going to do for ridesharing (short-distance carpooling and long-distance hitchhiking) what Zipcar had done for sharing cars. We were going to make

GoLoco

sharing a car trip easy, fun, and financially rewarding. Technology, great marketing, and branding would make it possible.

GoLoco would make use of all those empty car seats available in the 80 percent of cars that are occupied only by the driver. Branding is important to me, so I spent lots of time choosing the right name. GoLoco was fun to say, people could spell it once they had heard it, and you could make a case for the name making sense: go local, go low cost, go low CO_2. Getting the user interface and usability just right is critical, so I spent lots of money on a firm that had been responsible for some of Google's most iconic icons and page layouts. And because by this time I was well connected and respected, I could get attention and publicity at launch.

GoLoco was a fantastic idea, as currently proven out by BlaBlaCar, which launched in France around the same time and is hugely successful. People could easily post their own car trips. For example: *Leaving from the intersection closest to my house in Cambridge, MA, to the intersection nearest my daughter's apartment in New York City, departing noon on Friday, June 15 and returning Sunday at 4:00 p.m. on June 17th.* Both drivers and passengers could create profiles, with photos, links to their social media and blogs, information about languages they speak, and details of what they are interested in. Profiles could also include a very short audio clip (telling us, say, what you had for breakfast, or a joke) because we had learned from research that people are more likely to trust someone if they can hear the other person's voice. People could form groups that either would be open to all (the Burning Man group, the rock climbing group, the IKEA group) or private (the Arlington youth soccer group), and trips could be broadcast easily to the entire group. You could create trip alerts so that if anyone was ever going between your neighborhood and IKEA, or

New York, or Walden Pond, you would know about it. A map on your personalized home page would show you where rides that originated near you were going that day, letting serendipity guide your travel. You could pay for your share of the driving expenses online, without having to awkwardly hand over exact change for your share of the trip expenses (we would charge each party 10 percent of the transaction for doing so). And both passengers and drivers could say whether they would ride with the other person again, creating a trusted network.

I was proud of the product we launched with, and Steven Levy, the author of popular books about Apple and Google, broke the story about GoLoco in *Newsweek*: "If Chase has her way, GoLoco will be the behavioral equivalent of the Prius, zapping enviro-guilt while cooling off Gaia."[1]

We persuaded close friends and employees to create complete personal profiles to fuel our start. But all too quickly we learned that we had vastly overbuilt the website. Just about no one voluntarily created a profile. Nor did they want to put in street addresses (even though the auto-complete made it so easy). They just wanted to put in the city. Nor would they put in a specific time (such as 3:30 p.m.), or be willing to tell us how many seats they had in their car. How the heck did people expect to offer a ride or find a ride with so little information?

My engineers spent the next months undoing what we had just done—simplifying, simplifying, simplifying. Today we talk about building a minimum viable product. And with Zipcar, this is what we had effectively done because of our lack of money, time, and knowledge of the sector. With GoLoco, I was better financed and knew what I was doing—or so I thought. Wrong! It's hard not to overbuild your starting platform. You've given it so much thought! You've spent so much time doing surveys and focus groups! And even when you are trying to build what in your heart you believe is the absolute bare minimum to reach your audience, it is highly likely that you are still overbuilding.

Ready for another shocker? Most peer production sucks. I learned this the hard way with GoLoco. Individuals are not like companies, and they are new to this professional-grade peer production thing. Individuals are much more likely than companies to overpromise, underdeliver, miss deadlines, not follow through, and generally do shabby work. This is why eBay, one of the Peers Inc pioneers, realized it had to introduce ratings and commentaries. And my guess is that once the peer sellers understood the rules for engagement, their product descriptions, photographs, and on-time delivery rates improved dramatically. eBay itself, as a platform, probably also improved the end result by picking up as much of the work as possible, optimizing workflows, and improving information presentation. But this wide variation in peer production is exactly why it is so interesting. A simple normal distribution curve gets to the heart of the quality of peer performance by showing the number of people who participate at each performance level: low (some people will do this), average (most people will fall here), and high (a small percentage do this).

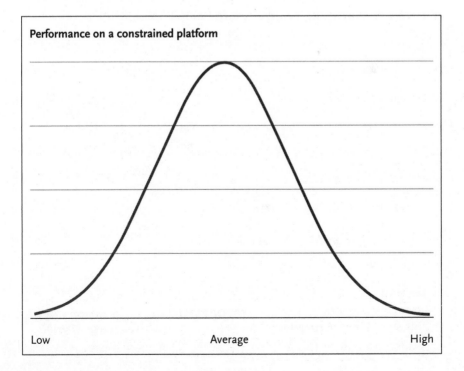

Performance on a constrained platform

Low   Average   High

My takeaway? Building a successful platform for participation is not easy. The goal is to engage the largest number of people while at the same time ensuring an adequate minimum quality. The platform builder (the Inc) must perform a very delicate balancing act. We could call it the Goldilocks principle: The Inc won't be able to guess right the first or even the second time, since it takes actual trial and error to figure it out, but once they've got it right, the fit will be very comfortable. It can take months or even years to finesse the amount of structure that works for both sides. How can the platform, the Inc, provide for each asset, process, regulation, and hurdle that could foreseeably slow peer participation? What is the minimum engagement required from the peers—as suppliers or as consumers—to make something interesting? Success and failure hinge on getting the balance just right.

The structure and complexity of the interface with the peers will determine not only if and how the peers will participate but also the potential for future innovation and thus market potential. The amount of structure built within the platform determines the amount of variation you let in (see the figure below).

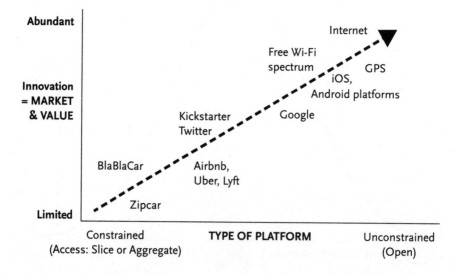

BlaBlaCar, Airbnb, and especially Zipcar are very closed platforms. Peers can operate only within constrained and limited choices,
resulting in relatively uniform collaboration (and products and
services). With GoLoco, only car trips can be shared; with Airbnb,
only beds. With Zipcar, people can choose the specific car and time
they want; they can make suggestions about improvements and complain about problems, but little more. Certainly variation and creativity creep in, but only to a certain extent. At the other end of the
spectrum are wide-open platforms with the least invasive and least
limiting requirements; iOS and Android platforms, the Internet,
open data APIs, and GPS are great examples. Their platform requirements are light—protocols and meta-rules—thus permitting the
widest possible variation and creativity. If the platform's goal is to
maximize innovation, the more open a platform is, the more variation you'll permit and the more innovation you'll uncover. Somewhere in between are platforms such as Twitter (do anything you
want with the 140 characters that will be broadcast for the world to
see) and Kickstarter (obtain almost any level of financing for any
kind of creative project). To increase innovation, you want to maximize flexibility and increase openness.

Figuring out the right amount of structure given your goals comes
back to the Goldilocks principle: try, iterate, learn, adapt. By starting small, you can ease your way into the right place and the right
balance. Why would three young guys with an idea that became
YouTube win out over Google Video? Faster learning on the fly and
more peer participation faster led to a platform where participation
was obvious, simple, and easy. YouTube's first home page, in February 2005, was geared toward online dating: *I'm a "Male" seeking
"Everyone" between the ages of "18" and "45."* People posting videos
tended to be using them to market themselves. Four months later,
YouTube shifted to become "your digital video repository" and invited people to both "search" and "upload your videos." Within just
two more months (still before its first venture financing), they set-
tled on three key components prominently displayed and equally
weighted on their homepage: watch, upload, share. These last two

actions are at the heart of a Peers Inc approach, since they invite direct peer engagement. By contrast, six months after Google Video's own launch (which was at the same time as YouTube), its beta website prominently displayed Google's famous empty search box, with a nice big link to "download video player" (downloading additional pieces requires an extra effort I generally avoid). Google Video was not yet thinking Peers Inc: no focus on inviting participation. It turns out that a significant part of YouTube's success was due to the fact that it made it easy to upload video in almost any video format. Google didn't. It was a full year later (June 2006) that Google Video finally announced its "New! Upload and Share Your Own Videos" link, too late to catch up. In August 2006, eighteen months after its founding, YouTube counted 19.1 million unique visitors. Google bought YouTube in October 2006.[2]

While both GoLoco and YouTube's first approaches proved wrong, and both companies scrambled to learn as quickly as possible, there are some critical differences. YouTube's platform was dramatically more open (users could upload any video.) and would therefore

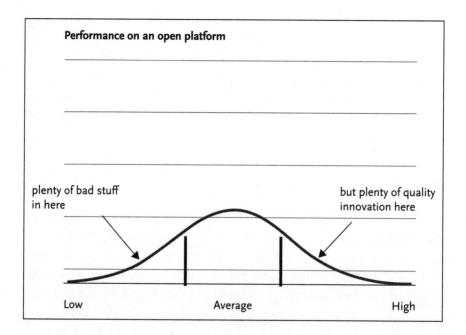

command a much higher value should it prove successful. Going back to the bell curve, we can also predict what YouTube's open and unconstrained platform would deliver: lots of bad-quality stuff (which we all know to ignore), lots of really innovative stuff (which we all enjoy), and a huge quantity of stuff that falls somewhere in the middle.

GoLoco, on the other hand, sought more consistency. We constrained our platform because we really only wanted to facilitate ridesharing. Had we started to see too many lackadaisical peers, it would have been simple to raise the standards, making it harder and more complicated to sign up. Chip Conley, Airbnb's head of global hospitality, told me that as the company and the number of listings has grown, they now warn and then delist nonresponsive hosts, or those with too many comments citing cleanliness as a problem. The difference between an unconstrained platform and one with more constraints looks like the next figure below. There is less variability with the constrained platform (every peer contributes basically the same way), so the difference between high and low performers is small, but there's also less room for innovation. Unconstrained

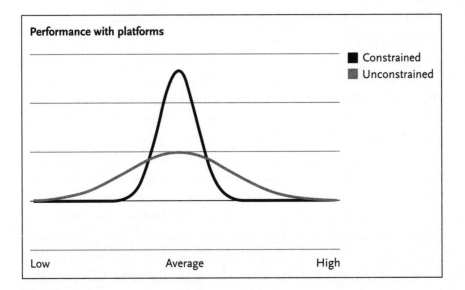

platforms will have result in more creativity (more of the good kind and more of the junky kind).

GoLoco failed because people in the United States were uninterested in ridesharing. It took a while for us to figure that out. Maybe we just had to work smarter. We narrowed our offering and targeted our marketing so that we might be able to force success in a specific niche and expand from that foothold, a strategy I highly recommend to start-ups seeking to build a critical mass. The smaller the niche, the smaller the critical mass needed to prove success. For GoLoco, we focused first on a specific geography (radiating from Boston, and the Boston-New York corridor), then on certain demographic market segments (working closely with universities to be their ridesharing provider; partnering with conferences, concerts, and sports events). Throughout the first year, there were glimmers of encouragement.

In late March 2008 I was asked to give a keynote address at the annual meeting of AIGA, the professional association for design. The conference theme was Design with a Conscience: "How can we become better stewards of the earth?—to our clients, to our community, to ourselves?" They also asked me to write an article about GoLoco for the pre-program newsletter, and I persuaded the conference organizers to include GoLoco as an option in the transportation and logistics section of the conference website. All the stars aligned, I thought. Everyone coming to the conference cared about sustainability. The venue could only be reached by car, and parking was $20 a day. We had created an AIGA group so that people coming in from the airport could share cabs, and people driving within California (a long, thin state with a major single highway corridor) could quickly find each other's trip. My article, sent out to all attendees, talked about the networking benefits of sharing a ride—and isn't networking a major reason to attend a conference? The result: Out of four hundred people attending, just two signed up to share a ride, and those two were a married couple. No matter how simple and easy we made our platform, there just were not enough people interested in sharing car trips. Two years into GoLoco, after several similar depressing doses of reality, I returned the unspent funds to investors. Breaking the disheartening news to investors over several months and crafting the final email were hard and unpleasant tasks. In the ensuing five years, I've felt validated. Despite dozens of earnest ridesharing start-up attempts in the United States, none have succeeded (although I believe in time, demand will come around in the United States). The moral? If there isn't demand for what you are creating, nothing I have to say in this chapter will help.

Steve Blank, a serial entrepreneur who began the Lean Startup movement, captured our experience succinctly in a blog post titled "No Plan Survives First Contact with Customers."[3] GoLoco's stumbling effort, with its back-and-forth interplay between founder vision and real-world experience, accurately depicts the importance of the "kernel," the first phase of experimentation. The Linux software information page provides a definition: "The *kernel* is a program that constitutes the central core of a computer operating system. It has complete control over everything that occurs in the system."[4] While you might have the notion that a Peers Inc company is highly democratic, with the peers always participating in meaningful ways, that's not necessarily true, or at least not all the time. During the controlled kernel phase, when the founders are first piecing together the platform, they necessarily exert maximum control, both forcing the participation to go where they want (or hope) it will go and watching closely to understand how actual participation is unfolding. If you allow a large and still dispassionate group of people to weigh in on too many decisions, you will never get the effort off the ground.

Linux, the open-source operating system that stands behind many of the world's smartphones, tablets, and laptops, is a prime example of the controlled kernel path for a Peers Inc organization. In 1991, Linus Torvalds conceived and created the Linux kernel. In August of that year, he issued a call for feedback on his code to a select newsgroup on Usenet. (Newsgroups are an early distributed bulletin board system first developed in 1980.) Five months later, he started the newsgroup alt.os.linux and widened the circle for comment and recommendations. Although the Linux kernel benefited from the contributions of thousands of programmers and had the outside appearance of democratic engagement, for many years it was

Torvalds alone who signed off on the formal "commits" to the code. Linux was nominally open, but in its formative stages it was tightly controlled.

In the early stages of Wikipedia's development, the debate over the right amount of founder control split up co-founders Jimmy Wales and Larry Sanger. Although Sanger couldn't afford to continue working without funding, he and Wales also disagreed about how to handle the real-world challenges that arise when anyone, regardless of expertise, can edit anything; Sanger wanted to be more restrictive and limit the ability to author articles to people formally vetted as authorities. Early in the second year Sanger left; Wales continued on, insisting on maximizing participation and letting anyone create an article.

Looking at today's most polished and successful platforms, we fail to remember that they all started with a clean slate, a glimmer in the founder's eye. Even the rule "Have no rules" is necessarily a decision made by the founders. Jack Hughes, founder of TopCoder, went so far as to say ruefully, "You ultimately need a dictator to insist that anyone can participate."[5] No matter how open they are, platforms for participation need unifying principles so people can understand what they are, and these principles of course also shape the trajectory of what is possible. I've spent a lot of time describing this first phase, because if you can get the kernel—the balance of structure with freedom—correct, you'll be ready for the next, thrilling stage.

EVERYBODY WELCOME (PHASE 2)

By the end of the controlled kernel phase, founders will have used their vision and power to shape the platform into something that feels like half a handshake: The hand is extended outward, and everyone who sees it knows exactly how to react. The platform is robust and attractive. The rules and culture are relatively stable. The platform is flexible, fair, and ready for expansion. While kernel building can take months (look at Instagram's success) or years (BlaBlaCar's platform needed more than four years to ripen), phase two is the giddy everybody-welcome phase, where the power and force of the incentivized peers come into play. This is when we start up the steep-growth part of the curve.

And here I leave the narrative of the failed U.S.-based GoLoco and begin telling the story of Frédéric Mazzella, my friend and founder of the successful French ridesharing company BlaBlaCar, who drove competently through phase two. Four long years passed between Fred's first vision and the development of a platform that could finally sing. He personally programmed the initial minimum viable product but knew that he would soon need to hire professional engineers. He too worked through the reality of sloppy peer production and learned how to improve the quality of peer-to-peer offerings. He experimented with several business models. And he had some very good luck (French rail strikes in 2007, and the 2010 eruption of the Icelandic volcano Eyjafjallajökull that shut down European air transport for eight days, stranding millions of passengers) just when he needed it; he was also well prepared to take advantage of that and make the service known.

In 2008, Fred introduced an online rating system for both drivers and passengers. This proved to be a key element in addressing fear and trust issues among prospective passengers. Year-over-year growth for BlaBlaCar began to accelerate: from 60,000 members in 2008, the community grew to 120,000 members in 2009 and 300,000 members in 2010. In 2011, the company introduced a business model with the right incentives. Drivers of long trips found it convenient and worthwhile to have passengers book and prepay seats via the website, reducing the hassle of chasing down prospective riders and also guaranteeing that they would actually show up, since they'd paid in advance. BlaBlaCar charges a 10 percent fee and applies the government-required 20 percent tax. Growth was exponential: 1 million members in 2011, 3 million in 2012, 10 million in 2013![6] BlaBlaCar raised $100 million in July 2014.

2014 proved to be a banner year for companies using this collaborative approach: over $3 trillion raised. Lyft raised $250 million, and Uber an astounding $3 billion. These are the companies that cracked the kernel platform-building stage, are experiencing the

exuberant growth of the everybody-welcome stage, and are therefore the ones who raised the most money. While a good fraction of
the value is likely the result of a bubble, the potential of the three
Peers Inc miracles to deliver—based on fast-paced growth, fast learning, and speedy low-cost localization—is worth a lot to investors.

In the summer of 2014, I was at a roundtable meeting at the Aspen
Institute. One of the participants suggested that the huge valuations for Peers Inc companies gives these startups large amounts of
"cheap" capital to play with, and therefore the ability to buy growth
rather than earn it. Lyft and Uber are fierce competitors in the new
app-based medallion-free taxi market. Both have experienced fast
growth and expansion in the few years since their founding (Uber
in 2009, Lyft in 2012). And now both are engaged in price wars, each
reducing fares to attract passengers and lowering their commissions
to attract peer drivers. Neither has any competitive intellectual property. Uber's competitive advantage was once in the deals it had
negotiated with local limo companies and individual drivers. But
nothing prevents drivers from agreeing to drive for both companies
or prospective passengers from having both apps on their smartphones. It is my experience with Zipcar and its competitors that
customers choose based on a combination of convenience (the technology), price, and proximity. Both Uber and Lyft have business
models and apps that appear to work; can the market sustain both?
Buying (bribing) users too early in a company's life cycle will just
eat up a lot of money and won't produce anything lasting. Doing so
later is indeed possible, but it can be a very risky strategy depending on a company's ability to defend that lead. I'll talk more about the
Uber/Lyft battle when I discuss the last phase, later in this chapter.

In all cases, the "greasiest" platforms, those with the least friction, win out. WhatsApp, the text messaging service, grew at many
times the pace of Skype (and Twitter, Instagram, and Facebook).
While the communications services offered are not identical, both
WhatsApp and Skype are examples of the Peers Inc framework:
leveraging excess capacity (users' existing PCs and smartphones),
building a platform for participation (the product apps), and requiring enormous peer participation (downloading those apps and

giving them permission to use and access the relevant devices). WhatsApp's growth was faster in large part due to the extreme simplicity of participation requirements (see the figure below). WhatsApp co-founder and CEO Jan Koum made the brilliant (he told me the "laziest") decision to repurpose users' existing phone numbers from people's contact lists as unique identifiers. This lets WhatsApp immediately identify for you all of your contacts who have downloaded the app and can receive your messages without any further effort from you. Skype, as you know if you've used it, chose the annoying path of requiring people to create an entirely new name for their Skype account, making it harder to create an account and harder to use each and every time you want to connect with someone new. Once again, platform ease and simplicity are the keys. You can also see in the graph below, how getting the platform right can take time, before the lift happens.

Depending on the goal and structure of the effort, large amounts of participation will create new problems. For GPS and the Internet, the world can accommodate an almost infinite number of peer

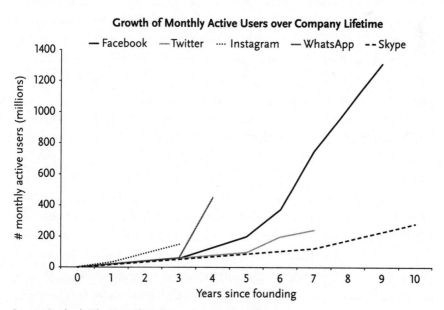

Growth of Monthly Active Users over Company Lifetime

Sources: Facebook, WhatsApp, Skype, Twitter, Instagram, comScore

innovations. But at a certain point, filters need to be introduced. Imagine the usefulness of the Web without an online search engine. Yet this is the case with apps. The millions of available apps are very hard to browse, and if you're looking for a particular app, it's hard to find if you don't know its exact name. As Internet consultant Clay Shirky said, "It's not information overload, it's filter failure."

The everybody-welcome phase doesn't end—you are always hoping to keep expanding the number of collaborators. In retrospect, this phase feels like the naive heyday where everyone is really excited to be part of this new platform. But it soon gets replaced by other, more pressing concerns.

POWER IMBALANCE (PHASE 3)

Phase three is about navigating power imbalance. The rules of engagement between the Inc and the Peers have been established long enough, and the benefits are clear enough, that we see the rise of power players who've figured out how to succeed at the game—sometimes making it difficult for newcomers and potentially threatening the smaller and much more numerous peers. Other times, the Inc-owned platform has become so successful that it forgets the fact that this is a collaboration. This is when we must return to our initial city metaphor and remember a delicate and complex ballet of collaboration is what makes the whole thrive. The value sharing between the Inc and the Peers is the most vulnerable link.

Bruce Schneier is a brilliant cybersecurity technologist. On Twitter, I stumbled across a T-shirt for sale that said, "Bruce Schneier is so smart he can factor prime numbers." Best of all, Bruce tells good stories about the evolution of the Internet (which operates in the Peers Inc framework). He talks about how excited and joyful early users felt when they realized that the Internet gave power to individuals, and made possible all the things that we know come with that: the ability to create content, services, and products without permission; boundless creativity and innovation uncovered; and fast growth for meritorious ideas. Bruce explains how it was individuals, not companies, that first conquered this new platform, because they are nimble. Since then, and particularly in the last decade, institutions such as Comcast, Verizon, and AT&T have seen the promise and learned the rules, and they are slowly beginning to dominate.

The first half of this chapter explained how successful platforms continuously evolve to meet the needs of their participants. What happens if the participants are no longer small but big, and the platform's rules begin to favor their needs? Slowly we will see that power can also shift away from the distributed and back toward the institutional. As Bruce puts it: "This is a competition between the quick and the strong."[7]

This potential for platform capture by power players is increasingly visible as the first Peers Inc organizations move toward maturity. Lending Club (founded in 2006) and Prosper (founded in 2005) are the thriving leaders of peer-to-peer lending. Lending Club is the significantly larger company. As of the end of October 2014, Lending Club had facilitated over $6 billion in consumer and business loans to more than 400,000 borrowers. About 80 percent of those borrowers were refinancing existing debt at much lower interest rates, with payments an average of 29 percent lower than what they were paying credit card companies or banks.[8] Investors, who could be people like you and me, are happy to put some of their money into peer-to-peer lending because they make better returns on this money than if they put it in a certificate of deposit or savings account. Like other Peers Inc organizations that have perfected their platform, business has accelerated: over $3 billion worth of transactions (half of the total) were done in the first three quarters of 2014 alone.[9] Prosper has about 35 percent market share in the industry. And it too is experiencing phenomenal growth rates: Prosper took eight years to attract the first $1 billion in loans, and then, within just six months, they crossed the $2 billion-in-loans milestone.[10]

However, both Lending Club and Prosper, which started firmly as peer-to-peer lending marketplaces, now mostly facilitate loans from institutional lenders, not individuals. At Prosper, more than 80 percent of the loans made in March 2014 were financed by hedge funds, pension funds, asset managers, sovereign wealth funds, and foreign banks.[11] And at Lending Club, that number—the percentage of loans fulfilled by institutional lenders—was about 70 percent.[12] In October 2014, institutional investors issued $177 million in loans, three-and-a-half times more than they had in October 2013.[13]

Larry Summers, secretary of the treasury during the Clinton administration and now a Lending Club board member, said, "Lending Club's platform has the potential to profoundly transform traditional banking over the next decade."[14] The question is, transform it into what? A different cover on the same deal flow? Or a totally different group of lenders?

In some city markets, Airbnb has seen the same takeover: professionals using the platform to market their apartments, condos, and houses. In early 2014, after a battle of several months, the New York State attorney general received data on New York rentals from Airbnb for the period from January 1, 2010, through June 2, 2014. The attorney general's analysis, released in October 2014, drew on the anonymized data of almost half a million stays in over 35,000 unique places, where the stay was for less than thirty days and the room was not shared. Ninety-four percent of Airbnb hosts had one or two units for rent, and that group had earned 63 percent of the income for the period analyzed—$280 million (think about what that amount of money meant to the individuals renting out their rooms or apartments). But the remaining 6 percent of "hosts" were renting between 3 and 272 units (clearly not individuals renting out their own apartment or a room there) and were responsible for 37 percent of the total revenue—$168 million. The top-grossing host, the one with 272 units, charged an average of $358.19 a night and grossed $6.8 million. Each of the top twelve New York City operators had revenue greater than $1 million. There were more than a hundred "power hosts," with ten or more units listed.[15] Shortly after turning the data over to the attorney general, Airbnb went through its New York listings, identified 2,000 that were clearly from institutions, and took them off the site. Airbnb says it removed them because they didn't reflect Airbnb's brand or service aspirations. It is unlikely that any of the top ten earners remain on the platform. From Airbnb's perspective, when it was deep in the everyone-welcome phase, the goal was to make adding a listing as easy as possible. Today, the company has moved beyond that. "It's not just vetting listings coming in," said Chip Conley, Airbnb's head of global hospitality and strategy. "We want to make certain kinds of listings not happen."[16]

A few more examples. Twenty-year-old Linux, fueled for years by the tireless efforts of thousands of engineers, now sees 70 percent of its accepted improvements coming from engineers working for IBM and Samsung. And YouTube's top ten videos last year were all from professional media makers.

So what? Does significant participation by bigger entities matter? As always, the right, if annoying, answer is that it depends. As Chip describes it, Airbnb has never made it easy for professionals to use the site, despite requests. "We don't intend to support power users," he says. Airbnb's goal is to "cultivate the kind of users we want," the ones who fit their branding of "Belong Anywhere"—with emphasis on the word *belong*. "Belonging means making a personal connection. If we were to institutionalize that, we would lose some of the spirit and the values of the company," he explains. So it's not just a question of whether the big players play; what matters is how the platform responds to their existence.

A similar thought was articulated by Ed Cone, a columnist for *CIO Insight*. In his essay "Decoding the Professionalization of Linux," he writes:

> Linux is not now, and cannot be, owned or controlled by IBM. Linux is a brutal technical meritocracy, and there is no senior manager at IBM who can say, "I don't care what the kernel engineers think, I want this." They can't put it into the product without appealing to people who don't work for them. If they announced a strategic change in the kernel they would be laughed out of the room. They have given up the right to manage the projects they are paying for, and their competitors have immediate access to everything they do. It's not IBM's product.[17]

Doc Searls, senior editor of *Linux Journal*, says: "Dan Frye, who runs systems development at IBM and employs many Linux kernel hackers, once told me it took six years for the company to learn that it couldn't tell those hackers what to do—and that in fact the situation was reversed: The kernel hackers were really the ones in charge. This is not a matter of governance, but of authority, influence, and constructive working-together in which all parties contribute what they are in the best position to contribute. The kernel hackers, as peers, do what they do best, while IBM, as an Inc, does what it does best. The logic of this is AND, not OR."[18]

Linux's entire authority structure is built around "what's good for the kernel." Linux kernel developers can improve the code as long as it is good for every possible use, with prejudice toward none. Having kernel development peers (the engineers) working for Incs is good for both because learning can move in both directions, provided the respect is mutual, as it is with IBM. It's true that individual start-ups have less ability to affect a broad foundational code base such as Linux. On the other hand, they are able to use hundreds of thousands of open-source code bases to build whatever they please. When those Harvard undergraduates started coding Facebook, they turned immediately to existing open-source tools.

As an Inc, Airbnb is responsible ultimately to its board of directors, many of whom are investors and who could choose to change the vision if it proved more profitable. Lending Club and Prosper are already adapting their platforms to meet the needs of the large institutions. In each case, however, Incs will have an advantage if they heed the lesson from IBM: that there are goods that only peers can bring to the table, and it is best to respect that fact of life in our new networked world.[19]

Much of the strength of the Peers Inc framework results from the diversity of the participation. If you take away the diversity, so too goes the resilience and redundancy; the innovation, creativity, localization, and humanity; the rapid co-investment of idle assets; and the recursive learning at hyperspeed. Hedge funds and institutions transfer their money in and out of investments in huge lump-sum transactions that can be destabilizing. If left to participate, institutional hoteliers don't have the time, inclination, or insight to offer rentals that are distinguishable from standard large hotels, eliminating the peer-to-peer competitive advantage. Borrowers and renters will then be back in the world of faceless suppliers whom they don't really care about or identify with. Default and damage rates will go up. Engagement and new ideas will go down. Engineers employed by IBM and Samsung will necessarily be working on the select topics and problems that IBM and Samsung care about, not the wide world of possible Linux uses. Linux software will naturally evolve in directions most useful to the largest corporations with the largest number of engineers using Linux. Doc Searls writes, "Kernel development is . . . reactive, not proactive." As a platform builder, I know personally that it is much easier to deal with one big company than with a thousand small ones. But a good platform removes the advantage of the larger players by making dealing with small entities just as easy. The reason why the hourly rental strategy at Zipcar succeeded was that we designed the platform (and the pricing) to make sure that we—the company—were indifferent between eight hourly rentals and one daily rental. The hourly renters were just as welcome as those booking for a longer term.

The issue of significant disequilibrium among the peer group can also arise when select peers become wildly successful. This power disparity puts the platform in many tricky situations, most of them leading to difficult choices.

On Facebook's tenth anniversary, it had 1.23 billion active monthly users. So much participation is hard to get your head around. The Facebook ecosystem includes more than 9 million apps. Nine million! Unfathomable. I also learned from the pages geared toward developers that they "support over 80 payment methods including Visa, MasterCard, PayPal and mobile in more than 50 countries."[20] Put yourself in the mind-set of the CEO of one of Facebook's most popular apps—say, Farmville. Facebook updates its system twice a day. Any one of those updates *could* break the way things work on your app. And while you're thinking about this, just imagine if Facebook decides to change its rules for engagement in some more fundamental way. As Farmville CEO (or, more accurately, the Zynga CEO who created Farmville), you're going to worry about your dependence on Facebook, and also think about ways to reduce your reliance on it. Now flip to Facebook's point of view. Wow, wouldn't you hate to see Farmville take its hours of user activity elsewhere? Facebook is going to work extra hard to make sure that Farmville gets everything it needs—or *might need*. It is a difficult thing to keep supporting the biggest, most successful peers, because pleasing them can lock the platform against change. The more Facebook shapes its evolution to Farmville, or apps like Farmville, the more likely it is to shut out the options for apps that are not Farmville. It also might be doing things that inhibit the way most users use Facebook: posting status updates, pictures, and links, and reading about their friends. One of the best attributes of a Peers Inc structure is the ability to embrace experimentation, and thus adaptation and evolution. Once a platform starts homing in on a few of the biggest players, it immediately closes out certain pathways.

Play this scenario out from the vantage point of the small individual lenders on Lending Club and Prosper. If the company starts making it easy and convenient for the big institutions to get first dibs at the best-rated loans, won't that mean that the little guys will be left to pick up the less desirable leftovers? Yes. And platforms frequently advantage one type of player over another. Cory Ondrejka, formerly vice president of engineering at Facebook and chief technology officer of Second Life, told me he has been in meetings where they were discussing the impact of Facebook's dependency on some other company's platform, which then caused them to reflect on how the successful members of their ecosystem feel about dependency on Facebook.

The platform creator has a number of ways in which it can deal with very successful peers. What it gives, it can take away. Twitter is a wonderful example of the promise of the Peers Inc paradigm—delivering incredible growth and innovation—and also the complicated corners the model can paint itself into. Twitter opened the doors to its simple platform in 2006: Get yourself a Twitter handle and broadcast anything you want as long as it is 140 characters or less. Nick Bilton, of the *New York Times*, wrote a blog post, "Why Are People So Upset with Twitter? Let's Grab a Bite" that used a terrific metaphor to illuminate the interaction between platform and peers:

In 2006, a small restaurant called Twitter opened for business. This wasn't your typical restaurant. Twitter didn't have its own chefs creating food. Instead, it invited anyone from the public to come into its kitchens and freely use the stove, pots, pans, plates, and knives. . . . Soon, word spread, and Twitter was bustling with people. . . . Twitter grew so quickly that it started to have major problems dealing with all the customers. . . . So Twitter came up with a plan: it told people that they could take the food being made in Twitter's kitchen and give it away by creating new places for people to eat. Twitter called this the application programming interface, or A.P.I.

Soon there were food trucks, delivery services, meal messengers, all taking what was coming out of Twitter with its A.P.I. and redistributing it to people all around the world. . . . As things grew, some decided to take hefty sums of money from investors to build specific businesses around Twitter.

But Twitter itself had yet to figure out a revenue model. The management team was replaced.

The new boss, Dick Costolo, realized that if the company wanted to make money, it would need to stop allowing all the food trucks and delivery services from taking everything made at Twitter. . . . This, understandably, incited the ire of everyone. The trucks parked in the street were understandably upset. They had spent years building a reliable service to get Twitter's wares to people. Now, they were at risk of being shut down. . . .

The people who had come to Twitter in the early days also felt duped. . . . So who was at fault in this tale? Really, everyone. . . . But most of all Twitter, which changed its decisions and strategy midstream, confused almost everyone, often hurting those who helped make Twitter successful and popular.[21]

While Twitter shut down some of its APIs, which is the ultimate betrayal for participating peers, there are many other ways a platform can mistreat successful co-creators. They can send cease-and-desist letters or capriciously interpret their own rules to close down successful apps that get too powerful, as in the case of AppGratis. John Koestler of VentureBeat so elegantly wrote up this story that even though I know the protagonist well, I can't improve on this succinct telling of the scandal:

> AppGratis CEO Simon Dawlat spoke out today about his flagship app being pulled from the iOS app store. And what he has to say should make every developer very, very nervous.
>
> One week ago, Apple approved his app. Two days ago, Apple banished AppGratis from the iOS app store.
>
> It's hard to overstate or overemphasize that previous statement. It's hard to express the confusion that such a reversal causes. It's hard to understand how Apple can expect to treat developers who invest millions of dollars in apps that benefit Apple's platform and not have a reaction that comes back and bites them where it hurts.[22]

AppGratis reviews apps and features a different one for free each day. Starting from scratch, Simon built his company up over three years with an enormous amount of physical effort, long hours, great strategic thinking, good humor, and ultimately the help of forty-five employees. Apple effectively shut them down overnight. AppGratis wasn't breaking any of Apple's stated rules, but it was changing the way people discover apps. So why did Apple really do it? Perhaps AppGratis was too successful; it had 12 million users. (The Android platform, unlike Apple, doesn't have an approval process. AppGratis continues in the Android world.)

Many (not all) platforms have visibility into peer activity on their platform. A platform could decide to buy the co-creations that are most successful, likely garnishing 60–80 percent of the activity in that market (which Twitter has done as well). By mixing platform and content, the platform can no longer remain impartial. In doing so, it risks stunting further growth from co-creators, who will become wary of using a platform that may also be their main competitor. In fact, this is what is happening on the Internet. Service providers, who provide us with access to wired and wireless Internet infrastructure, the physical platform over which the Internet effectively runs, are buying up content providers, creating a real conflict of interest. And this is what is happening when Microsoft or Apple or Google buys and absorbs, or simply replicates, the most successful applications on their platforms and starts offering them up embedded in their platform. Apple didn't like the success of Google Maps and its dependence on it, and so it built its own mapping software. Google's domination of our laptops comes from the convenient (and free) bundling of Gmail, Google Docs, Google Calendar, and Google Drive, taking out lots of companies that were providing these services independently.

And although peers as collaborators are critically important and powerful as a whole, as individuals they are expendable. In the earliest days of a platform's life, the Inc fights to attract and preserve all those small efforts. Individual peers have power. But once the platform is big and strong, the participation by any one random individual is irrelevant.

In May 2014, disgruntled peer co-creators, aka Uber drivers, felt that the platform they were using, Uber, wasn't paying enough attention to their needs. Several hundred of them joined the newly created App-Based Drivers Association. Because drivers are independent contractors, this can't be considered a union, but it is effectively the same. Driver Daniel Ajema from Seattle commented, "They call us partners, and basically we demanded a true partnership."[23] Other Uber drivers who feel helpless echo these sentiments: "We want the company to understand that we are not just ants" and "Uber's like an exploiting pimp. [It] takes 20 percent of my earnings, and they treat me like shit—they cut prices whenever they want. They can deactivate me whenever they feel like it, and if I complain, they tell me to fuck off."[24]

For the peers, the upside of the Peers Inc model is that they are autonomous and can choose when, how, and where to participate: In effect, "You are not the boss of me!" The downside is that there is little today that legally binds the platform to act consistently or fairly. For the Inc, the upside of the Peers Inc model is co-investment by the peers with their assets, good ideas, and diversity. The downside is that, unlike with employees, the company or the institution can't force peers do anything: again, "You are not the boss of me!"

How much leverage do the peers actually have? It depends on when and where. Emily Castor, director of community relations at Lyft—and the primary conduit between drivers and the executive team—says that keeping peers happy is paramount to their success:

> Drivers have a great deal of leverage over our product and business model. As a platform, we rely on them to provide great experiences to passengers and ensure ride availability. For that reason, we are extremely responsive to driver feedback and are constantly striving to keep drivers as happy as possible.
>
> On peer to peer platforms, "supply" is an ephemeral thing. Providers have options, and we do not have the coercive power of traditional employers. Instead, we survive by providing the most attractive platform and most rewarding experience for our community. This pressure has the function of giving a great deal of influence to everyday participants, especially since we provide such open, transparent channels for them to communicate with us and each other.
>
> Platforms that are not responsive to the desires and well-being of their participants will evaporate, as providers flee to the myriad other options for flexible income generation.[25]

Will all successful platforms become monopolies? It depends on how they decide to share power (and how they were financed—which is Chapter 9's topic). As Lyft and Uber battle it out, drivers and passengers can use both apps. Switching costs for the supply-and-demand side of this marketplace are very low. That said, while any particular market could likely support both companies (and drivers can driver for both), will customers know about both? When Simon Dawlat's AppGratis was cut out of the Apple app store, he could continue with Android users but lost access to about half of his potential smartphone market. Users are unlikely to choose an Android phone simply so that they can benefit from AppGratis. Unloved crafters on eBay were the impetus for the 2005 launch of Etsy, which was specifically customized for them. In 2013, $1.35 billion worth of sales passed through Etsy en route to its sellers.[26] And eBay lost a multibillion-dollar marketplace because it didn't care enough to support peer creators.

Not all platforms tend toward monopoly. Some do; some don't. Platforms that are open, minimalistic, and decentralized—open APIs, protocols, simple rules—leave users so unconstrained that there is no possible way to have the binding constraint of a monopoly. How a platform was financed, and therefore who owns it, will also dictate its likelihood of exercising monopoly if it has the option. A discussion I had with entrepreneurs on this topic led to a lack of consensus. Some platforms (such as cloud computing, credit card processing, and mail servers) lack barriers to entry or protective intellectual property, and therefore they have competitors. For peers, using these platforms is much cheaper than building those assets on their own. I can attest to this, having built so many pieces for Zipcar and having bought them for my last company. And then, "when we don't like the platform, we can just go elsewhere because we haven't invested in the assets—switching costs are much lower than if we'd built it ourselves, and sunk costs are much lower likewise," one CEO told me. In the old siloed economy, where everything was single-purpose and closed, investments in infrastructure and devices could lock users in for a very long time; think of all the states and countries that have written fifteen-year contracts with tolling system vendors that require every driver to purchase a $30 transponder to pay for tolls electronically—a device in actual use less than a minute a month. Meanwhile, every driver has a cell phone in his or her pocket that could make electronic payments. But some platforms for participation deliver infrastructure *and* significant network effects. In other words, the value of the service goes up the more people participate. Zipcar, for example, is useful if there is just one car parked near your house, but when people in another city make it possible for you to rent cars there too, there is added value to you, albeit a marginal one. For BlaBlaCar, on the other hand, all the value is derived from network effects: Ridesharing only works when lots of people are participating. These network effects are powerful and can make it very hard for a new entrant to enter the market and go up against an established company with a very large network.

The pinnacle in a pure capitalist economy is creating so many barriers to entry that no one else can really compete. That makes for an effective monopoly, yet one without government intervention or regulation. One way to stave off regulation is to act nice. If your co-creators aren't complaining because they are fairly treated, well served, and heard from, then maybe the platform won't need regulation but it truly is self-regulating.

As we start to see more mature Peers Inc companies, we are also recognizing the huge problem with old-fashioned but unrecognized monopolies. Monopolies don't adapt. They build high walls around themselves to keep all that value in for themselves. Meanwhile, the world around them evolves, creating workarounds and black markets, until one day there is a chasm between what the monopoly provides and what the real world wants. (Automobile, telecommunications, and fossil-fuel industries, are you paying attention?) Once the gap is too big to transition slowly, change happens in big ugly disruptive jumps. Why spend the time to build a Peers Inc company only to throw away the benefits? If during the power disequilibrium phase the Inc doesn't give power back to the peers, the company will lose the peers, and the gains that come with them.

POWER PARITY (PHASE 4)

The solution to building a long-term sustainable organization is to seek power equilibrium, the last stage and an ever-shifting almost-steady state. As Bruce Schneier, the cybersecurity expert, puts it, "Between the quick and the strong, what we need is a stalemate. We need a proper balance between institutional and distributed power. The more we can balance power among various groups, the more stable society will be."

Our platform has moved through the stage of early founder vision and control, through the burgeoning excitement of rapid adoption, and into the swamp of power capture and difficult choices. As the platform gets stronger, it must make overt and significant efforts to continually invest and share power with peer creators. Remember, we are looking for power parity, a dynamic yet stable end state. The platform doesn't need to give away too much power, or do it too quickly. The goal is to keep all the parties in balance, continually making adjustments so as to maintain a kind of power stalemate.

Reid Hoffman, the successful investor and co-founder of LinkedIn, said in an interview that LinkedIn works hard to deliver value to all sides: "The individual matters, too. It's not just [LinkedIn's] interests. It's not like, 'Well, it's only as long as it's good for my interests.' No, no. Your interests, our interests, and how do we align them? That's the really key thing."[27]

The ways to share power and value start to become obvious as you think them through:

Permit data portability. This is most easily done by using open standards. It is the biggest switching cost and barrier to exiting your platform. Remember that hokey saying you first read in seventh grade: "If you love something, set it free. If it comes back, it was meant to be"? If your platform is really as great as you think it is, people won't leave. But you'll have to work harder to make that true.

The platform should be an advocate for the peers. In the beginning, I'm sure this is true within the company. But as the effort grows, individuals inside the company have other work to do and lose sight of this. That's the time to create a position for someone whose job it is to think about this. When that person's voice isn't being heard, it's time to add more staff or rules to protect minority interests to make it so. Again, all of this requires increasing escalation and effort.

Airbnb has created a group of seventy-five "trusted testers" drawn from their 30,000 "superhosts," those with the most experience. These testers participate (unpaid) in vetting design and rule changes, as well as making recommendations. Airbnb's fifteen largest markets also have dedicated community managers as an on-the-ground resource to connect the company more closely to its hosts.

Give peers the ability to communicate with each other and organize. Daniel Ajema had to work hard to find drivers who shared his views about Uber's practices, as Uber didn't give him a way to find and communicate with other drivers. On Facebook, by contrast, users are constantly airing their grievances and circulating petitions about practices that make them unhappy by making Facebook groups and sharing them widely on the platform. The activity of the aggrieved is all out in the open. Facebook sees it happen and can address peer-related problems when they start having traction. (In fact, there are many Uber driver groups using Facebook to connect.) The alternative is to have unhappiness turn into anger and come to light in one big boiling eruption or mass exodus.

Just as I was thinking that Airbnb was the right size to begin to facilitate organizing by its hosts, it introduced Airbnb Groups: "online communities created and organized by Airbnb hosts around a specific topic or interest." Within a year, 25 percent of hosts had joined at least one group.[28] As one would expect, most groups are focused on topics salient to hospitality: "Making Guests Feel Special"; "Sustainable and Eco-Conscious Hosts and Travelers"; "Hosting 911"; "House Swap." In just over a year, hosts had created more than 2,000 groups. Interestingly, hosts who participate in groups have ratings 15 percent higher than those who don't participate.

In July 2014, a poorly vetted change was introduced into the thumbnail descriptions of Airbnb listings. The change removed the number of reviews each specific listing had because guest feedback showed that they didn't understand the purpose of the number. Hosts were furious. From their perspective, the number of reviews distinguished experienced hosts from inexperienced novices. Chip Conley had given out his email address months earlier during a talk broadcast to hosts, and within hours a dozen groups had posted how to get in touch with him. By the next day, hundreds of hosts had texted and emailed. Within twenty-four hours of the change, Airbnb returned the review number to the listing descriptions, and used design to clarify its meaning. Thirty hosts active in this write-in effort were invited to become part of Airbnb's trusted testers.

Share best practices with all peers. This is another example of a complete reversal from the playbook of traditional capitalism. In the old days, companies would build value by keeping their best ideas to themselves. In the collaborative economy, and particularly with the Peers Inc framework, everything you can do to make your peers grow and succeed only adds to your own value. The success of platform and peers is totally intertwined. Best practices can be shared in many different ways. The platform uncovers a new way to learn something and then institutionalizes it within the platform, as Duolingo does when it has a new understanding of how people learn a language better. YouTube and Etsy hold conferences, webinars, and blog Q&As to get the word out. And, as many software companies have figured out, facilitating and encouraging user groups to ask and answer questions among themselves can be a very effective way to provide answers to the huge diversity of existing problems, because if the group is large enough, someone somewhere has also had a given problem and solved it.

Increase transparency. Cory Ondrejka, former vice president of engineering at Facebook, noted "As you get big, one challenge is to continue to be trustworthy and transparent enough so that people don't spend so much time worrying about how to get off your platform."[29] At a minimum, we need transparency around data privacy, especially who owns the data and what happens to it.

Transparency around algorithms lets us know how things are actually calculated. Uber's "surge pricing" policy during high-demand times could absolutely benefit from transparency. Uber explains that it increases the price of the fare to attract enough drivers to meet the peak demand. According to Uber, to meet the need of those seeking a ride home from an August 8, 2014, concert outside of San Francisco, the regular fare (around $60) needed a fivefold surge price increase (resulting in fares between $390 and $470) to attract enough drivers. I'd love to see the numbers behind that curve. How many drivers opted in at double the usual fare? How many more would only show up at the triple offering? And what additional percentage of the total was added when the price went from four to five times the regular rate? Passenger insight into that calculation might have reduced the outrage expressed on Twitter, Facebook, and in the press. If surge pricing is needed to address passenger demand, surplus supply seems like the parallel feature for drivers. As Daniel Ajema, organizer of the App-Based Driver Association, wrote me, "Uber wants to have unlimited number of drivers in their system, and argues that market supply and demand will take care of any problem there might be. We, on the other hand, believe having unlimited number of drivers on the street will prevent each driver from making a living. Slicing the pie into an unlimited number of pieces will not affect the company's overall income, whereas drivers' income will be reduced as they scramble for a limited demand base." Uber could restrict drivers from signing in when there are more drivers than demand, and it could offer an hourly wage floor, as does Favor, a marketplace for small tasks.

Transparency around process, what happens next and why, gives relief from uncertainty. Ajema notes, "We are aggrieved for the lack of notice and communication about what the company plans to do in matters that directly affects us." Likewise, many expelled Zipcar members contacted me (when I was no longer connected to the company) to ask me to intercede on their behalf so that they could get back in. Zipcar needed to be much more clear about the process by which people could get themselves back into the company's good graces. And transparency around code—sometimes even open sourcing—is the ultimate in transparency, for engineers at least, because it lets them know exactly what is happening.

All of these ideas and practices are captured in a different framing by a hero of mine. Well, Elinor Ostrom is not just *my* hero, but one for others as well, since she won the Nobel Prize in economics in 2009 for her analysis of economic governance especially for commons. Lots of us have heard about the tragedy of the commons: When people share a resource but don't own it, everything goes to hell because they don't care. As you know, this was not my experience with Zipcar, which proved to be a shock to investors and business pundits. And it was this reality that led to the founding of dozens of other successful sharing-economy companies. Ostrom identifies "common pool resources," which have two characteristics: they produce a steady stream of benefits accruing from the resource, and it is very difficult to exclude individuals. You can see how this maps very closely to what is happening within the Peers Inc model. The platform for participation absolutely produces a steady stream of benefits, and the peers are free agents who opt in. Some Peers Inc companies are able to exclude certain people; at Zipcar, for example, we were able to exclude people with bad driving records. But if we think about GPS, or the Internet, there is almost no ability to exclude, and so the definition of common pool resource fits very well. While this is not a perfect mapping in every case, it comes quite close, with the platforms becoming commons for those co-creating on them.

Ostrom died in 2012. I don't think the reality of this new kind of organizational structure had yet crossed her mind. Her fieldwork—looking at sustainable long-term management of pasturelands in Africa and water irrigation systems in Nepal—seems distant, yet her findings are very pertinent, especially her discovery of commonly held resources where there was no "tragedy." One question guided Ostrom's research: "Were there practices for the long-surviving institutions that are not there for the failed systems?" Decades of research led her to codify eight "design principles" for stable local common pool resource management. These principles ensure that the participants have power over rule making and feel fairly treated. While I think it may be too much to ask many private platforms to hand over this kind of control to the participating peers, the desired outcomes are good to keep in mind. Here are the principles:

1. Define clear group boundaries (to exclude parties who are not entitled).
2. Match rules governing use of common goods to local needs and conditions.
3. Ensure that those affected by the rules can participate in modifying the rules.
4. Make sure the rule-making rights of community members are respected by outside authorities.
5. Develop a system, carried out by community members, for monitoring members' behavior.

6. Use graduated sanctions for rule violators.
7. Provide accessible, low-cost means for dispute resolution.
8. Build responsibility for governing the common resource in nested tiers from the lowest level up to the entire interconnected system.

These rules make good sense, and some seem self-evident and should be familiar to those of us who live in democracies ("Ensure that those affected by the rules can participate in modifying the rules"). Others surprised me by making the list, but with more thought, also seemed just right. In a world in which our professional (and sometimes personal) lives are laid bare, we need to establish clear rules for forgiveness (see rules 6 and 7). A vengeful evaluation by one pissed-off person can ruin the reputation that someone has built over years. And the person himself can ruin his own reputation with one really stupid decision. Somewhere, somehow, we have to build in the ability for mistakes to be corrected and for the rehabilitation of reputation over time. This is something we were only just beginning to understand while I was at Zipcar. Members whose actions put the safety or welfare of the whole community at risk would be warned, monitored, and ultimately barred from driving if the problematic behavior continued or was serious enough. I remember very clearly the first person we kicked out (she had returned a car knowing the brakes weren't working—she'd run over a plastic bag that had somehow inhibited braking—but hadn't bothered to tell us), and the day two months later when she came into the office begging for a second chance. We didn't give it to her. That said, at the time I hadn't appreciated the need for clear guidelines about how such people could rejoin.

As befits such a powerful new kind of engine for generating wealth, Peers Inc enterprises will eventually have to address the degree to which peers share both the power and the enormous value created when a platform becomes a smash hit or a ubiquitous standard. During the early stages of development and the everybody-welcome phase, there is a fairly equitable deal between the platform and the peers. As we saw earlier, the platform company takes on a lot of risk and works very hard to perfect the platform, and the hard-to-attract peers use the service because it really suits them. The platform is small, and the peers have lots of choices.

COMMUNITY BUILDING FOR POWER SHARING

Community building was a significant part of Zipcar's early success and a key part of my future strategy for the company, one that I didn't get to execute. I've avoided discussing it so far because community isn't an obvious fit for every Peers Inc structure. For Whats-App users or companies built using GPS, it is hard to imagine that any of those peers would have an interest in forming a community with all the others. But if we think of those platforms as common pool resources, and if those resources are threatened—say, the U.S. government changes its mind about sharing its satellites—suddenly we can completely imagine GPS-using peers wanting to organize and form a community. This chapter is all about staging certain execution elements over time. Once a platform—a kind of standard—becomes widely adopted, we almost always see business associations formed around these standards to protect the common interests of the businesses using that standard. There are thousands of these associations, ranging from behemoths such as the American Petroleum Institute to the more esoteric Independent Book Publishers Association and Personal Watercraft Industry Association. There is not an exact parallel here, but in the Peers Inc model, the size of the peers can be very, very small relative to the size of the institution creating the platform.

Just like business associations, a peer community provides a whole host of benefits to both Inc and peer: meeting others in the network, sharing of best practices, exploring new ideas, and problem solving in an informal, low-pressure setting. We can see all of those things happening in Airbnb's groups. And a new NGO, Peers.org, is trying to serve as a convener and service provider to support freelancers working in the collaborative economy. Ultimately, a happy community absolutely encourages viral marketing, by far the cheapest, most authentic, most distributed, and most targeted form of marketing possible.

The FOSS movement provides some nice examples of what is possible when peers form a community. As has been hinted at in this chapter, peers aren't like employees, in that their work, thoughts, and actions are wholly their own, so the Peers Inc model can be a double-edged sword. FOSS projects often have highly transparent, rough-and-tumble cultures where discontented coders can "fork" the project, making a split in the platform code, with some peers veering off to greener pastures. As a result, FOSS projects are required to constantly manage the Peers Inc power balance, typically through community, in order to succeed.

Drupal, like many other FOSS projects, had a very humble start. Its founder, Dries Buytaert, created the seed while completing his computer science PhD at Ghent University. Since being hatched in Dries's dorm room in 2001, Drupal has attracted a global community of coders, now grown to more than 1 million members and close to 30,000 active code contributors (for perspective, that's roughly two times the size of Linux community) spanning more than two hundred countries. Drupal has evolved into an enterprise Web content management platform that now powers over 2 percent of the world's websites, including many prominent sites in a wide range of industries: mainstream media (Economist.com, FoxNews.com, MSNBC.com), business (GE.com, Pfizer.com, JnJ.com, TeslaMotors.com, Timex.com, Zipcar.com), technology (RedHat.com, Box.com), entertainment (Grammys.com, Zynga.com), banking (ING.com), museums (Louvre.fr), sports (NBA.com), education (Columbia.edu, TeachForAmerica.org), and government (WhiteHouse.gov).[30] In addition to the hundreds of thousands of independent engineers, the platform has also spawned many Drupal companies around the world. The largest, Acquia, was founded by Dries in 2007, has raised more than $100 million in venture capital funding, and was named North America's Fastest-Growing Private Tech Start-up in 2013.[31]

As Drupal's peers grew in number, the community established the Drupal Association in 2009 with the mantra "Come for the code, stay for the community." The association is responsible for helping Drupal flourish by providing community infrastructure, events, and collaboration (including codes of conduct and other rules). The stability it has provided allowed Drupal to evolve to a point where it now competes with traditional software created by the likes of Adobe and Microsoft. The community continues to produce hundreds of Drupal events around the world, the largest of which are world-class technology conferences that attract thousands of attendees. Drupal is not alone in this regard either, as other well-known FOSS projects, such as Linux and WordPress, have massive communities of peers and a flurry of annual events.

Despite these many success stories, the technology landscape is littered with tales of FOSS that failed by not providing engineers with a way to organize and evolve productively, frequently suffering a tragedy of the commons and becoming mere footnotes in the history of the Web. The bigger and more successful the platform, the more it is perceived as a common pool resource, and the more its peers feel entitled to a say. I'll talk more in Chapter 7 about how and when government might play a role in protecting the rights of peers.

Last year Facebook experienced a public relations fiasco: the aftermath from the results of an experiment it had let researchers conduct inside the Facebook community. For one week in January 2012, data scientists skewed the news feed of almost 700,000 Facebook users so that they saw either happier or sadder news. At the end of the week, those who had seen happier news feeds themselves posted more upbeat status updates; those who had seen the more pessimistic news feeds posted more negative updates. The report, "Experimental Evidence of Massive-Scale Emotional Contagion through Social Networks," was published in the June 2014 issue of the *Proceedings of the National Academy of Sciences of the United States of America*.[32] Danah Boyd, a principal researcher at Microsoft in the area of social media, commented on the fallout that had filled Twitter, Facebook, blogs, and the mainstream media for days: "What's at stake is the underlying dynamic of how Facebook runs its business, operates its system, and makes decisions that have nothing to do with how its users want Facebook to operate. It's not about research.

It's a question of power." Indeed, it all comes back to power. If this new structure has effectively created a new class of common pool resources, those participating want and expect their share of the power. Boyd continues, "More than anything, I want to see users have the ability to meaningfully influence what's being done with their data and I'd love to see a way for their voices to be represented in these processes."[33]

To conceive of a long-lived Peers Inc organizational structure, power parity must necessarily be the end state.

SEVEN

For the People

Engaging Government

CHAPTER 6 concluded with the important point that power parity between peers and Inc is a requirement for a stable long-term collaboration. Democracy is itself the successful embodiment of this requirement. In the last two centuries, democracies have produced longer-lived regimes than other forms of government because the people, through their votes, have been given power to make the rules about public goods and the laws that govern their economic self-interest. Democracies will ultimately fail when they are no longer democratic and the government Inc no longer shares power with the peers. In this chapter, we'll cover just two government roles: government as a creator of platforms (the creative uses of these are left in the hands of the people/peers who are closest to the needs and problems) and government as a protector and champion (regulator) for the people.

GOVERNMENT AS CREATOR OF PLATFORMS

One of the best examples of a government unlocking excess capacity is when the United States opened up the space-based Global Positioning System, which was originally built to aid in deterrence of nuclear attack during the Cold War. It was in response to the tragedy of a Korean Airlines passenger plane shot down by the USSR in 1983 after the plane strayed into prohibited Soviet airspace, and 269 people were killed. These tragic deaths could have been avoided if the pilot had had access to GPS. So President Ronald Reagan issued a directive making GPS freely available for civilian use, once it was sufficiently developed, as a common good.[1]

The U.S. government initially configured the GPS platform to determine positions with a one-hundred-meter resolution—adequate for determining whether you were in another country's airspace, but not that useful if you were lost in a city. In 1996, President Bill Clinton announced that the U.S. government would stop its intentional degradation of the civilian GPS signal—called Selective Availability— to change the resolution from a hundred meters down to twenty meters by 2000. And in September 2007, it stopped degrading the signal at all.

Reading very old press reports offers the delicious possibility of laughing at very wrong predictions. But in that March 1996 announcement, U.S. transportation secretary Federico Pena nailed it when he said, "Today, not many Americans know what GPS is. Five years from now they won't know how they ever lived without it." The Clinton administration believed that the move would quadruple sales of global positioning systems to $8 billion a year and create 100,000 new jobs by the year 2000.[2] In fact, by May 2000, when the GPS signal degradations were removed there were 4 million GPS users worldwide. The government then predicted that the market would "double in the next three years, from eight billion dollars to over 16 billion dollars."[3] And in 2013, ten years beyond the prediction window, there were more than 2 billion global navigation systems installed and $200 billion in revenue directly related to the global navigation satellite system.

I have a strong visceral image of my life before GPS. Burned into my memory is the image of my daughter Cameron in Paris in 2003, finding her way to "look-sees" and fittings for designers during her first fall fashion week as a model. I see her from across the street as I arrive at our designated meeting space and time. She is sixteen. A heavy drizzle is coming down. The stone buildings and empty street are wet, an unfocused sea of gray. Rivulets move through the gutters. Her slight figure is at an angle, amplified by the umbrella wedged under her armpit, akilter, water dripping onto her lower back. She hunches over a damp and dog-eared paperback map book of Paris. One hand holds both the book and an open subway map trailing earthward. Her schedule, with times, names, and addresses of people to see, printed on a white sheet of paper, pokes folded, rumpled, and sodden from between the book pages. She is not dressed for rain, or for 40°F weather. On her shoulder is looped a large leather bag filled with an oversized and very heavy portfolio of photographs and a pair of six-inch heels that she will change into immediately before any appointment. She speaks no French and has no phone.

Before GPS-based navigation systems we had printed maps. Some readers might remember a time when AAA members could request a TripTik for a planned road trip. AAA staff would collect a series of maps along a route and use a big green highlighter to trace the route from New York City to Chicago via Cincinnati, for example. The maps would be assembled into a spiral-bound notebook and mailed to you. Every gas station sold maps, and you could buy big books of detailed maps of each state and of the whole country. Every car had piles of these maps in the glove compartment, though it often seemed that the map you really needed was never handy because you had lent it to a friend who never returned it or it was unreadable from all the folds, creases, and rips that had developed from overuse.

Today our stacks of dog-eared and out-of-date maps have been replaced by GPS navigation devices and smartphone applications that shout out turn-by-turn directions with incredible precision. That pitiful bleak scene of my daughter is no longer a reality when we find ourselves as strangers in foreign cities or foreign parts of our home town. Our lives have indeed been transformed by GPS, smartphones, and real-time map applications. This significant improvement in our quality of life, like the tremendous economic activity surrounding these innovations, was only possible because of the size and scale of a government that unleashed the potential of the excess capacity embedded in its own assets and made them available on well-designed platforms for participation. Thank you! Without billions of dollars in R&D funding from the Department of Defense—an estimated $5 billion as of 1994—GPS never could have been developed.[4] Certainly no private enterprise, not even a multibillion-dollar behemoth such as GM or GE, had the resources and the wherewithal to achieve such a feat.

But—and there is definitely an important caveat here—it is just as true that government alone could not have produced the economic engine, innovation, and value creation found in the GPS ecosystem. It required the Peers Inc paradigm—leveraging of excess capacity (the R&D and the satellites), the platform for participation (the Standard Positioning Service), and the innovating peers to produce practical results on this scale, with this speed, and with this immeasurably large economic impact. While it took a government-sized institution to create it, coming up with the myriad ways this free location information might be applied was best left to the world's peers: tens of millions of individuals, associations, universities, start-ups, medium-sized enterprises, multinationals, and even other countries that are making use of and building on the availability of GPS. The Pentagon never would have envisioned the wondrously creative uses to which it has been put, including the geolocation of rhinoceroses, whales, cattle, pets, "lost" maple trees, children, extreme skiers, mountain climbers, bikes, cars, trucks, shipping containers, and, yes, even misplaced keys.

It could have been otherwise. The U.S. government could have decided to keep its military research to itself. It could have opened it up but made the interface incomprehensible or impractical (lots of examples of this happen as well). It could have decided that peers needed to get some form of permission in order to tap into the GPS network, or pay a fee to use it. Because it did none of the wrong things and eventually all of the right things, we have today a wealth of benefits and economic activity based on GPS.

These same precepts were at work when the government opened up another asset it had paid for: the Internet. Barbara van Schewick is not only a professor of law at Stanford Law School but also an associate professor of electrical engineering in Stanford University's Department of Electrical Engineering. Her research has focused on the factors that have allowed the Internet to serve as a platform for innovation, free speech, and decentralized economic, social, cultural and political interaction. Van Schewick identified four key factors underlying the Internet's success, all of which must be present:[5]

- Users get to choose which applications they want to use, without influence by the network providers.
- Innovation on the network does not require permission from the network providers.
- The network itself is blind to application or use. It doesn't know or care how it is used.
- The costs of innovation on the network are low.

We can see that these four factors were the foundation of GPS's success. The same is true of roads and electric and water utilities. End users of GPS (or roads, electricity, or water) can choose any device (or vehicle, lighting fixture, or dishwasher) they want. The innovating peers did not have to ask the U.S. government for permission. You don't need permission to receive the signals transmitted by the GPS satellites. And the cost of building a new GPS application is so low that even high school students can do it. The Peers Inc framework, and its success, stems from these same four factors, with some minor variation.

User choice. Of course, all users or potential users get to choose which applications they want (this is the free market at work). I can choose to put Lyft or Uber—or both—onto my smartphone. I can say no to a lift from any specific driver. This is critical not just to protect user choice but also to protect the potential for new applications. Peers providing services will stop participating if they think their potential for success, for fair treatment, is rigged from the outset. And this is why Mohammed, an Uber driver, told me he switched from working for a black car service to working for Uber: "I know I will get the call because I'm the closest car, not because I have seniority or am a friend of the dispatcher." Similarly, we talked in Chapter 6 about the concerns of the small lenders on Lending Club and Prosper, worried that their chances at the best loans would be diminished if the platforms were optimized for the institutional investors.

No permission. As noted, peer participation is on an opt-in basis. The impetus comes from the individuals or small companies themselves. Anyone can create a Twitter or Facebook account. Anyone can recommend code changes on Drupal. Some platforms do offer some well-defined constraints (Zipcar requires a clean driving record without any moving violations in the last three years, for example). Regulators who seek to regulate at the individual peer level (for Uber, Lyft, or Airbnb) should really target their regulatory efforts at the platform, not the peer level, in order to maximize the potential for participation. Instead of requiring every host or driver to fill out forms and get certified, this kind of oversight is better done at the platform level.

Low cost. The Peers Inc emphasis on leveraging excess capacity always makes participating very low-cost.

Application blindness. In Chapter 6 we talked about the range of possibilities when shaping a platform, from constrained to completely open, and how this defined how much innovation could happen. Right now, the Internet and GPS are wholly open platforms. It is this openness that has made for the infinite variation in applications. But some Inc platforms don't want a lot of variation or creativity or innovation, and so they constrain the types of participation possible. Prosper wants to make loans to creditworthy borrowers. Uber and Lyft want safe drivers with clean cars. Twitter, on the other hand, doesn't much care what you do with those 140 characters.

The French precursor to the Internet was called Minitel and was widely used. It didn't share these key characteristics. You needed a license to publish on it, and it was in every way a corporate and government walled garden. Almost nothing culturally interesting came from it. Certainly the enormous vitality, freedom, and openness of the Internet as we know it was nowhere to be found: it was not the computer networks but the openness that enabled the breakthroughs we have seen.[6]

When might it be a good idea for government to constrain its platforms? First, when they produce bad side effects and negative externalities such as pollution or congestion. None of us incur any penalty for hopping onto a federal highway (a platform on which we are the participants) during rush hour alone in our gas-guzzling, emissions-belching car, rather than taking the trouble to carpool or choosing a more fuel-efficient car that produces fewer fine particulates (directly related to many kinds of health problems). The government should be putting a price on congestion and pollution so that we take these into account when we decide how and when to travel, and so that we pay our fair share of the problems created that government now picks up the tab for. Second, government should constrain the asset when it can be used up or can't be shared effectively at the same time (called "rivalrous goods" in economic parlance). During droughts, for example, the government does this, banning the watering of lawns or the filling of swimming pools. Sometimes, in cities with very poor infrastructure, the government constrains use by only providing electricity or water at certain times during the day (as is done in the Gaza Strip). But for resources that are non-rivalrous and don't have negative externalities—GPS, the Internet, open data, open spectrum, and open devices, to give a few examples—governments have every reason (and the wherewithal) to offer up as many wide-open platforms as possible. These open platforms maximize the potential for participation and therefore deliver maximum innovation and maximum economic output. Government platforms should be based on van Schewick's four factors. Doing otherwise will directly reduce the utility of the platform, the innovation that follows from it, and the resulting economic activity.

In 2010 I was invited to be part of the secretary of commerce's newly created National Advisory Council for Innovation and Entrepreneurship. At the first meeting, Gary Locke, then secretary of commerce, opened the meeting with questions about what could be done to boost entrepreneurship in America. What more could the private sector do? What could the public sector do to help? And what were the opportunities for public-private partnerships? Seated around the conference room's long table were more than a dozen of my colleagues, newly appointed like myself. We were university presidents, venture capitalists, and entrepreneurs. Senior staffers and policy advisors from the Department of Commerce and the White House formed a concentric circle behind us.

There was just one problem: one significant sector was missing from the conversation. "What about the people?" I wanted to shout. "Why aren't we talking about the power of people to ignite and execute game-changing innovation?" As I wrote in my recommendation to the committee, way back in 2010: "Discussions about public sector or private sector solutions miss the power and potential of the 'people sector.' The Internet, wireless, and smartphones have been key tools in unleashing the potential of people. Open data, open devices, open radio will further accelerate it. 'People-powered' companies provide a speed and scale unthinkable in traditional business that will be required to meet the world's pressing problems."

One of my primary recommendations was to make "open" the default for federal technology procurements, rather than the de facto "closed proprietary" status quo. Proprietary systems have secret languages and secret rules, locking the government into an ongoing and expensive relationship with vendors. Collaborators can play in the proprietary space only if they have been invited in, have bought the certified stuff, use the product only in the recommended way, or have been trained based on vetted protocols. Ideas for new games or new ways to play the old games are unwelcome, not listened to, and impossible to incorporate. Examples of life stifled by the closed proprietary regime abound. A nice and irritating example that many will recognize is that for many years you had to throw away your "locked" cell phone and buy a new one if you wanted to change carriers.

In September 2014, the UK National Health Service (NHS)—the fourth-largest employer in the world after Walmart and the Indian and Chinese armies—got it right. They started using open-source software called noSQL to run their main secure patient database and messaging platform, named Spine.[7] Spine keeps all the nonclinical information for the 65 million people in Britain who rely on NHS.

The associated messaging service processes 1,300 messages a second in support of the database. The Health and Social Care Information Center (HSCIC), which runs the system for NHS, used to use Oracle for Spine. While it is yet too early to validate the claims, the new vendor says that the open-source software will be up to two times cheaper than the proprietary Oracle, and the associated infrastructure will cost just 5 percent of what the old one did. HSCIC is also hoping that its own local engineers will be able to fix problems themselves more quickly and cheaply, since they have access to the code. Sadly, the United States' Healthcare.gov database—supporting the needs of 94 million people—chose Oracle, with the associated cost and slow, closed, proprietary, and expensive means of addressing problems.

Open standards give us the ability to evolve over time.[8] Once we flip closed to open, we unlock the door to excess capacity. Once we move from closed to open platforms, new peers can quickly hook in and start improving things. Sure, proprietary systems can evolve, but the speed of evolution depends entirely on competitive pressures. No competition, no evolution. Most government contracts come with long lives: three-, five-, ten-, and even ninety-nine-year terms (to an Australian and Spanish consortium to operate and maintain the Chicago Skyway in exchange for keeping all the toll revenue). Why bother to innovate during the first seven years of a ten-year contract? Steve Crocker, one of the Internet's founding fathers, wrote a really wonderful piece for the *New York Times* that describes how the Internet's open standards were able to evolve over time. As he told me, "We had no idea when we started [forty years ago] that this is where we'd end up." Of course, who among us can predict the future? Open standards invite and encourage participation, variation, and evolution. Privately Steve wrote me: "Open standards become particularly important when they enable new products and services to be built on top of existing ones. Openness is not just about enabling others to build the same products and services and compete directly. It's also about enabling huge vistas of new inventions that bring the enormous expansion and payoff from new technologies." A friend offered a simple test: "If you think this is the final and best version, buy the closed proprietary system. If you think it will continue to evolve over time, go open."

Here's Steve's penultimate paragraph from his *Times* op-ed celebrating the Internet's fortieth anniversary: "As we rebuild our economy, I do hope we keep in mind the value of openness, especially in industries that have rarely had it. Whether it's in health care reform or energy innovation [or transportation!], the largest payoffs will come . . . from the huge vistas we open up for others to explore."

During the Obama administration, the United States has made great progress toward increasing openness. Aneesh Chopra, the country's first chief technology officer (responsible for government technology development), made open-source and open-standards technology procurement the norm. And as noted earlier, Vivek Kundra, the United States' first chief information officer (responsible for accessing and processing data), put into motion Data.gov, the repository for U.S. government data sets. Governments around the world now have formal recommendations, and sometimes laws, requiring open standards to ensure interoperability within governments, and between government and the governed.

In 2013, the consulting firm McKinsey published a study on the value of open data. It picks up on all three components I've identified as key to the benefits of a Peers Inc model. The study notes that "open data [is] a highly cost-effective source"; that's because it is leveraging excess capacity. It can deliver billions of dollars in potential annual value specifically because the data have been made "more 'liquid' (open, widely available, and in shareable formats)"—that is, turned into platforms for participation. Finally, for open data to "realize [its] value potential," "a vibrant ecosystem of developers will be necessary"—these are the participating peers. The report is effusive, noting that the best opportunities lie in seven sectors. In education, open data could enable approximately $890 billion to $1.2 trillion in value annually, with the largest potential benefit resulting from "identifying the most effective strategies and tools for teaching specific skills and knowledge" (think back to Peers Inc Miracle #2, tapping into exponential learning). In transportation, open data can reduce travel times, improve the efficiency of public transit and freight operations, and prioritize infrastructure improvements, for a value of $720 billion to $920 billion per year. In electricity, the value is produced by providing consumers and businesses with much finer detail about their own use, together with comparisons and benchmarks with their peer groups, resulting in as much as $340 billion to $580 billion in savings annually. Consumer products, health care, consumer finance, and oil and gas sectors bring the total to seven sectors and a potential $3 billion in annual value.

There is much more that governments should do beyond open data and open source. We need more open radio spectrum—consider the innovation on and explosion of uses for Wi-Fi in the tiny slices of spectrum the U.S. government has left free and open. We should open up more government-funded intellectual property. And outside of the technology realm, we should require that government procurements of schools, post offices, and government buildings ensure that the associated theaters, playgrounds, gyms, and parking be accessible to the greater community when they are idle. I've been in many state-of-the-art elementary school auditoriums that go unused 360 days a year, inaccessible to the surrounding town because use requires a "security detail" or passing through too many school hallways to get to the actual theater. If we want to build a better, more innovative, entrepreneurial, and adaptive future, we need these valuable low-cost resources to be made open, usefully organized on platforms.

From a taxpayer perspective, this all makes sense. Requiring open standards and Internet protocols expands the reach and value of taxpayer dollars. It means that our other investments—cell phones, personal computers, even plug-in hybrid cars—will one day be able to connect and interoperate. It means that innovators and business will be able to improve on past procurements and put this new infrastructure to work in other areas of the economy. There is so much sense in governments requiring as much openness as possible that the old way of doing things looks almost criminal. I can just imagine an angry headline from the future: "Using Public Dollars to Build Proprietary Systems?"

GOVERNMENT AS A PROTECTOR, CHAMPION, AND REGULATOR FOR THE PEOPLE

So far, my focus in this chapter has been on how to encourage, enable, and enhance the economic development of platforms: open things up, reduce interference, don't require permission, and maximize potential. The examples of co-creators working feverishly on these platforms have run the full gamut of possibility: companies (as in the GPS or open data context), devices (as in WhatsApp), and individuals (with their ability to play endlessly with open data). But now is the time to focus only on peers who are individuals. As more and more companies switch over to the Peers Inc structure, more and more people will become freelancers, working for themselves. What are the near-term and long-term implications for them?

Andrew Leonard, a business and technology journalist writing for *Salon* and *Wired*, has raised a widespread concern about the sharing economy: "The services built on top of these [platform] technologies become especially lucrative when their creators figure out ways to avoid taxes or safety regulations or insurance costs that their old-economy, non-'sharing' competitors are stuck with."[9] Leonard's assessment seems very straightforward, but it obscures the complexity that lies underneath. Who exactly are the "creators" avoiding taxes, safety regulations, and insurance? We know these services are being co-created. In the Peers Inc world, we have both big and small entities working together to produce the service, and individuals are both self-employed and also working under rules set by the platform. As Brian Chesky, CEO of Airbnb, said to me one day, "There are laws for people and there are laws for business, but this is a new category, a third category, people as businesses. Hosts are micro-entrepreneurs and there are no laws written for micro-entrepreneurs." Is this true?

The unfolding war between the app-based driving services, taxi drivers, their unions, and city governments illustrates the complexity of the regulatory situation. One sunny day in June 2014, 5,000 London taxi drivers (says Transport for London, the regulator, while the organizers claim 12,000) halted traffic in Trafalgar Square for hours to protest the unregulated Uber service.[10] Taxi drivers in Paris, Berlin, Madrid, and Rio de Janeiro mounted similar though smaller slowdowns, parking their vehicles in major intersections and immobilizing central business districts. The fight was between those who were abiding by the rules (the London cabbies) against those who had decided the rules no longer made sense and had gone off the grid (to drive unregulated for Uber). The congestion and media reporting were a boon to Uber. They reported nine times the number of app downloads between midnight and noon on the Wednesday of the London strike, compared to the same time period the week earlier. As they say, any press is good press.

If you are a law-abiding regulated and certified taxi driver, you have every right to be incensed by the enormous number of trips the unregulated services are siphoning off. The regulations you have to abide by control how, when, in what, and where you can earn a living. Unfortunately, some of these regulations are pointless and out-dated, serving the best interests of no one, or are blatantly anti-competitive, existing solely to prevent competition. What happens when the speed of innovation outstrips the pace of regulation?

Enter Dan Doney, chief innovation officer of the Defense Intelligence Agency, who explained this to me in a way I hadn't understood before. I met Dan when I was at the Aspen Institute in the summer of 2014. We were together in a roundtable of a dozen or so professionals with diverse sector expertise. One person would lead off a topic with a ten-minute exposition (I did the leading for two sessions for two roundtables with the Peers Inc thesis), and then we'd have a passionate roundtable discussion that tended to be dominated by a few people and featured lots of interruptions. As the discussions petered out, Dan would raise his name card into the polite vertical I-have-something-to-contribute position. In his tidy khaki pants and button-down shirt, he'd quietly say when called upon, "Let me draw a graph you might find interesting."

His graph links the characteristics of a platform, civil society, and IT governance. It showed me clearly what happens when we overregulate. Regulations (platform structure, laws, specifications) are designed to increase collective benefit but do so at the expense

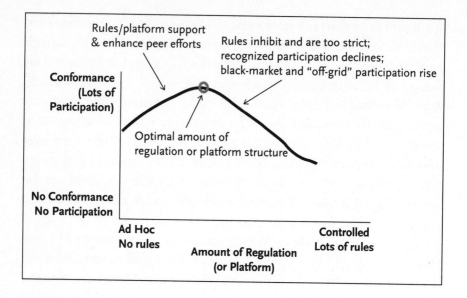

of individual freedom. For example, a speed limit is a regulation designed to enhance public safety. If a speed limit is too low (55 miles per hour on a desert highway, for example), few conform due to the mismatch between perceived benefit of the limit and the cost of increased travel time. Ironically, those who do conform to the limit may present a greater public safety risk due to a mismatch with the prevailing speed. Past a certain point, a more restrictive speed limit will cause a decrease in collective benefit. On Dan's graph, there is an optimal point: the exact right amount of organizing control (regulation, platform structure) where individual and collective interests are aligned. The whole is greater than the sum of the parts. People choose to conform (participate) for their own sake or at least for the benefit of the whole. But past this point, individual and collective interests begin to compete. In IT governance, this is the point at which the enterprise (the government, the business, the institution) competes against mission delivery (its own goals). As I looked at the graph, it became evident: having some rules (some structure) encourages me to participate, but having too many rules (too much structure) discourages me.

Taxi regulations are full of outdated rules; hence the success of Uber and Lyft. Washington, D.C.'s Taxicab Commission chairman, Ron Linton, said that "Uber's service is illegal because its drivers do not give passengers a receipt as they exit."[11] That's true only if you define a receipt as a piece of paper. Everyone who uses these services pays by credit card from a preestablished online account and receives an email receipt in real time, pretty much as they close the door of the vehicle. In Miami, no limousine can legally respond to a call in less than fifteen minutes, in order to protect the market for cabs you hail in the street. In New York City until very recently, it was illegal to measure distance for fares with anything other than the one city-approved device, something that might have made sense before the existence of smartphones and GPS (not approved). London started regulating hackneys (the legal word to describe the combination of driver plus conveyance for hire) in 1636—almost four hundred years ago![12] The number of carriages was limited to fifty back then. Since 1865, the city has required that all drivers pass "the Knowledge," a test that ensures they actually know their way around London—all the streets, all the sights, all the best routes. This raised the status of the cabbie profession (relative to what is in America, for example), and drivers take great pride in their knowledge. The millions of London passengers who have since traveled efficiently from point A to point B are surely appreciative. Today, "[Knowledge] applicants will usually need at least twelve 'appearances' (attempts at the final test), after preparation averaging 34 months, to pass the examination."[13] Today, of course, we also have GPS and smartphone apps. The taxi drivers protesting that June in London should really have been protesting against their taxi licensing commissions for having such a costly—and outdated—requirement.

As Dan pointed out to me, "Regulators think that by exerting more control, they will increase compliance. At some point, the opposite is true, a point you may see as counterintuitive. The heavy-handed rule maker is fighting the participants." At a certain point many will choose to break the rules and go off the grid—like the subset of Uber drivers who were formerly part of the regulated industry.

Dan continues, "At this point, the benefits of all the rules are lost, and best practices can't spread, as they are hidden from central authority (or a platform). This is known as 'shadow IT' in the tech world, and as 'black markets' in economic terms. Worse still, these limits constrain solution possibilities, impacting creativity, innovation, and agility." The graph is equally instructive if we use it to think about how much structure to use in platform building, as discussed in Chapter 6. Structure is necessary to derive benefit. If it doesn't offer structure, it isn't a platform and isn't helping organize things. That said, the more structure (constraint), the fewer people will be interested in using it. As anyone who has designed forms and measured participation knows: every field you add causes more people to drop out.

Most of the mismatches between regulations and today's reality that I've described here result from new technologies that make the old ways—which once made sense—obsolete now. Government regulations were built over decades to fit the dominant framework of corporate employer and employee. Insurance, housing and zoning regulations, labor and safety laws, and our entire tax code were built in response to needs of the times and were based on some clear distinctions that today are no longer so clear. When we had lots of small-scale industry that was noisy and polluting, we developed zoning laws to appropriately separate these activities from residential areas. When, after World War II employment transitioned from small local efforts to increasingly large offices, factories, and retailers, there was less need to protect smaller, more independent efforts and more need to protect the rights of workers now lost in the rise of multinationals. But today more work is being conducted productively and effectively by smaller entities and in a diverse range of locations. We have entered a blurry era in which there's no sharp line to be drawn between what is and isn't corporate or private. Technology has opened up a whole new world of sharing of assets, time, and skills, all empowered by platforms. While government and regulation move slowly, the pace of innovation on platforms is quick.

Many platforms were built precisely for this purpose: to make it easy to experiment, adapt, and evolve. And it is one of the reasons we love them and value them and want to encourage them—because they match today's pace of change. Entrepreneurs can leverage the Internet, Wi-Fi, smartphones, GPS, global maps, electronic payment systems, and the marketing reach of the Apple app store, and presto: Uber, Lyft, Sidecar, Hailo, and other competitors from around the world exist. Speaking as an entrepreneur, I feel like some rules just shouldn't be applied until the new company has reached some critical mass. As Michael Pollan pointed out in *The Omnivore's Dilemma*, regulations developed for factory farms have made it impossible for small farmers to slaughter animals for sale. Food and Drug Administration requirements include things like a separate bathroom for exclusive use of their inspectors. Pollan makes the point that proximity and scale change the nature of the relationship between producer and consumer. Unlike the factory slaughterhouses, those who purchase meat from small-scale providers can see where the animals were slaughtered, know people who have purchased the meat, and have direct and obvious recourse should there be a problem. Small entrepreneurs have to be incredibly responsive to their consumers, even individual ones. Weighing down these specks of economic activity that are just barely able to cobble together the means to get started feels like overkill. Once they have traction and a transactional volume that can produce enough negative outcomes to bother regulating, yes, they should be held to higher standards. I'm being overly broad here, and the devil is in the details, but I'm convinced we can find a way to regulate with a more fine-grained approach that is appropriate to the risk.

The taxi lobby likes to paint the unlicensed vehicles and their uncertified drivers as unsafe. But if we look more objectively, we find three other mechanisms that are doing the task.

- First, regulations targeted at protecting individuals already exist and come into play. In many states, every car is required to pass a safety inspection every year or two.
- Second, the platforms have established their own quality and safety standards in response to consumer demand. In the United States, Uber, Lyft, and Sidecar do a real-time

background driving check on their drivers, excluding those with bad records (just as Zipcar does), and run criminal background checks as well.

- Third, and perhaps most significant, these platforms have a new policing mechanism to tap: the rating and comment fields, which apply to both the peer-supply and peer-demand sides of the transactions. Instead of a one-time government check, passengers rate drivers (and drivers rate passengers) after each trip, giving continuous feedback that appears in real time on the driver's (and passenger's) profile. Low ratings (such as for rudeness, bad driving, or lack of street knowledge) can cause drivers to be dropped from the service.[14] When has a taxi business ever done that?

Airbnb finds itself in the same situation as Lyft and Uber with respect to the clash between regulation targeted toward industry and Airbnb's small-scale provision of services. Should city governments regulate Airbnb or the homeowners? Should a bedroom rented on Airbnb be required to have the same sprinkler system as a four-hundred-room hotel? Aren't existing fire codes, created to protect families sleeping in their homes, sufficient to protect visitors also sleeping there? How does the risk of fire in an Airbnb lodging compare to the risk of fire in a large hotel, and if there is a difference in risk, does that increase the need for government oversight? Harkening back to Barbara van Schewick's principles, we know that regulators should err on the side of lightening the load for the peers, to let participation be permissionless, and to push regulation up to the platform where that makes sense. "I want to live in a world where people can become entrepreneurs or micro-entrepreneurs, and if we can lower the friction and inspire them to do that, especially in an economy like today, this is the promise of the sharing economy," said Brian Chesky, Airbnb CEO. For regulators, he has a request: "Don't kill something wonderful before knowing what it is."[15]

While I think existing laws cover car safety and residential fire safety at these smallest units, if you were a passenger in or the owner of a car used for an UberX, Lyft, or Sidecar trip, you did have a valid reason to be unhappy. For months (in fact, for well over a year), each trip was completed with totally inadequate insurance. Some regulations do protect the best interests of the consumer and the worker, and these companies were ignoring them. I pin the blame on the platforms, not the peers. Car accidents will definitely happen given enough miles traveled; I have experienced more than my share. The UberX, Lyft, and Sidecar platforms incorrectly assured the drivers that their personal car insurance would cover these remunerated (meaning they were now considered commercial) trips; in fact, drivers and passengers would be uninsured in worst-case calamities. Today, these companies have all scrambled to get adequate insurance from recalcitrant insurers. Maybe the better adjective, ironically, is "risk-averse" insurers. My experience with Zipcar, GoLoco, and Buzzcar is that insurance companies don't like to insure things with which they have no experience. It took me months (and sometimes years) of persuasive cajoling to get insurers to write affordable policies to meet my newfangled needs. Brian Chesky said, "There are no laws written for micro-entrepreneurs." I think what he had in mind when he said that was right-sizing regulations surrounding the provision of service. I see it in another light. We need to bolster the rights and protections afforded to these micro-entrepreneurs. Those driving their cars without adequate insurance coverage were misled by the platform to the benefit of the platform and the detriment of the peer.

Once upon a time, this country, like every country, had a much larger informal economy. As wealthy countries transitioned from an agricultural economy to an industrial one, they regulated away most of the informal economy, which is now much smaller and hidden. Governments see the informal economy as unsafe, unreliable, and just plain chaotic. Productivity gains and the ensuing rise in standard of living came with the purchase of capital assets—machines, tools, factories—that only companies could afford. It made sense to favor this kind of productivity. Poor countries that still have a large informal economy strive to do the same in their central business districts, ridding their cities and economy of this uncontrollable blight and pushing the informal economy to the edges and slums, where it remains an important part of the total economy. The Peers Inc structure transforms the economic logic and this once-sound societal-benefits argument. Remember, platforms give individuals the power of the corporation at very affordable prices (often for free). Productivity and quality-of-life gains are now not necessarily achieved only through government support of the big and wealthy. Peers now have access to the means of production themselves. We don't have to stifle the informal economy, because platforms organize, improve quality, and even self-regulate. In Chapter 10, I profile G-Auto, an example of an Indian company that is cleaning up the disorganized auto rickshaw market.

But for all that, the rise of the micro-entrepreneur requires reworking and rethinking laws that protect them and their rights to earn a living wage and to work in a safe and healthy environment. Is the Peers Inc paradigm just another way to outsource labor? The desire to deny employee status is a challenge worldwide. Walmart has famously limited staff hours in order to define workers as part-time contractors and not employees eligible for certain types of benefits. And as recently as August 2014, a federal court of appeals ruled that FedEx's 2,300 California delivery drivers were in fact employees and not independent contractors. Prior to the ruling, because these workers were not technically employees, FedEx avoided paying millions in payroll taxes. And because they were not employees, FedEx didn't need to meet the standards imposed by fair-labor laws, such as minimum wage, overtime, or family medical leave provisions. The difference between independent contractor and employee will mean hundreds of millions of dollars to FedEx. And on the difference between contractor and employee hinges the applicability (or not) of worker protection laws that have built up over the last hundred years.

According to the Internal Revenue Service, "employees" get benefits, expect a long-term relationship with the employer, and perform work that is a key aspect of the business. Peers do all of this but don't get benefits. Is this a bum rap? Let's look a little closer.

Employers control things such as how a worker is paid and whether expenses are reimbursed, and they provide the tools required to get the job done. Here we find murkiness. Many peer platforms do set rates, like the peer taxi services and TaskRabbit. And how exactly does one define "tool" today? A significant part of the platform's purpose is to provide access to the tools that make production vastly simpler and easier.

Employers control what the worker does and how the worker does it. Quality constraints and standards for participation enacted by the platform (be a good driver, maintain a good rating) make it feel like platforms could in some circumstances actually be exercising a lot of control around work production. But there is a key defining distinction. For any and every engagement with the platform, peers' participation is wholly up to them. It is opt-in, each and every time. Both Uber and Task Rabbit have at times compelled their drivers or taskers to accept certain jobs, and therefore they are likely crossing the legal line back into employer status. Autonomy and independence are what distinguish Peers Inc from franchises.

Peers Inc is the atomization of the company. From a government perspective, a primary benefit is that people can now create their own jobs. In Chapter 4 I introduced the idea of peer power and the many benefits of this new way of working, but it is time to look hard at the potential downsides of this economic model. Just as in the current economy—I think of the FedEx case and the Walmart workers—there is great potential for sidestepping fair-wage and labor laws. I think of the new Uber driver who purchased his car through a lease with Uber so that he could drive a new vehicle appropriately insured for the task, but who then received a single four-star rating (out of five stars, which hardly seems bad), which pushed his average below the required 4.6 stars and means that he is summarily excluded from the platform. No more passengers to pick up, but still with $400 monthly lease payments, and no recourse with Uber. And just like in the industrial economy, there will be too many people vying for the lowest-skill jobs in this new collaborative economy. We will have too many freelance taxi drivers, too many places to stay, too many errand runners, and wages will fall. The wages of higher-skilled laborers, whose work doesn't need to be done locally, are also at risk. Platforms facilitate globalization, leveling wages around the world. The engineers, graphic designers, editors, and architects in Delhi will be competing with those in Detroit, Dubai, and Durban. And finally there are the passion jobs, in which artists, musicians, and writers now work for free or almost free on platforms that expose their work (all those blogs, crowd-sourced news sites, and artist marketplaces). These last are putting enormous pressure on career professionals to retain full-time jobs.

Thirty-four percent of the U.S. workforce, 53 million Americans, are working as freelancers. "Nearly eight in ten (77%) freelancers said they make the same or more money than they did before they started freelancing—indicating that freelancing can be an even more lucrative career path than traditional jobs. In fact, more than four in ten (42%) said they already make more than before they started freelancing."[16] The Peers Inc model, with its ruthless efficiency of each entity sticking to what it does best, is speeding up the transition to an independent workforce. So what's a government to do when faced with the explosion of Peers Inc efforts?

RECOMMENDATIONS FOR SUPPORTING THE PEERS

First, do no harm. Permit the small-scale experiments to happen. We need trials. New platforms that succeed and become big enough should be examined more closely, remembering that the tools needed to oversee and protect the public good are radically different from what they were in the nineteenth century. If regulation is necessary, the first instinct should be to put pressure on the platforms, preserving the fluidity of the peer economy. Better to tell taxi-like platforms what needs to be done than to require each and every participating peer to ask the government for permission. However, there is a nuance to this recommendation. Regulators also need to remember that platforms don't and can't control the peers—this is the key defining positive and negative of their position.

In 2011, U.S. lawmakers put forth two bills—the PROTECT IP Act (PIPA), introduced in May, and the Stop Online Piracy Act (SOPA), introduced in October—that would have required U.S. websites (the platforms) to police user-generated content (from the peers) for copyright and intellectual property infringement. The penalty for permitting illegal content to appear would be immediate shutdown of the platforms—removing them from browsers and search engines, and disabling credit card processing and advertising revenues. Action against the two bills gained momentum in December of that year. It continued into 2012 and culminated in a coordinated action when 115,000 websites joined in the protest, citing inability to control the peers. The English-language version of Wikipedia, one of the most trafficked sites on the Web, was the most radical, going dark for the day. More than 3 million people emailed Congress, 4.5 million signed a petition organized by Google, Twitter recorded at least 2.4 million SOPA-related tweets, and lawmakers reported that more than 10 million voters contacted them to protest the bills. On January 20, 2012, the bills died. While SOPA/PIPA were misguided, platforms are the right locus for requirements (like negotiating insurance for independent taxi drivers) that benefit from scale (such as the lower costs that come from collective buying power) and from smoothing across large populations (such as the promise of risk mitigation across a large group).

Second, governments should make tax and regulatory compliance easy and workable for both parties (unlike SOPA and PIPA, in which the penalty far outweighed the crime, quite counter to Elinor Ostrom's rules 2 through 7, described in Chapter 6). As should be clear by now, the wealth and benefits of the platform and of the peers are profoundly tied together. Without the peers, the platforms are like old ghost towns, without value. Without the platforms, the peers cannot be as productive, nor can they contribute their ingenuity and learning to the whole. Both sides need to contribute to these social benefits. Harking back to Dan Doney's graph, governments need to provide peers with a simple way to be part of the formal recognized economy and pay their share of taxes. We must minimize regulations that might discourage them from joining the mainstream economy, and platforms need to make it easy to pay the appropriate taxes. Peerby, BlaBlaCar, Airbnb, and others operating in countries where a value added tax (VAT) is required apply this lesson. There has been a lot of controversy over Airbnb host payments of hotel taxes. On its website, Airbnb counsels its hosts to pay them where they are applicable, and in some cities the platform has made agreements to apply this tax to the guest's bill. As of October 1, 2014, Airbnb has been applying the 14 percent hotel tax to all stays in San Francisco. The city and Airbnb anticipate this will add $11 million a year to the city's tax base.

Third, my boldest policy recommendation as far as the United States is concerned is that labor standards, worker's compensation insurance, health benefits, sick leave, vacation time, parental leave, pensions, disability, and child care rights need to be granted to every citizen as a right, as is the case today in many European countries. Some people will work full-time on one platform, while others will work simultaneously on six different platforms. In all cases they are self-employed and so are not covered by the rights and benefits that society has agreed ought to come with employment. As the number of autonomous workers grows—and the 53 million Americans today considering themselves freelancers is a very hefty number—it no longer makes sense to tie benefits to full-time employment. In fact, the reverse is true. We need to make sure that these benefits are available to everyone, despite fragmented sources of income.

Lastly, government needs to protect these collaborating peers with a platform-independent contractor's bill of rights. Successful platforms have effectively become common pool resources: the platform is producing a stream of benefits to the peers who are reliant upon it. At a minimum, peers collaborating on these platforms should be able to own, control, and remove their own data. Rules for engagement with the platform should be spelled out in understandable ways (not buried in terms-of-service agreements), equitably applied, and changeable only with adequate notice. The Apple Store's treatment of Simon Dawlat's AppGratis by suddenly changing the rules of engagement should be stopped. A sentence I read in a paper exploring value sharing in user-generated content contained this sentence, which is wholly applicable to this situation: "The architecture of participation sometimes turns into an architecture of exploitation."[17]

There should be some recourse for the driver who leased a car from Uber and was then banned by the company from using the platform. For the GPS platform, the Department of Defense was required by law to "maintain a Standard Positioning Service (as defined in the federal radio navigation plan and the standard positioning service signal specification) that will be available on a continuous, worldwide basis." If platforms don't want to abide by a government-enforced contractor's bill of rights, they can self-regulate by giving power back to the peers, as discussed in Chapter 6. Remember that the end-state for a long-lived platform is power parity, achieved through data portability and privacy, increased transparency in internal rules and processes, and a forum for peer advocacy and sharing of knowledge. The ultimate in power sharing is to apply Ostrom's principles, giving peers the power to establish their own rules. Platforms that do right by their peers will naturally institute these rules, since they know that peer participation is voluntary and they need to treat them well.

EIGHT

Embracing the Change

Evolving Legacy Institutions

THE STANDARD & POOR'S 500 lists the five hundred most valuable companies in the United States, based on market capitalization. Dick Foster, a retired McKinsey consultant, studied their average life span.[1] It is a sobering tale that reminds us just how fast-paced business innovation has become. In 1937, the average tenure of companies on the list was seventy-five years. By 1960, it was sixty-one years. In 1980, thirty-seven years. In 2000, twenty-six years. Today, it is an average of fifteen years.

Innovate and adapt, or disappear. That disappearance might be the result of bankruptcy, or it might come about because of acquisition. In either case, the company is no longer its own master.

If the above incites fear, the following will trigger greed. Recent research used the last forty years of financial data for the S&P 500 to examine how business models have evolved over time, and which were the most successful. The researchers compared four business models, Asset Builders, Service Providers, Technology Creators, and Network Orchestrators, which closely mirror Peers Inc. Their findings were published in the *Harvard Business Review*: "Our analysis indicates that as of 2013, Network Orchestrators receive valuations two to four times higher, on average, than companies with the other business models . . . we also found that Network Orchestrators outperform companies with other business models on both compound annual growth rate and profit margin."[2]

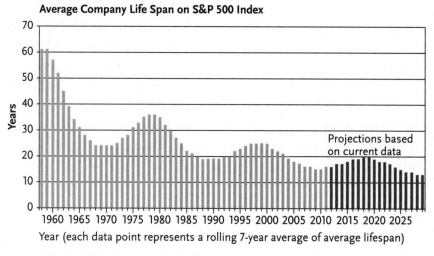

Average Company Life Span on S&P 500 Index

Projections based on current data

Year (each data point represents a rolling 7-year average of average lifespan)

Source: INNOSIGHT/Richard N. Foster/Standard & Poor's

I think life expectancy on this list will continue to decline as the economy switches over to the Peers Inc model. Thereafter, company longevity is likely to increase as platforms get ever larger and more powerful. These institutions, these Incs, will be faster, smarter, and stronger than traditionally organized companies. And if they can manage to pass through the first three phases of controlled kernel, everyone-welcome, and power imbalance, and arrive on the other side, settling into a state of power parity, they could be there for a long time.

Both mainstream analysts and upstart innovators have recognized the power and inevitability of the Peers Inc paradigm. Dan Bieler, a principal analyst on Forrester Research's Business Technology Futures team, writes that "rising customer expectations and faster product life cycles are forcing companies to adapt to a new style of business: 'the collaborative economy.'" Bieler continues, "Collaboration not only connects customers, partners, and employees in the context of a single issue or incident; it can also be a massive driver of innovative new products, stronger business growth, and ultimately even improved social welfare. As a result, companies, industries, and entire economies that used to operate in silos will have to open themselves up and embrace the collaborative economy."[3] Dries Buytaert, the founder of Drupal, has observed that "society is undergoing tremendous change right now—the sharing and collaboration practices of the Internet are extending to transportation (Uber), hotels (Airbnb), financing (Kickstarter, Lending Club), and music services (Spotify). The rise of the collaborative economy, of which the open source community is a part, should be a powerful message for the business community. It is the established, proprietary vendors whose business models are at risk, and not the other way around."[4]

THE OLD INDUSTRIAL APPROACH

Merriam-Webster defines *legacy* without value judgment as "something transmitted by or received from an ancestor or predecessor or from the past." The definition Google offers up includes the meaning when the term is applied to computing: "denoting software or hardware that has been superseded but is difficult to replace because of its wide use." This is where the term picks up some negative connotations. Our lives, world, and economies are all constrained by things that are currently used widely, even as many of those things are inexorably being replaced. So what is holding our institutions back? Legacy. People occupying "C suites"—the CEOs, CFOs, and COOs—have a vested interest (and a lot of assets invested) in doing things the old way, since the highest margins typically come from milking the same old cash cows . . . at least until a competitor kills them.

Institutions have internalized lessons that no longer apply, and they continue to rely on strategies that no longer make sense. They are molded by regulation and cultural forces that themselves are becoming obsolete. Industrialization, followed by automation, has led us to value conformity and uniformity above all else and in every situation. The Peers Inc framework lets us apply that drive with more discretion. The industrial process taught us that tight control delivered the highest precision and quality (something we still want in the manufacturing of things such as smartphones, light bulbs, and refrigerators, and which can be achieved using tools such as Six Sigma). Managers sought to eradicate variation through this centralized control. The bigger the company, the greater the urge to centralize. I remember case studies from my business school strategy classes during the mid-1980s that encouraged an enlightened flexibility. If a centralized company was failing, then it should decentralize! If it was failing and decentralized, then of course it should centralize! Nowhere was there a hint of the idea of distributed networks. Their beauty hadn't yet reached the professors teaching at business schools. Further away still was the understanding that distributed structures scale best of all. This, one of the many lessons the Internet has taught us, had yet to be analyzed by academics and internalized.

All legacy institutions believe deeply in command and control as the right management tool. Command-and-control cultures are extremely risk-averse. The biggest of these companies *know* that the smartest people work for them, and that those people are the *only* ones who really understand the complexities of their business. If innovation or variation manages to find its way in, the corporate culture antibodies swarm in and soon put an end to it. In *Democratizing Innovation*, Eric von Hippel writes, "The ongoing shift of product-development activities from manufacturers to users is painful and difficult for many manufacturers."[5] Most big companies today won't be able to make the transition from value creation based on induced scarcity to value creation based on shared abundance. In the industrial economy, most value is created based on goods and services that are protected by patents, copyrights, and trade secrets and controlled by and accessible only through employees or certified representatives. Such a worldview did (and will for a short while longer) result in profitable businesses. But Peers Inc reveals that we can get much more value out of resources by sharing them, letting them be used more efficiently (slicing and aggregating), and making them available for new value creation (opening them up). We also know that the wide world of diverse peers will deliver more innovation, customization, specialization, localization, co-investment, learning, resilience, and redundancy than will ever be possible with a set number of employees.

CHANGING THE WAY THINGS ARE DONE

I appreciate that openness is frightening. For most people, opening up assets—letting strangers play in your yard—means a loss of control, a loss of quality, and lost value in a hard-won brand. Facebook, Google, Twitter, and Wikipedia succeeded because they realized that the benefits of opening themselves up to engagement by anyone outweighed the problems.

Openness also brings up the free rider problem. "In economics," according to the website Investopedia, "the free rider problem refers to a situation where some individuals in a population either consume more than their fair share of a common resource, or pay less than their fair share of the cost of a common resource."[6] But Nicholas Gruen, an economist who has worked closely with the Australian federal government—most recently on two task forces on innovation and Government 2.0—figured out that for this new class of companies, free rider *opportunities* were much larger than the cost of free rider *problems*. Wikipedia succeeded because Jimmy Wales believed that more people would contribute valuable articles to Wikipedia than would vandalize them. This is the Peers Inc paradigm at work: Opening assets up delivers more value and more innovation than keeping them under lockdown. New ways to address bad actors—reputation and trust systems—do change behavior and minimize negative contributions, as they did for eBay sellers, Airbnb hosts, and Uber drivers, who become more conscientious and professional in response to the potential for bad ratings. Examples of institutional courage to adopt the new rules for value creation abound.

The capacity of the Peers Inc model for generating jaw-dropping value is evident to most executives. When they see a company going from zero to a multibillion-dollar valuation, they can't help but think how it might work for their business. But they face a conundrum. Peers Inc requires the opening up of long-guarded assets (data, patents, know-how, expensive assets) and entrusting these to outsiders with no guarantee of return. And to top it off, Peers Inc's most valuable assets—the peers' talent, creativity, and drive—are the very things that are the least manageable and least predictable. So how do you spark the necessary change when your institution is deeply conventional and has been for decades? Dan Doney (head of innovation at the U.S. Defense Intelligence Agency) explained to me that "virtually everything in a bureaucracy resists change. It is always 'We need to stick to the plan.' But innovation requires creative destruction—that is, the free flow of resources from ideas that are falling behind to new and better ideas. To embrace this principle, an organization must decentralize decision-making, delegating to the edge as much as possible. Our mantra: Start small. Scale fast. Fail cheap." Regardless of whether you are big business or big government, this is sound advice.

Create Pilots out of Edge Cases, Expand with Success

The Defense Intelligence Agency has 17,000 employees, two-thirds of whom are civilians, and a budget of about $4.4 billion a year.[7] Dan sought to establish a platform for innovation reform, focusing internally first, seeking ideas that lay within the organization before attempting to incorporate practices, methods, and capabilities from outside. By surfacing ideas from within, bottom-up, rather than top-down, he created impact quickly and with minimal cost while generating buy-in from a skeptical workforce and management—support that would be needed for the follow-on strategic reform that would come later.

The biggest engine for innovation inside an organization, Doney believes, is the "mission edge": those closest to the institution's customers. DIA's mission edge consists of a workforce responsible for delivery of intelligence products to senior policy makers. Every day, service members in combat roles creatively solve problems at the speed of crisis and conflict. But without supportive models, these solutions don't grow and expand to enterprise best practices. To adapt to the constantly changing needs of customers, who in turn are responding to ever-changing threats, those at DIA's mission edge are the best "feelers" to sense emerging or disruptive trends such as the impact of social media on traditional intelligence activities.

Solutions and practices emerging from edge environments (where the peers are) are often dismissed by the center of the organization, which tends to be caught up in the problems of yesterday. The people and departments responsible for research can come to believe that they have cornered the market on innovation. To counter this, Dan established a small internal innovation fund and process, designed to surface and support ideas and methods developed by the peers closest to the action. The process Dan took within a huge government agency reminds me very much of that used by the vastly smaller Quirky. The platform provides a formal path to convert original ideas and creative practices into broader impacts through presentation, evaluation, and if necessary financial support. A key feature is "crowd refinement," which engages anyone in the workforce interested in triaging and improving emerging ideas. Because it is so public (within the agency, that is), the process of crowd refinement serves some important functions that help head off the anti-change antibodies of big organizations. First, it minimizes the possibility of conflicting initiatives or solving a problem that has already been solved. Second, it aligns the idea creator with an entity that has the means to implement the proposed solution. And lastly, it creates a grassroots movement of supporters vested in the initiative outcome—critical if the change is to be adopted. Ideally, this process of crowd refinement yields organic execution: Participants decide to act on good ideas with no need for management engagement. But the process has a built-in "relief valve." If a significant idea requires more enterprise coordination or commitment than can be mustered through a bottom-up process, it is presented to senior executives representing the breadth of the organization for a crisp up-or-down vote. For ideas that will demand big substantive changes, this ensures that top-level endorsement for reform is on record.

With the creative energy of the workforce unleashed, the DIA's platform-validating victories came quickly. One small idea drove changes to deployment policy that let young military families plan around agency needs, providing the families with a much-improved quality of family life. Another solution that was truly "out-of-the-box thinking," according to Dan, may address a significant national security gap when validated (though he won't give me details). Some ideas that yielded significant impact weren't even really new. Employees suggested the adoption of capabilities that had proven valuable in previous settings. Once identified, they were fielded quickly, yielding major impact without risk. This bottom-up process produced quick wins within the Department of Defense and has given Dan the momentum he needs to introduce more fundamental changes based on models successful outside his organization.

In Chapter 3 we explored the first experiments with open data: Peter Corbett and Vivek Kundra's invention of Apps for X, which exploded around the world. The U.S. Army got its start with the first small step of Apps for the Army, launched in early 2010. "We're building a culture of collaboration among our Army community to encourage smarter, better, and faster technical solutions to meet operational needs," said Army chief information officer Lieutenant General Jeff Sorenson.[8] Reluctant to let the world at large have access to their data catalogues, they opened up the competition only to Army soldiers and civilian personnel. Especially with large employers, this internal action is a safe way to engage a lot of people—significantly more than would have been identified as in-house experts in the old thinking—and prove internally that openness does result in tangible value that outweighs the feared downside. In just seventy-five days, the Army had fifty-three apps. At that time, the average software procurement cycle in the U.S. government was twenty-four months. With Apps for the Army, no security clearances and vetting had been needed; this was truly agile development and rapid deployment.

The Army's pilot of the approach had worked. Just one year later, in 2011, the Army opened up the challenges to the public, hoping to capture both the tech industry and independent developers.[9] And in 2012, the stepwise progression to increased openness continued with the announcement of the Apps Marketplace. Lieutenant General Susan Lawrence, the Army's subsequent chief information officer, described the Marketplace as "the center of Army efforts to radically reduce the time to deliver applications across the force. This prototype is a first step in establishing and exercising new submission and approval processes that will eventually enable Army members, organizations, and third-party developers to release applications for Army-wide distribution."[10] Today, the Army has more than one applications portal, with apps on basic training, uniform guides, bugle calls, medevac protocols, emergency navigation systems, and many more.

GlaxoSmithKline offers up an example of leading with a small "edge case" that doesn't threaten the whole organization. GSK's foray into open innovation is both pragmatic and revolutionary for a big pharmaceutical company. Their rationale for this collaboration is very clearly and narrowly defined, no doubt appeasing any internal naysayers who are opposed to this new open approach. The goal: "To encourage innovation targeting diseases of the developing world—where there is not the same potential commercial return as in developed countries—we have changed the way we think about intellectual property and the way we work with others."[11] Taking aim at neglected tropical diseases such as dengue, rabies, and Chagas disease, as well as malaria and tuberculosis, GSK has opened up some of its own data, patents, and expertise in labs that it is financing collaboratively with other research institutions. The hope is that by working together, "a critical mass of knowledge around neglected diseases" will result in long-overdue progress. GSK takes a page from the FOSS copyright approach: "A prerequisite for granting access to the data is that the researchers agree to put their findings into the public domain, thus encouraging further collaborative research by the scientific community on this challenging disease [malaria]."

Engage Others' Minds by Publishing Problems, Not the Solutions

Sascha Haselmayer is founder and CEO of Citymart, a firm that works with cities to increase their capacity for innovation and entrepreneurship. He tells a tale of two cities—St. Paul, Minnesota, and

Stockholm, Sweden—that provide a black-and-white contrast of the old way of doings things and the new.[12] Both cities wanted to do something for people who are blind.

St. Paul released a detailed RFP for a cool new technology they had learned about. At intersections throughout St. Paul, blind people can find posts with a big button that when pushed will announce the street intersection. The cost for the system? $4.5 million.[13] As Sascha points out, blind people lost alone in a city is a very rare event. But the St. Paul blind community did give the mayor the White Cane Award, to express their thanks for the attention he gave to a group of people whose needs are all too often ignored.

Stockholm had a different strategy. Instead of an RFP in quest of a solution, they announced the problem they wished to solve: *We want to make the blind in our city more independent. What solutions do you propose?* They got many responses, and co-funded the development of a system called e-Adept, integrating various technologies in a co-creation process with the blind. Coincidentally, I experienced a demo of e-Adept myself on a visit to Stockholm, where I was giving a talk. I was culturally, geographically, and linguistically blind since I don't speak Swedish and know nothing at all about the city geography or its public transit system. Using e-Adept on a smartphone, I was able to put in my origin and destination. The app provided me with turn-by-turn directions through the city. I was instructed to cross at crosswalks (unlike my usual jaywalking self); it brought me down into the subway, through pedestrian tunnels to the right train, and then out the other side. A blind Stockholmer said of e-Adept, "This makes me 90 percent less disabled." Price tag: $4.5 million. e-Adept was able to accomplish so much for relatively little because it leveraged people's existing devices and all their embedded capabilities, as well as existing mapping software.

The moral of the comparison between St. Paul and Stockholm is that if cities and companies want to solve a problem, they would be far better off publishing the issue they want to tackle, rather than requesting a specific solution, particularly since the institutions usually have limited expertise in the problem areas. A survey of government procurement agencies found that 68 percent of the time, RFPs and contracts stemmed from word-of-mouth recommendations about the solution. Citymart, which was working closely with the city of Barcelona, wanted to correct that bias. Barcelona had been promoting itself as a destination city to entrepreneurs for years. It seemed clear to Sascha that if cities were going to invest in attracting entrepreneurs, "they should prioritize and invest in companies that solve their own problems."

This is exactly the same strategy that Nick Sinai, deputy chief technology officer in the White House, was describing for what the U.S. government is doing to promote the use of open data. In Chapter 3's discussion of data.gov as a platform for participation, I withheld Nick's last point: "The president has articulated a variety of national priorities—from transforming health care to addressing climate change." That is, the president was specifically prioritizing the problems he wanted to address. Nick continues: "We need to encourage the public's participation in addressing these priorities through a wide variety of open innovation mechanisms, such as grand challenges, crowdsourcing, incentive prizes, and citizen science. We've found that open data combined with these open innovation mechanisms can uncover unanticipated solutions and spur economic growth from the private sector. What is truly exciting is how the private sector is doing all sorts of creative things with open government data." What the White House is doing at a national scale parallels what the city of Barcelona was trying out at a city scale.

Over the course of several years, Barcelona had run twelve open challenges. Hackathons and challenges are absolutely great for unearthing a lot of creative ideas. The cities and companies that sponsor these end up with impressive statistics that they can cite: how many people got engaged, how many ideas were generated, how many apps created, in how little time. In fact, the Apps for Democracy story is an example of this. But idea and prototype generation are a far cry from a robust product or service with a business model that delivers longevity. This gap in the hype had been bothering me for a long time. Citymart and the city of Barcelona looked more closely at that gap—between great idea and dependable service—really analyzing the city procurement process and conducting a survey of 1,000 start-ups. There were two important findings that shaped the next step. First, the city incurs significant procurement costs (time and money) to convert the ideas generated by challenges into actual pilots. And second, innovative ideas are usually generated by small, hungry, focused companies who go on to spend 42 percent of their annual budgets on prospective city clients.

Barcelona's innovative solution was to create a challenge platform that combined open problems with a promise to nurture best ideas through to pilot implementation, with real revenue guarantees. The city wrote the contracts carefully, with milestones, so that failed ideas would fall out without cost to the city. But it also means that successful ones continue straight through. "The combination of challenge plus procurement," according to Sascha, "is saying the city is committed to solving this problem. And they are looking to partner with those most committed to finding a solution. Small start-ups are the most aligned; they specialize in addressing very narrow problems. Big companies go broad." To create the 2014 Barcelona Open Challenge, they found €1 million in funds (which is a drop in the bucket for a city the size of Barcelona) and went to six departments to develop their problem challenges. The six problems included automating the detection of road surface problems, reducing bicycle theft, finding ways to monitor pedestrian traffic flows, creating support systems with the goal of reducing social isolation, incentivizing local commerce through technology applications, and developing tools for digitizing museum collections and archives. Typically RFPs run 150 pages for each procurement. This one was thirty-three pages for all six problems—less than six pages per problem.[14]

The city not only publicized the challenge in the required government procurement outlets but also made use of Barcelona's communications and PR engine. This included ads on buses, in subways—whatever the city had access to. They logged 55,000 views of the online challenge (25,000 within the city, and 30,000 worldwide). The city received 130 submissions from twenty different countries.[15] By "linking the budget to the problem statement," says Sascha, "we moved citizens much closer to the problem." In fact, a number of new businesses were created in the city simply in order to respond to the challenges. The results of Barcelona's Open Challenge are still unfolding, but we know that they will necessarily result in at least six companies with out-of-the-box solutions providing competitively priced solutions needed by the city.

Michael Bloomberg's foundation created a Mayors Challenge (another platform for participation) that was equally open, inviting cities around the world to compete for one €5 million grand prize and four runner-up prizes at €1 million each. Michael Bloomberg is a man committed to improving the quality of life in cities, and he has the resources to play a role in making this happen. One hundred and fifty cities from around the world entered, including Barcelona. The Barcelona entry—to create a digital and community "trust network" for each of its at-risk elderly residents—was one it had received in its own Open Challenge (with its own much smaller prize of ~€180,000). In September 2014 the announcement came: Barcelona had won the grand prize!

Needless to say, Barcelona's winning solution is Peers Inc. Like many countries, Spain's population is aging. One in five residents of Barcelona is over sixty-five (by 2040, one in four will be), with a resulting increase in social isolation. The winning solution will build a platform that creates a new trust network for individuals, comprising family, friends, neighbors, social workers, and volunteers. The platform will organize and facilitate care, making it faster and easier for everyone to communicate and fill gaps in care.[16]

EMBRACE THE CHANGE RATHER THAN FIGHT IT

When peers try to break into an institution's inner sanctum, the institution can choose to embrace the opportunity—or it can choose to aggressively push back. First, two stories of companies that chose to fight peer participation, with unsatisfying effect.

Clay Shirky, a New York University professor and author of *Cognitive Surplus* and *Here Comes Everyone*, tells a story about a small local bakery in Manhattan, with just the one storefront, that was sent a cease-and-desist letter by a major media company. The baker

had acquired a printer that could take any photograph and repro-
duce it as a sugary frosting on a cake: graduation, wedding, and retirement photos, images of Susie on her third birthday, and, yes,
your six-year-old's hand-drawn image of a favorite cartoon character. From the media company's' perspective, this copyright violation
would pollute and spoil its brand, and was unfair usage. The bakery
chose to restrict its images to only an approved set rather than let
people bring in whatever they wanted for reproduction on top of a
cake they were buying. This is not a satisfying answer to a six-year-
old who wants to decorate his own cake however he pleases.

John Hagel, co-chairman for Deloitte's Center for the Edge, told
me a similar story. Back in 2006, a woman from Malaysia who was a
huge fan of IKEA created a website with the URL IKEAhackers.net
and started collecting interesting examples of what people had done
to modify IKEA furniture. Over time, a large community of like-
minded individuals gathered there, exchanging ideas and design
results, and learning from each other. The site grew to such a scale
that the woman, Jules Yap (a pseudonym), left her day job and
started accepting advertising to support her efforts to manage the
site. In the summer of 2014 IKEA issued a cease-and-desist order
insisting that Jules transfer the URL to the company because of infringement of its trademark. After extensive negotiations, it finally
agreed to let Jules keep the URL but insisted that she stop accepting advertising on the site, depriving her of her only source of income. For IKEA's management team, the problems of openness
outweighed the opportunities of openness.

Lego took the exact opposite route. In the late 1990s, its market
share had begun to decline as a new generation of children was attracted to electronic and video games. After unsuccessfully trying to
launch some new products, the company turned to another source of
creative talent—the passionate users of Lego products. In 1999, it
launched Mindstorms, a robotics kit, and soon noticed that a number of users had hacked into the software for the kit. While these
hacks were technically a violation of Lego's copyright, the company
realized that many of the hacks significantly improved on the performance and features of the software. Lego decided to join forces

Photo Credit: Christophe Vidal

with these hackers and provide them with tools and advice to help them pursue their hacking initiatives. As a result, Mindstorms became one of Lego's most successful products. Since then, the company has undertaken a broad range of initiatives to encourage and support hackers who seek to modify and enhance the core Lego product offers.

The sugar printer copyright fight feels like the leading edge of the battles that will be fought as 3-D printers find their way into local markets. Lego, Hasbro (My Little Pony), Disney Princess, and Crockpot have all developed a more future-oriented and productive way to deal with their brand and copyright through Open Brand APIs that let peers print and exploit the brand and share revenue from the result. Here is an example from Christophe Vidal of his 3-D-printed 70-millimeter-tall interpretation of Spitfire, a "sandstone" My Little Pony, as permitted in a licensing agreement between Hasbro and Shapeways, a 3-D printing company.[17] Christophe is a peer producer on Shapeways' online store platform, which is much like Etsy for the broader maker community.

As an industry, 3-D printing is still in its infancy, but it is clear that Peers Inc will necessarily be the organizational paradigm. Companies will provide the 3-D printers, basic materials, and patterns. Peers will deliver on the variation—the source of innovation in printer customization, improvement on materials, new uses, tweaks on standard patterns, and likely new business models. Perhaps most exciting, from an innovation standpoint, is the ability for peers to "send" to one another the precise specifications for physical 3-D objects, enabling very rapid iterative prototyping across great distances.

The natural progression toward increased openness, beyond the licensing of a previously closely held brand asset, is to get rid of that legal protection altogether. Elon Musk—founder of SpaceX, co-founder of PayPal, and currently CEO of Tesla Motors—made just such an announcement in a blog entry on June 12, 2014. "In the spirit of the open source movement, for the advancement of electric vehicle technology," he wrote, Tesla was opening up all its patents. Musk understood that like in FOSS, where it is well appreciated that more minds are better than fewer minds, more rapid innovation demands more access. "If we clear a path to the creation of compelling electric vehicles," he said, "but then lay intellectual property landmines behind us to inhibit others, we are acting in a manner contrary to that goal." Patents were initially created as a means of promoting innovations—if promising technologies and approaches were written down for all to see, they could be quickly licensed and more widely adopted than if the inventor alone tried to expand. Musk's blog notes this: "Maybe [patents] were good long ago, but too often these days they serve merely to stifle progress, entrench the positions of giant corporations." It's true that patents feel particularly important for fragile start-ups trying to demonstrate value and raise capital. Musk recognizes this, but goes on to point out the greater value found in openness:

> We felt compelled to create patents out of concern that the big car companies would copy our technology and then use their massive manufacturing, sales and marketing power to overwhelm Tesla. We couldn't have been more wrong. . . .
>
> We believe that Tesla, other companies making electric cars, and the world would all benefit from a common, rapidly-evolving technology platform.
>
> Technology leadership is not defined by patents, which history has repeatedly shown to be small protection indeed against a determined competitor, but rather by the ability of a company to attract and motivate the world's most talented engineers. We believe that applying the open source philosophy to our patents will strengthen rather than diminish Tesla's position in this regard.[18]

Tesla's share price rose 12 percent in the week following this announcement (a period when there were no other major new announcements from Tesla).

It is worth noting here that IBM, Microsoft, and others have made cross-licensing agreements for their patents. They agree not to litigate over the huge areas where they are each infringing on each other's patent portfolio. This does increase the number of minds that can access and find value in that intellectual property, but that innovation is restricted to the companies that are sharing these patent portfolios. They should take the next step and open them up to all.

John Hagel and his co-chair at the Center for the Edge, John Seely Brown (who is also on Amazon's board and was director of the famed research center Xerox PARC for two decades), offer another way to think about patents. Companies used to build their businesses by monetizing stocks—hard fixed assets like factories and heavy equipment. Hagel and Brown show that *knowledge* stocks—trade secrets, patents, licenses, copyrights, know-how—are depreciating at an accelerated rate because new knowledge in the world at large is increasing at such a rapid rate. It is no longer enough to have some knowledge and rest on your laurels. The world's knowledge will quickly pass you by. Hagel and Brown tell companies that they need to move "from monetizing stocks to monetizing *flows*"—that is, making money on the transactions, the service, the new value creation.[19] So Elon Musk opens to the world the static intellectual property bound up in Tesla's patents, because that is not where the value lies. The value lies in building on that base of knowledge, in engaging the hearts and minds of as many people as possible so that Tesla's best guesses about electric cars and batteries become the foundational standard on which a new industry is built.

Imagine Your Entire Ecosystem to Be Potential Co-creators

When Elon Musk made Tesla's patents open, he didn't know from which corner breakthroughs would come—and he still doesn't know. It may be from competing fledgling electric car companies or from existing car manufacturers in the United States, Europe, or Asia;

from focused engineering PhDs or from a self-taught hobbyist making herself known from some unlikely geography. Peer participation is opt-in and without guarantee. We have to rely on the belief that the diversity of approaches stemming from large numbers of participants will bear fruit.

Sainsbury's, a UK supermarket chain with 161,000 employees and over $36 billion in gross sales, opened itself up for outside assessment and ideas from its economic peers, including its archrival. For five days in September 2013, Sainsbury's put itself under the microscope, with 155 corporate sustainability experts from across business sectors—including a direct competitor—reading and rating the company's sustainability strategy. This was no small thing, given that Sainsbury's has a lot to protect. It holds a 17 percent market share and does 23 million customer transactions a week.[20] It was the first time that a major company had opened up its sustainability strategy for peer review. The process was run by The Crowd, which independently laid out Sainsbury's 20x20 Sustainability program (twenty goals to be achieved by 2020). Through an online appraisal, these peers provided 1,162 ratings and 689 comments. They concurred that Sainsbury's was "significantly" ahead in two out of ten of its self-proclaimed goals: its sustainable strategy for fish resources, and the way it engages with communities and society.

But a gap analysis revealed a lot of room for improvement, particularly in "building a sustainable supply chain" and "engaging customers on sustainability."[21] So Sainsbury's conducted a survey of its customers. Sixty-eight percent said they did care about sustainability issues. Sainsbury's then launched an advertising campaign on the "Value of Values," pairing identical pictures—bananas, cups of tea, ham sandwiches—with the tagline "Same price, different values." One of the bananas and cups of tea were acquired through fair trade practices, the other not, and one ham sandwich was EU-sourced and the other locally sourced within the United Kingdom. In the middle of 2014, Sainsbury's archrival, Tesco, launched a product comparison campaign comparing prices on store-brand items between the two stores, claiming that Sainsbury's was consistently more expensive. Sainsbury's complained to the Advertising Standard

Authority (ASA) that they were not fair comparisons, pitting fair-trade tea against non-fair-trade tea, sustainably sourced salmon against salmon that was not sustainably sourced. The ASA rejected the complaint, saying only price mattered. Sainsbury's then took the unusual step of seeking a High Court review of the ASA's decision. Alex Cole, the head of external affairs at Sainsbury's, wrote in a blog post at the time, "It is in many ways thanks to the wisdom of the crowd, that we decided this is a battle we should take up on behalf of our customers and our suppliers."[22] Sadly, in early November 2014, the ASA returned with a decision against Sainsbury's saying that price, not source or fair trade, was the relevant comparison for most shoppers.[23]

Véronique Laury, the forty-seven-year-old CEO of Castorama, a home improvement business based in France, electrified me when I heard her speak about the strategic vision for her company.[24] She, like Tesla and Sainsbury's, sought to expand the pool of company of collaborators. "In business, we used to talk about being [either] a business-to-business company or being business-to-consumer. These words aren't meaningful anymore. I think the company has to become an H2H company—human to human. That's the future." Her goal was to break down the barriers between Castorama's customers (53 million of them), employees (12,600 of them), and tradespeople, and build an ecosystem among them. Competencies must be exploited, wherever they might be. People working in her stores have expertise, but there are times when customers know more than they do. So, said Laury, "we want them to work together, growing the market, growing the number of people to facilitate sharing, interaction, learning." In retail, Laury said, "we are obsessed by the competition. We hide everything . . . [but] if you want to have any form of leadership, if you want to be the leader, you have to share, because you will get contribution from others."

Her strategy for Castorama, announced from the stage, had six important elements:

- Create a wiki of home improvement solutions.
- Work closely with start-ups and learn from their processes.

- Create a system of skills bartering among and between the public and employees.
- Hold "bar camps," conferences whose topics are user-generated on the fly.
- Create MOOCs—video instruction courses.
- Move toward 3-D printing for tool repair rather than discarding repairable items.

A compelling vision statement is one thing, but had she executed? Four months after hearing Laury speak in May 2014, I Googled "castorama.fr," and the leading search recommendation after the store name was "castorama.fr/votreavis," with the last element translating as "your opinion." The skills bartering site (Les Troc Heures) seems like it is living and breathing: 2,400 people signed up to trade skills in the greater Paris area, 650 in Lille. While it is too early to evaluate the impact of collaborative strategy, the industry's response to her alternative progressive vision surprised me. Castorama's parent company, Kingfisher, one of the United Kingdom's hundred largest public companies, recruited her as CEO of the entire business in September 2014. As Laury said, we are moving "from a consumer society to a collaborative society."

"WE CAN'T": WHY CHANGE IS PARTICULARLY DIFFICULT

I have a lot of empathy for big institutions. While I have no experience moving these big ships, I have been collecting success stories. But here are the reasons I'm given for why change is hard.

We can't change because the market forces short-term thinking. The problem caused by quarter-over-quarter reporting requirements of public companies—the metrics of Wall Street—is well known. If a company invests significantly in new pursuits that will take years to pay off, today's balance sheet looks bad and their stock price suffers. New investments that take time to deliver are punished in the short term, and they also carry risk: Is this new approach actually going to pay off? Repeating what worked in the past is always the least expensive, and in the short run it's going to give you the most profit for just the same reason. But that produces a vicious circle of slow erosion of value over time. It seems that only the strongest CEOs are able to place big bets and rely on cross-subsidization from existing revenue streams to finance new ideas. And it appears that these CEOs are most often founding CEOs. Steve Jobs's early years after he reclaimed the helm of Apple were greeted miserably by the stock market, which couldn't imagine or quite believe in his promises about the iMac, then the iPod, and then the iPhone. Ditto Jeff Bezos at Amazon, who ran the company in the red for its first four years, reinvesting all the while in service of his grand vision.

Short-termism is indeed a problem for public companies. Other than changing SEC reporting requirements, I can only add that one of Peers Inc's greatest attributes, is its ability to deliver lots of low-cost experimentation at the fastest possible rate (remember the three miracles from Chapter 5).

We can't change because we are heavily regulated. This is a real problem in so many ways. Companies fight off regulation for years, but once they've submitted to it, they typically enjoy a nice guaranteed profit stream that they then aggressively defend. Electric utilities fighting against the incorporation of electricity from local solar or wind power are a good example. A unified electric grid (the platform) with peer-financed hardware investments (solar or wind) contributing their unused excess capacity (land, rooftops, and power) to the whole makes so much sense for all the reasons we know: co-investment by others, the ability to scale quickly, resilient and redundant energy sources, and the ability to learn from the running of hundreds of thousands of experiments simultaneously (which locations and equipment deliver under which conditions). Yet from the electric utility's perspective, every kilowatt generated by a peer, through a peer's investment, is power not generated by the utility's own existing sunk-costs power plant, for which they are allowed remuneration. But now that cleaner low-cost solutions to energy generation exist, state regulators should be looking closely at utilities' rate setting and investment returns with an eye toward enabling more innovation, experimentation, and resilience to enter the system. Likewise, it is this same regulatory rigidity that is causing so much trouble in the licensed taxi and livery industry and in the hotel industry around the world, as we've discussed in other chapters.

We can't change because our size exposes us to too many lawsuits. We have much more to lose than small upstarts. This is absolutely true. Uber and Lyft are pushing the envelope. When they both started, they had little to lose and everything to gain. They now have a lot more to lose. In the early race between Google Video and YouTube, YouTube ignored potential copyright issues from video content providers. Google Video couldn't afford to do that.[25] When I was exploring peer-to-peer car sharing, I spent more than a year figuring out how to provide appropriate insurance for the individual car owners. My research included many meetings with regional insurance providers and with the Massachusetts commissioner for insurance. I learned that the state's auto insurance laws forbid using your personal car for commercial purposes. So I launched P2P car sharing in France, where I could get the insurance I wanted (and needed) to protect car owners while their car was being rented out. Meanwhile, right in my backyard in Cambridge, Massachusetts, a recent Harvard MBA graduate launched RelayRides, doing exactly what insurance regulators had told me was illegal as far as my own business was concerned. I was struck by the fact that a young guy with no reputation was willing to do something that I, fifty years old with both personal and reputational assets, would never consider. Meanwhile, it took the state of Massachusetts four years to issue a warning to consumers about the insurance gap.[26] With the rapid pace of change happening today, rigidity, protectionism, and outdated rules serve neither regulators, the regulated, nor the public well.

Underlying all these claims why companies can't do something is the question of how companies can be nimble at scale. This is what legacy companies should be thinking about constantly. Nimbleness is the asset, I tell entrepreneurs, that wins out over the money and scale of established companies. And it is the nimbleness embedded by the peers in the Peers Inc framework that they bestow to the Inc.

Sometimes, the underlying issue is often not *We can't change* but *We won't change*. Legacy companies usually fight to protect the status quo, and to be fair, this is the easiest choice, since they are weighed down by their existing hard and soft assets—buildings, employees, processes, and know-how. The weight of these legacy assets are responsible for the decreasing life span of companies on the S&P 500. Many people have written about the need for big companies to reinvent themselves and the difficulty of doing so, perhaps most prominently Clay Christensen (*The Innovator's Dilemma*) and Dick Foster (*Creative Destruction*). We can think about the music industry, which was just about ready to collapse under the pressure of Napster, a platform that unlocked the excess capacity found in other people's music, until iTunes came up with a business model—a platform—for selling single songs quickly and easily. This gave the music industry another decade. Spotify and Pandora, however, advanced the business model yet again. Not only do I not need to buy a whole album when I only want one song, but since I can listen to any song I want at any time through a subscription service, I don't feel the need to own music at all.

Jeremiah Owyang, formerly an analyst at Forrester Research covering peer-to-peer models and how companies respond, is now founder of Crowd Companies, a brand council that offers research and strategic advice to companies seeking to become part of the collaborative economy. He has a simple four-phase circular path that explains the transition from the old industrial approach to the new one: Product → Service → Marketplace → Platform. Jeremiah has documented how many large companies are already making the transition. The first transition, from product to service, is what Zipcar did: making durable goods available as a service. In the second transition, companies create marketplaces, which enable buyers and sellers to transact around their brand. In addition to the obvious Airbnb example, Patagonia, Ikea, and Levi's are all offering used-goods marketplaces where people can get "gently loved" apparel and furniture from other customers. Their efforts illustrate a brand's commitment to sustainability, offer proof of durable products, and create brand loyalty for a potential upsell. Lastly, the third transition is the creation of a platform that opens itself up more broadly to peer creation of the products themselves (as seen with Quirky and GE, profiled in Chapter 4).

PLATFORM ECONOMICS: WILL ECONOMIC EFFICIENCY LEAD TO A LESS FAIR SOCIETY?

What happens to the economy as Peers Inc structures expand and grow?

As Airbnb grows, value is being created in three significantly new ways. One, the platform itself adds a lot of value by organizing the excess capacity. Two, each peer adds value (and, generally speaking, a peer will participate only because it is worth it to him or her). This is the nature of the company's innovation: taking an underutilized resource (spare bedrooms and temporarily empty apartments) and pressing them into use for the benefit of their owners. At the same time, Airbnb is cutting the price of travel for visitors. Regular hotels may feel some pressure, but that is only to be expected when a resource as large as a million spare bedrooms is made available in a new market. The third source of value is created by the *group—the aggregated* peers making a network—and this has enormous value. It is this third part of the value pie that the Incs generally eat as well. Venture capitalists recently valued Airbnb at $10 billion in 2014, surely taking this network value into consideration.[27]

At first, everybody seems better off. But if we explore all possible outcomes of a quickly growing platform, we see that many midrange hotels might go out of business as people opt for Airbnb for everything except the luxury market. Full-time jobs in hotels will be lost, and the wealth will be distributed between homeowners making additional money as independent contractors and Airbnb, the platform operator, sitting in the center making a healthy profit.

In the future, these kinds of collaborations between efficient platforms and participating peers will spread to all walks of life. Let's see what Roxane Googin, a leading technology analyst who advises fund managers who move billions of dollars, said in a recent issue of her newsletter, *High Tech Observer*, about where this will lead us.

The concentration effect is extreme. The centralized processing engine [what Peers Inc calls a platform] is a bear to develop, but once it works, the next transaction is effectively free. It therefore devours all the less efficient and smaller scale operations because it is both cheaper and more effective. Then, the profits of all the failed companies, along with the difference in efficiency between the manual and the automated business, accrue to the center. And, it learns. If managed correctly, it becomes a recursive learning machine that just gets more effective with every measured mistake.

This is what I've called miracle #2, exponential learning. As the platform starts to really perform, the tendency is for larger platforms to eat smaller ones because of network effects: We all want to use the short-term rental service with the broadest possible range of rooms advertised, or be on the social network that has most of our friends on it. The winners keep winning and tend to wind up with monopolistic power. She continues:

It soon grows beyond replacement. Just look at how even after [Microsoft] management wasted billions of dollars on Bing, it is still failing against [Google], while [Google] never even missed a quarter. Thus, hyper efficiency, automation, wealth transfer and income inequality go together. In addition, this concentrating quality has all the power of the gravitational pull of a black hole.

That is because in this model, with a relatively fixed cost for the central processing engine, he with the most transactions wins. Not only are all transactions amortized against a similar fixed base allowing for lower end prices, but the biggest engine gets smarter, faster. Thus, in their desperate race against each other to be the number one transaction engine, any emerging giants quickly obliterate mom and pop operations without blinking. In the end, we have one gigantic processing engine that learns the most since it covers the most events, providing the least inexpensive, yet effective, transactions. While extremely effective from a macroeconomic perspective, this model lays waste to the small business model that supported our great middle class.[28]

As you can see, she is discussing the same phenomenon as the Peers Inc framework—the scale of growth, the potential for hyper-learning, and the inevitable efficiency of it. But where Roxane sees the demise of small business, I see the rise of micro-business. In Roxane's scenario, everything becomes automated and computerized by the platform. In my thinking, some platforms are in fact people-centric partnerships, opening up the possibility of a new localized, customized, specialized economy as delivered by the people. Platforms have unleashed the talents of artists and craftspeople (Etsy), musicians (SoundCloud), freelance administrators, accountants, and logisticians (eLance-oDesk), illustrators (Behance), cooks (Feastly), dog sitters (Rover), caregivers and babysitters (Care.com), errand runners (TaskRabbit), editors, programmers, designers, and videographers (Fiverr.com), communities of knitters (Ravelry), and gardeners (GardenWeb). This list could go on for pages, as we all know. All of these people now have newfound agency, new corporate powers, and access to a marketplace. These are examples of platforms that do not simply aggregate a commodity such as spare bedrooms but act as marketplaces for genuinely creative people to find audiences for their work—the same job that record companies and movie studios started out doing.

But the Peers Inc organizational structure, as enabled by technology, does result in a certain inevitability of outcome. The platforms will exist, and they will grow and increase in power for many years to come. While some activities invite a greater degree of human interactions than others, most will become so efficient that people will be removed from the transaction altogether. The increasing use of automation is showing up everywhere, and it's a trend that intersects with peers and platforms more every day.

Most of the incredible productivity gains of the last forty years have been unevenly distributed. Each year *Fortune* publishes data on executive compensation. Beginning in the mid-1970s, executive salaries began to outpace salaries for everyone else by a factor of three to one. Over recent decades, the richest 1 percent of families received 70 percent of the increase in average household wealth.[29] So how will we distribute the productivity and efficiency gains that will result from the Peers Inc collaborations? The worst-case form of the platform economy—with the productivity gains of the platforms

going almost exclusively to the platform owners and with significant unemployment—is unthinkable and unstable. We know that
every big change results in winners and losers. We don't want to end
up with the almost-everyone-loses-everything alternative. Governments have always had to restrict monopoly power, and it has been
a major aspect of life in American business since the days of the rob-
ber barons of the railroad industry and the epochal breakup of Ma
Bell in the in the 1980s. Right now we have the opportunity to guide
this transition, redesigning these businesses not just to centralize
wealth and power at the platform level but also to build new structures for democratic control of big asset bases. The implications of
the Peers Inc transition on companies play out differently than for
people.

When I left Zipcar in 2003, I started educating myself more about
urban transportation. I realized that in cities, where 50 percent of
the world lives now and most will be living in the future, the vast
bulk of vehicles on the street will necessarily be shared. There is no
economic rationale to have cars that are used 5 percent of the time
taking up valuable and heavily subsidized real estate for parking
the other 95 percent of the time. Once vehicles are shared, we only
need about a tenth of the number we currently have. The move to
shared-cars-only cities is almost certainly inevitable, particularly
when the self-driving car arrives. Technology makes it simple, the
economics of pay per use are preferable to consumers, and cities will
increasingly require it because of parking space constraints.

Back in the mid-2000s, I couldn't figure out why the car companies didn't see this (today, they all do). Why weren't they adapting
faster? In part for all the reasons I've outlined in this chapter, and in
part for a reason I hadn't appreciated. In 2007, I was asked to participate in a conference at Ford on the Future of the Car in 2030. I
was excited to be there. Finally I'd get to tell the Ford executives
what they should be doing! I remember sitting with earnest and
thoughtful senior executives over lunch thinking, *Robin, you are so
naïve.* Hearing how vast the Ford ecosystem was, it was obvious
that the 181,000 people who work at Ford, not including the broad

network of suppliers and dealerships, cannot turn on a dime. Big companies have limited flexibility.

Likewise, employees have inadequate flexibility. In November 2008, when the three American car manufacturers sat before Congress and begged for help to avoid bankruptcy, I was opinionated then too. I thought that instead of using government money to prop up the companies, the money should have been applied to guarantee health care to every employee for the next decade, or until they found another job. So many people in the United States stay at their unsatisfying jobs due to their family's need for health coverage and other benefits. People can't try their hand at any of the Main Street businesses, nor high-growth ones. They can't explore other passions; they can't tentatively find other employment. We need to make it possible for people to change, to make full and effective use of their assets and talents, without risking the welfare of their family (particularly in key areas such as health care) in the process.

The lack of flexibility for both company and worker is true in different measures in most of the wealthy countries. U.S. employees are tied to full-time employment with one employer in order to maintain needed benefits. In France, which has national health care, once a person is hired and passes a probationary period, it is almost impossible to fire someone, building in rigidity for employers. If we want our economies to experiment, adapt, and evolve, to keep pace with technology, innovation, and environmental pressures, we need to reduce the stickiness of the labor force to the benefit of both the Peers and the Inc. Right now we leave good people in economically unproductive industries, unable to get out and start something new. And in other ways make it very difficult for employers to adapt quickly to changing environments.

What if all (or almost all) work was done by independent contractors in Peers Inc platforms? Both business and labor would gain from the new fluidity and responsiveness. Employers could respond more rapidly to market forces; workers could diversify their income streams and transition from dying industries or boring jobs in an adaptive way that was much more in their control. The "job for life" that was the hallmark of corporate America in the 1950s has been gone for close to two generations. Way back in Chapter 1, I talked about the economist Ronald Coase and his work showing that companies grew bigger in order to avoid transaction costs grounded in lack of information. The corollary to this insight was his prediction that as markets become more efficient because of better information flow, companies will tend to get smaller and smaller. Our platforms are such places, where tiny little companies (often independent contractors) find each other and interact, together creating larger economic processes But in a genuinely efficient platform economy, in which assets and labor flow to the most productive uses, the job-for-life benefits package provided by private companies evaporates.

Some countries seem to have figured out a way to deliver balance, giving both companies and people flexibility. For the ninth year, *Forbes* magazine ranked 146 nations on eleven different factors to produce a list of the "Best Countries for Business." For the fourth time (2008, 2009, 2010, 2014) Denmark came up in first place. According to John Weis, an economist at Moody's Analytics with an expertise on the Danish economy, Denmark's pro-business climate stems in large part due to its long-standing policy of "Flexicurity," a multipronged approach supported by the European Commission. Flexicurity combines flexible and reliable contractual arrangements with lifelong learning strategies and adequate social benefits, supporting the needs of both employers and employees. "The model encourages economic efficiency where employees end up in the job they are best suited for," says Weis. "It allows employers to quickly change and reallocate resources in the workplace."[30] All the while, Denmark is among the most productive economies in the world.[31] True, it has one of the highest tax rates to pay for these benefits and commitment to retraining,[32] but it is also ranked as the "Happiest Country" in the United Nation's 2013 World Happiness Report.[33]

Can these policies (also implemented in other Nordic and northern European countries) be adapted to accommodate a fully flexible workforce? Let's go back to one of Roxane's sentences: "Hyper efficiency, automation, wealth transfer, and income inequality go together." While this has been the path of least resistance, we just saw that tax and employment policies can in fact deliver both higher growth rates and adequate income equality. But can these policies work in an environment of increased unemployment? I recently talked to a CEO of a telecommunications company that had been sitting on a technology improvement that would not only dramatically reduce the company's costs and improve customer service but do so by reducing the company's workforce by 40,000 people. Self-driving vehicles, which are coming much faster than people realize, will take away the need for drivers around the world. This will be painful everywhere, but devastating in megacities such as Mumbai and Lagos, where millions of people earn their living from driving. The least skilled and the least educated will likely not find new full-time employment. Even with the optimistic and inevitable forecasts that new technologies will open up new economic frontiers, we all know the difficult truth: In real time in defined geographies, job losses do not equal job gains one for one. We can see this future and have time right now to produce a different outcome.

A more efficient economy is also an economy that creates fewer jobs and does away with job security. Given a generation, the platform + peers structure could result in as big a change in the basic construction of our economies as the invention of mass production in factories did. We need to create new social mechanisms to spread out the gains of the new platform economics—perhaps even a Basic Income allotted to every person, in addition to the Flexicurity principles. Without this, the social consequences could be dire, bad enough to upset the entire applecart in time. National basic income schemes are getting serious consideration even in fiscally conservative nations like Switzerland, which has a national referendum scheduled in 2015 on the topic following a successful citizens' initiative in 2012. Much better for us to get off on the right foot: a maximally fluid and efficient economy that makes full use of our social, material, and technical possibilities, with the necessary safety nets. Basic income is the long-term answer to the increasing precariousness of ordinary people in a global economy that can shift their jobs to the other side of the world in a heartbeat.

How would we pay for these benefits? We know that when employers outsource labor, even within the same country, they do so to avoid paying for health insurance, worker's comp, disability insurance, and retirement benefits (remember the FedEx case in the last chapter, where the company claimed—and lost—its California delivery drivers were independent contractors). All these services have to be paid for by somebody; the costs are simply being moved to the shoulders of the government. Thomas Piketty, the economist who burst into public consciousness with his bestselling book *Capital in the 21st Century*, calls for a global wealth tax that is impossible to evade by changing jurisdictions. This seems like a radical proposal indeed, but given the spread of multinational corporations and offshore profits, can multinational taxation be far away?

Other models might include a value-added tax (VAT), a luxury tax, or, better yet, a carbon tax. The more you consume, the more you pay. It would be hard for either companies or individuals to hide from a global carbon tax, particularly if the tax was collected at the point where the carbon was mined or drilled rather than at the point of use. Using the revenues from a global carbon tax to protect and reinvest in the environment, as well as provide for national basic incomes, could compensate for damage to the environment we all share. This would set up the right system of incentives for rapidly decarbonizing the global economy while giving ordinary people the economic freedom and support that they need to be genuinely productive in this new world of ours. What could be better?

Next up, more revolutionary ideas: how Peers Inc could democratize power. As Cory Ondrejka, former vice president of engineering at Facebook, asked me: "What is the role of corporations and governments in a world where individuals have superpowers?"

PART III

Transforming Our Future

NINE

Who Has the Gold?

Democratizing Power and Wealth

I GREW UP THINKING about economic development though a lens that celebrated American capitalism and democracy. My father was an American diplomat, a World War II veteran awarded the Purple Heart, and a genuine patriot. He taught me to never let an American flag touch the ground when we lowered it at sunset, and to fold it into a tight triangular packet for careful storage. I lived and breathed firsthand the acute differences between the chaotic poor street life of the cities we lived in and the calm, green, abundant America of our vacations. I went to business school so that I might apply business discipline to big-budget international public health projects.

As an entrepreneur, I found that these early experiences constantly focused my inquiry. Would I have been able to start Zipcar in Africa or the Middle East where I had grown up? What were the roots of the differences in economic infrastructure? What caused some companies to increase economic opportunity, while others seemed to diminish it? The ideal of capitalism I perceived as a child seems a far cry from what I understand today. American capitalism has moved from an industrial path that grew a middle class to one that seems to be increasingly taking the ugliest, most extractive form, reversing those gains.

It's essential that we bring economies back to a more sustainable distribution of productivity gains. In economist Thomas Piketty's

2014 bestselling *Capital in the 21st Century*, his analysis found that the top 10 percent of Americans in 2010 owned 70 percent of the capital, trending toward the extreme capital inequality last observed in 1910 monarchical Europe. Today, in the countries experiencing the most economic equality (like Norway, Denmark, and Hungary as measured by the Gini coefficient), the top 10 percent control about 50 percent of the capital, an amount considered "medium inequality."

In the fall 2014 issue of the *Journal of Post Keynesian Economics*, Pavlina R. Tcherneva, an economist at Bard College, updated Piketty's data through 2012 and looked at which groups got the benefits of economic expansion. In the postwar expansion of 1949–1953, the top 10 percent of Americans received 20 percent of the economic gains. In the most recent expansionary period, 2009–2012, the top 10 percent took in 116 percent of the gains, meaning that the bottom 90 percent saw a decline of 16 percent. Even more striking, during this same period the top 1 percent got 95 percent of the income growth.[1] So we can conclude that the 2008 financial crisis resulted in losses being socialized (the U.S. taxpayers financed the $3 trillion bailout), while the gains were privatized and allocated to the top 1 percent.

If wages had kept pace with productivity gains since the 1970s, on average they would have doubled! In fact, productivity rose more or less continuously between 1945 and the present, but wages remained flat from around the early 1970s. For whatever reason, the rich got richer, the poor got poorer, and the benefits of improved productivity were not widely shared.

Chapter 8 concluded, as did Chapter 5, with a strong prediction that we are going to see a significant part of the world economy transform into platforms (the organizing structure) and peers (the participants). Peers Inc is going to bring incredible productivity and efficiency gains. If capitalism is broken and productivity gains aren't shared, that leaves the 99 percent of us with a very unpleasant outlook. This cannot become the template for the Peers Inc transformation. We have to find a better way.

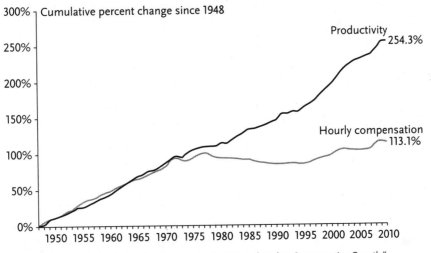

Source: Lawrence Mishel, "The Wedges Between Productivity and Median Compensation Growth," Economic Policy Institute report, April 26, 2012

This chapter examines Peers Inc financing options, and gives a deeper look at those that bypass both government and venture capital, leaving power and value distribution in the hands of the peers.

GOLDEN RULES

When I was CEO of Zipcar, an advisor once asked me, "Robin, have you heard of the Golden Rule?"

Yes, of course I had: "Do unto others as you would have others do unto you."

"No, no. It's 'He who owns the gold rules,'" he said, making clear the reality of capitalism.

Capital will always be important. As CEO of Zipcar, I served as a buffer between the pure capitalist instincts of most of my investors and the much more values-driven company I was creating. But Zipcar could achieve its goal of simple, seamless access to a car only if we had the investment of a lot of money. We needed to build a complex technology platform, and that would not come cheaply. It required many millions of dollars and many investors. Building the technology that was the foundation of Zipcar was not something I could do myself, cajole my friends to do, or finance on the back of the company's cash flow.

So a charge I find particularly frustrating, and particularly naive, is that the platform owners—the founders and investors—are unfairly benefiting off the backs of the hardworking peers. Building a solid, elegant platform is a prerequisite to peer collaboration. Zipcar ended up needing to raise about $67 million before it broke even. BlaBlaCar had spent $13 million, wasn't yet profitable when it raised its last $125 million, and likely won't be profitable for the next few years. Yet millions of drivers are reducing their travel costs by sharing expenses with millions of passengers, who are themselves traveling more cheaply than they would by any other alternative. Airbnb's financials aren't public, but it is likely that it wasn't at the break-even point yet when it began its B (second) round of financing, with a total of $120 million raised.[2] People who claim that Airbnb shareholders are getting rich off the backs of hardworking hosts haven't thought through what it costs to build a successful platform (tens of millions of dollars, maybe hundreds of millions). Nor are they appreciating that while investors see zero returns for many years, the very first Airbnb hosts are making money off each and every transaction. It can take hundreds, thousands, even tens of thousands of transactions before a platform breaks even. Remember that the U.S. military had invested several billion dollars in GPS before the government made it open to the public. Even the most efficient platform builder I know, Jan Koum, co-founder and CEO of WhatsApp—with just fifty employees supporting the more than 50 billion daily text messages of 450 million users when it was bought by Facebook in January 2014—had its expenses exceed its revenues by $10 million in the 2013 calendar year.[3] Still, I do think platform creators get more than their fair share of the value created. In addition to their well-earned piece, they are also getting the value created by the network effect, despite the fact that this is wholly created by the peers.

Regardless, platform building needs to be financed. Most platforms fail. In order to accept this risk, investors—who pay for something before the product or service is realized—demand their hefty fraction of ownership. No investment is risk-free. Very low risks get low compensatory incentives, and very high risks get very high rates of return. Certainly there is a lot of room for argument about whether founders and investors are being compensated fairly or proportionately for the real risks, or whether we are taxing real gains adequately, but the principle is sound. This is how capitalism works. When you start building a platform, you can't know whether it will be successful, nor really be sure of its ultimate trajectory (remember the controlled kernel stage, discussed in Chapter 6). Many types of companies are impossible to finance by bootstrapping, which involves using earned income to grow the business. And there are times when competitive pressures can force companies that might have been able to grow organically by using their own revenues to instead expand faster and therefore bring in outside capital in order to compete. Some platform founders and their investors can have good intentions about the values they want to embed in a company, but hypergrowth, requiring lots of capital, can dramatically curtail the power and therefore the flexibility of the founders and undermine their intentions. Ultimately, those who finance platform building will control it.

The Peers Inc framework thrives when peers are motivated to contribute. Platforms that do not adequately reward peers, value their contributions, and invest in their innovative potential will fail in the long term. Yet capitalism—with private investors interested in getting their money out of their investments as soon as possible and public company stock prices dependent on quarterly earnings—doesn't care about the long term. Restating this chapter's guiding question: How do we finance platforms to permit large investments while also making sure that peer power is preserved and peers as a group share in the significant value created from the collaboration?

FINANCING OPTIONS FOR PLATFORM BUILDING

Broadly speaking, there are three options for financing the building of platforms: public financing, private investment financing, and crowdfunding. Each choice has different implications for how power and value will be shared with the participating peers over the long term.

The public sector can finance it. The most basic and foundational platforms (public goods) have been and should continue to be financed by government with our tax dollars, and made freely available to everyone. All of our basic utilities—roads, water, electricity—are effectively platforms for participation. The government provides the platform, and we (entrepreneurs and consumers alike) bring our cars, sinks, and the cornucopia of devices that plug into outlets. It is easy to see how the Internet, the World Wide Web, GPS, data.gov, and the Wi-Fi radio spectrum are all public goods. Often government financing does come with strings attached. In many states, federal financing of highways requires that the state mandate use of seatbelts or specific speed limits. Sometimes these government rules feel appropriate; sometimes they feel unnecessarily restrictive.

Every time I see Vint Cerf (one of the Internet's founding fathers) and Tim Berners-Lee (creator of the World Wide Web, the visible part of the Internet), I am struck by their personal humility and life choices. Instead of figuring out how to cash out on the government-funded research that led to their inventions, they tirelessly work to ensure that these public goods remain public. I thank them again and again for the way they advocate for these government-financed efforts to remain open, free, and neutral. I also shudder to think about what the privatized alternative future might have wrought (although U.S. Federal Communications Commission rulings have pushed us ever closer to living that reality: In 2014, 85 percent of Americans had just one or two broadband service providers to "choose" among).[4]

The private sector can finance it. Advocates for pure unregulated capitalism, where the only thing that matters is money, will build platforms that maximize shareholder value. If platforms are funded and run to please traditional private sector investors, particularly those looking for short-term gains, things that have no financial value (known as externalities), such as social benefits and environmental damages, won't enter into the calculation. The power and income inequality that exists today will likely continue, and the innovation potential of Peers Inc will fall short. These platforms will lead short (if profitable) lives.

"Benevolent dictators" are cited as an alternative to bottom-line-focused CEOs. Google and Facebook come to mind. Their founders were able to retain majority control, giving them leeway to manage far more than simple shareholder value. CEOs who choose to deliver on a triple bottom line (people, planet, profit) are great . . . except that they eventually have to leave. Google's motto "Don't be evil" is only as good as Larry Page's interpretation of it. And even benevolent dictators are still dictators.

A few companies—including Zipcar, in my opinion, but also BlaBlaCar and Etsy—will always deliver significant social and environmental benefits no matter how they are financed or who runs them, because they necessarily deliver positive externalities. No matter who owns or runs Zipcar, it delivers more car happiness with dramatically fewer cars, fewer parking spaces occupied, and fewer overall vehicle miles traveled than if people owned their own vehicles. For most companies, however, ensuring that they will treat employees, customers, and the environment well in the long term, regardless of who is CEO, is definitely not a given. Absent taxes on negative externalities (such as pollution) or reporting requirements that promote transparency for public companies while making longer-term investments or changes in our tax codes that spread productivity gains more equitably, platforms that are financed and controlled by investors will continue the trend toward increased income inequality and lack of concern over environmental deterioration.

In 2011, Michael Porter, a Harvard Business School professor and a leading authority on competitive strategy, and Mark Kramer, a consultant on philanthropy strategy, wrote an influential piece for the *Harvard Business Review*, "Creating Shared Value: Redefining Capitalism and the Role of the Corporation in Society." They say, "The capitalist system is under siege. In recent years business increasingly has been viewed as a major cause of social, environmental, and economic problems. . . . [Corporations] remain trapped in an outdated approach to value creation that has emerged over the past few decades. They continue to view value creation narrowly, optimizing short-term financial performance in a bubble while missing the most important customer needs and ignoring the broader influences that determine their longer-term success." Porter and Kramer make a business case for "the principle of shared value, which involves creating economic value in a way that *also* creates value for society by addressing its needs and challenges."[5] While waiting for that shift in business culture to happen, the beneficial corporation, or B corp, has emerged. It is a new organizational structure, legally recognized in twenty-seven states, with social and environmental goals, as well as financial ones, tied into its formal requirements. The North Face, Patagonia, Etsy, Warby Parker, Seventh Generation, and Change.org are B corps that you might recognize. Their CEOs can come and go, but these companies still need to meet all three requirements that are built into their charter: financial, social, and environmental.

Peers require substantial trust in the platforms they use as the basis for their economic livelihood (see Chapter 7). The conventional for-profit company may find that there are substantial costs in gaining and maintaining the trust of the very people that it relies on for its inventory of assets to share. The B corp and similar cooperative corporate forms found in Europe (such as the United Kingdom's industrial and provident society) may provide the necessary backbone of trust by legally binding the administrators of the platforms to do what is best for the peers, not just the investors. The result of this approach is for-profit companies that peers can trust to represent their best interests, even if there are occasional tensions as short-term and long-term interests clash.

People can crowdfund Peers Inc platforms. At first glance, cooperatives and employee-owned companies would appear to be people-financed platforms, but they are usually different. Employee-owned companies were typically financed and built in the usual way by private risk capital and then later sold to employees. They are also not open to participation by just anyone. You can only join an employee-owned company by being hired. For GPS, the Internet,

Etsy, MeetUp, and Lyft, *anyone* can join (or try to join—Lyft does exclude people with a bad driving record or a criminal record). As for co-ops, they are typically built over years, which is not necessarily a bad thing; they're just not what this book is about. While some co-ops are really big—the Seikatsu Club, combining thirty-three consumer cooperatives in Japan, has over $1 billion in annual sales, and Mondragon, a federation of worker cooperatives in the Basque region of Spain, employs 75,000 people in 257 companies—their organizing structure is not built for rapid scaling.

While impressive, these older cooperatives are using standard industrial-age operations with different ownership models, not the new postindustrial internal structures this book is about. Mondragon and Seikatsu won't ever benefit from the three Peers Inc miracles of exponential growth, exponential learning, and finding the right person. There is, however, an opportunity for a new cooperative ownership model that makes use of underutilized assets and leverages technology. The rest of this chapter explores how we might finance high-growth, high-potential Peers Inc platforms from their inception in such a way that the community of peers retains ownership and control in perpetuity. Can it be done? I see inklings of the potential path ahead.

GIFT CROWDFUNDING AND EQUITY CROWDFUNDING

The Peers Inc structure has enabled a new class of crowdfunding for all kinds of efforts, unleashing, organizing, and empowering small-scale funders. We'll follow Caroline Woolard, a Brooklyn-based artist and organizer who founded the Trade School, a platform for participation in which anyone in the New York community could sign up to teach a one-session class, which was offered free to anyone who showed up to attend. She successfully raised money using Kickstarter several times.

Kickstarter and Indiegogo (among others) let people contribute money to projects of all kinds without taking any equity. Instead of equity, donors are given a range of thank-you gifts depending on how much they've contributed. In 2010, Caroline co-founded a community experiment in a small storefront in Brooklyn, where people took classes in exchange for barter. Over the course of thirty-five days, eight hundred people participated in seventy-six single-session classes. As Caroline describes those first courses, the topics ranged from "Scrabble strategy to composting, from grant writing to ghost hunting. In exchange for instruction, teachers received everything from running shoes to mixed CDs, from letters to a stranger to cheddar cheese."[6]

A year later, the Trade School decided to turn to Kickstarter again to raise $9,000 to repeat the experiment for a longer period of time and to pay for some materials and a staff coordinator. Successful for a second time, the idea attracted attention from cities around the world. Trade Schools were opening in Oakland, Singapore, London, New Delhi, Sherbrooke, Jamaica, Purchase, Guadalajara, Cardiff, San Francisco, Bangkok, Paris, San Francisco, New Haven, and Milan, and all of them were seeking advice and support of the original group in Brooklyn. So the team turned back to Kickstarter to raise $10,000 to reimburse the freelance engineers and designers building an open-source Web platform that would make the lives of volunteers in all those cities much easier.[7]

Since 2009 Kickstarter has funneled nearly $1.4 billion to more than 70,000 projects, which are usually small, one-of-a-kind efforts.[8] It's great for pilots or small projects, but not enough to get a platform through the controlled kernel phase. While the Trade School's Kickstarter efforts did finance the individual projects, it was not enough to develop a robust, sustainable platform.

Other crowdfunding alternatives—Angel List, Startup Crowdfunding, and MicroVentures—offer equity stakes, and therefore raise more capital and provide a longer runway for entrepreneurs. Since each individual investor is small and there are many of them, this kind of financing likely reduces the amount of control the investors can exert. North American baby boomers—many of whom were once 1960s activists—will be shedding $30 trillion in financial and nonfinancial assets over the next thirty to forty years.[9] The new crowdfunding platforms make it easier for them to choose triple-bottom-line investing.

Using no-equity crowdfunding to understand market demand or create a pilot that is then followed by equity funding or a successful acquisition has raised moral outrage in some circumstances. Oculus Rift, the company producing a virtual-reality headset, raised $2.4 million on Kickstarter. A year and a half later, Google bought the company for $2 billion. The headline of an article from *Verge*, an online magazine, asks: "If you back a Kickstarter project that sells for $2 billion, do you deserve to get rich?"[10] Had a $300 "gift" to Oculus Rift been a typical Series A investment, it would have resulted in a return of $43,500.[11] Sure, the people who backed the project did so with eyes wide open. But that differential makes you think twice about the fairness of it.

Equity crowdfunding, in which all of those small donations would have been for a tiny equity stake in the business, is illegal in many jurisdictions because of the long history of fraud being perpetrated on small investors by people promising get-rich-quick schemes. In the United Kingdom, CrowdCube is pioneering equity crowdfunding models that blend early-stage investment with traditional crowdfunding approaches. The United States passed the 2012 Jumpstart Our Business Startups (JOBS) Act, which included an easing of Securities and Exchange Commission restrictions on investors to allow for smaller-scale funding. Pieces of the legislation are still coming into effect, so it is still too early to see how it will play out. But investment communities made up of small investors will likely still face the same kinds of issues that companies with more traditional investors have: how to balance the needs of the peers with the needs of the investors who finance the initial platform construction.

GPL AND CC: PROTECTING COMMUNITY-BUILT ASSETS FROM PRIVATE EXPLOITATION

There are two examples of clever manipulation of existing patent and copyright laws that give us some interesting tools and ideas about how we might more fairly distribute the value created by peers in a Peers Inc organization.

The first, General Public License (GPL), is an example of how innovative licensing can prevent the privatization of community-built assets in perpetuity, and sometimes expand them. In 1989, Richard Stallman of the Free Software Foundation invented the General Public License (GPL) for use with free and open-source software. According to Black Duck Software, the leading provider of systems to manage open-source software development, fully 54 percent of open-source projects in 2013 were associated with Stallman-created GPL licenses.[12] GPL states that you can use a piece of open software any way you like, including improving upon it and selling it for profit. The only catch? Any of the code you develop must include the original piece of code that was open-sourced, and any of your improvements must carry the same license (or one that is even less restrictive). The implications of this are really far-reaching. GPL is like the Midas touch. Anything that King Midas touched turned into gold; any code that leverages code created under a GPL is now also under a GPL (or even freer). With GPL, you can't ever privatize what was community-built.[13] Sometimes a company doesn't want to do the right thing, because it believes its competitors won't play nice either. With GPL, every company knows that every other company is legally bound by the same rules.

The second example, the Creative Commons (CC) license, enables individuals to give their copyrightable content away freely for others to use for noncommercial purposes, but requires permission and sometimes compensation for material that is used for profit. In 2001, Lawrence Lessig, Hal Abelson, and Eric Eldred invented the Creative Commons license for print, music, photo and video materials. Its purpose was to give individual creators "an agile, low-overhead and low-cost copyright-management regime, profiting both copyright owners and licensees."[14] With CC, you can allow anyone to use your material for any purpose, or to add some restrictions (for example, "If you are going to use this commercially, you need to tell me and license the use from me").

If we go back to the Oculus Rift story, the application of these kinds of licenses might have prevented the donors from feeling that they had been abused (and might also have caused Oculus founders to choose a different source of financing). Kickstarter and other donation funding sites might consider creating some simple rules, like GPL and CC, that could quickly and easily cover these low-likelihood financial windfalls.

J. P. Rangaswami, an open-source advocate and most recently chief scientist at British Telecom and then Salesforce.com, thinks about how we can apply these ideas to the analog world—that is, not to code but to atoms, physical stuff. Imagine if we could have a common data standard (like the way we write dd-mm-yy, 11-16-14) for our assets: cars, buildings, favors from me. I could attach a Creative Commons–like license to that object. Then I could let you use my car for free if you are running a personal errand less than five miles away, but if you are delivering pizza, you'll pay me. Or we could combine CC and GPL attributes: Lots of people build a barn together and we give our labor for free but specify that anything done inside that barn can't be commercial but is necessarily free in perpetuity (though we'll let you earn enough to keep the barn well maintained). Is there embedded here a virtuous circle that contributes and expands community benefits and also provides the right incentive structure? Could there be some benefit so profound and tangible (say, this barn hosts programs that educate teenagers to become hardworking engineers) that the private sector decides it wants to pitch in and support it out of self-interest? FOSS is just such an example, where the private sector has become willing to finance a wholly free and open resource.

FOSS: A CASE FOR PLATFORMS THAT ARE CROWDFUNDED AND THEN ALSO PRIVATELY FINANCED

The most exciting possibility for crowdfunding platforms is what is happening in the free and open-source software movement. Earlier I mentioned that in the 2008 financial crisis, gains were privatized and losses socialized. With FOSS, however, gains are socialized (the entire community benefits from improvements to the code) and losses have been privatized (individual companies succeed or fail based on how they apply the code). Instead of using money from individuals to build a platform, the FOSS movement is built on in-kind free labor, and then later supported in part by the private sector. This is an important development because some FOSS platforms—Linux, MySQL, Drupal, and Mozilla—have become large enough to challenge and in many cases supplant the former alternatives, which were privately financed and closely held. The FOSS example holds important clues about the way forward.

Timothy Lee, who has spent twenty years doing quality assurance on open-source software, considers the private sector's inability to influence Linux as a positive development. Even companies whose salaried employees are working full-time on open-source code have been unable to break the culture of meritocracy that guides open-source code evolution. Lee writes:

> What makes the open source model unique isn't who (if anyone) signs the contributors' paychecks. Rather, what matters is the way open source projects are organized internally. In a traditional software project, there's a project manager who decides what features the product will have and allocates employees to work on various features. In contrast, there's nobody directing the overall development of the Linux kernel. Yes, Linus Torvalds and his lieutenants decide which patches will ultimately make it into the kernel, but the Red Hat, IBM, and Novell employees who work on the Linux kernel don't take their orders from them. They work on whatever they (and their respective clients) think is most important, and Torvalds's only authority is deciding whether the patches they submit are good enough to make it into the kernel. . . . There is no "central management" for the Linux kernel, and it would probably be a less successful project if there were.[15]

Ed Cone, a writer and now head of technology for Oxford Economics, notes "how radical it is to have IBM and Novell effectively collaborating with no contractual agreement between them, and no right to expect that their programmers' work is going to be contributed to the kernel if people external to those organizations don't like it. And that's a huge change."[16] Yes, it is. The private sector is the servant of the community. No guarantees, just a promise of access to high-quality adaptive software in which each peer collaborator receives more value than he, she, or it contributes. That's the Peers Inc way.

Private financing can provide significant financial support for established community-built platforms. Once a FOSS "code base" has become successful and widely adopted, the private sector's reliance on it means that these leading companies will contribute resources— money and engineers—to improve the code for their own self-interest. Such was the ultimate result of the dramatic and horrifying announcement on April 7, 2014, of a bug discovered in the widely used security software OpenSSL and dubbed Heartbleed. The cybersecurity expert Bruce Schneier called it "catastrophic": "On the scale of 1 to 10, this is an 11. Half a million sites are vulnerable"—that's 17 percent of the trusted servers on the Internet.[17] However, despite Schneier's gloomy assessment, a fix for the bug was posted within hours of the announcement. It turns out that only one independent engineer earning a mere $20,000 a year had been working on the OpenSSL code, and donations financing this key piece of Internet security amounted to only about $2,000 a year. On April 23, Jim Zemlin, the executive director of the Linux Foundation, spent all night calling potential donor companies, and by April 24 he had the funding to announce the creation of the Core Infrastructure Initiative. Thirteen companies—Amazon Web Services, Cisco Systems, Dell, Facebook, Fujitsu, Google, IBM, Intel, Microsoft, NetApp, Rackspace, Qualcomm, and VMware—together committed more than $1 million per year for three years to resolve the funding gap faced by the OpenSSL FOSS team.[18] The private sector had stepped in to finance the ongoing improvement of a free and open-source platform.

Another example of private money following on a community-built platform without corrupting it is GitHub. Four million engineers currently collaborate using GitHub to provide code hosting and revision-tracking management. In a 2013 interview, GitHub president and co-founder Tom Preston-Werner explained how the founders were able to control their destiny because they had been able to grow and build the platform without venture money for the first four years: "[We were] optimizing for the happiness of the team members and customers. . . . Money was a natural by-product, but it doesn't start with money."[19] By the time they went out to raise capital ($100 million in their one and only round of financing), GitHub had proven the success of its approach. Preston-Werner continued, "We had already proven that our philosophies worked. . . . Now the VCs [venture capitalists] ask, 'How can I get involved and what is it going to take?' We've flipped the conversation."

FOSS is a remarkable and novel way of financing, building, controlling, and governing a Peers Inc platform that mostly overcomes the negative power and control issues associated with private- or even government-financed platforms. (I say "mostly," because the governing committees can still become inbred: Both Wikipedia and GitHub have been criticized for being unwelcoming to participation from women, for example.) It is the peers themselves who are building and governing the platform. But FOSS does have what feels to me like structural failures in certain areas, just as capitalism suffers occasionally from "market failure." The Achilles' heel of FOSS and other community-built platforms is that the nub of the shared platform— the core, the kernel, the organizing principle—requires the focused, dedicated, full-time commitment of someone in order to get created.

I think of this as the "volunteer coordinator problem." While you might have plenty of volunteers to do the work, someone or some entity has to do the heavy lifting of creating the organizational backbone. This job is typically too big, too hard, and too full-time to be ripe for execution by the opt-in peers (indeed, this was the topic of Chapter 3, which discussed why Incs are usually the platform builders). Certainly we all might be able to come up with an example of someone who did this for free; consider the "benevolent dictators" who are the founders of many of the FOSS platforms.[20] But we know that this a rare event.

Another necessary role of the volunteer coordinator is the burden of responsibility—making sure that things get done and keeping them moving forward. Volunteer and part-time labor doesn't internalize this. Curiously, I experienced this responsibility on/off switch while writing this book. When I was working on it alone, I internalized the reality that no progress would be made if I didn't make it. But whenever I had serious editorial help, I instantly felt like certain issues were no longer my problem, and so I slacked off. Because of this weird, counterproductive feeling, I realized that if I was going to get this book written on schedule, I had to work by myself and count on myself. I don't have an answer for how we can finance the volunteer coordinator outside of traditional financing mechanisms. I leave the problem unsolved.

The second problem lies in platform governance. No matter who does it, centralization is a weakness, especially in the distributed Peers Inc world. In fully distributed networks (the Internet is the most familiar example), there is no core, no single point of weakness. Intelligence is distributed throughout the system. This is something of a holy grail in the networked world. Lately, an example of a wholly distributed and crowd-financed platform has emerged: Bitcoin. It is a critically important example of what is possible.

BITCOIN: A CASE FOR A DECENTRALIZED SCALABLE PEOPLE-GOVERNED AND -FINANCED PLATFORM

Imagine if people could make their own money. We've all done it as children—crayon bank notes or games with the cash from the Monopoly deck. But, generally speaking, money comes from central banks such as the Federal Reserve, the European Central Bank, or the Bank of England. We know at some level that most money is electronic, so what exactly is it that central banks do that is so difficult? The hard part is not creating the money but getting people to believe in it: that it has value, that this value will maintain over time, that you can confidently store your personal effort in it so that you can use its stored value when needed. Historically, that ability has always lain with governments.

Incredibly, some anonymous, enterprising hackers figured out a process that gets people to believe. The experiment is going on right now, and billions of dollars of this new currency—the market capitalization is currently at $5 billion—have been created, traded, bought, and sold.[21]

Bitcoin is a currency that has been created by the people (well, engineers) for the people. And like FOSS, it is a real-world example showing that significant, valuable, and resilient platforms can be financed, built, and self-governed without the involvement of any private sector or government help. It provides a successful model for how Peers Inc networks can be entirely owned and governed by peer collaborators. Right now there is an explosion of ideas, innovation, invention, and excitement as a result of the Bitcoin experiment. People are applying the principles, code, and experience to arenas well beyond just currency, trying to solve many of the challenges raised in the second half of this book. Let's start with a very brief background on Bitcoin.

In 2008, Satoshi Nakamoto wrote a paper about a digital currency, called Bitcoin. "Satoshi Nakamoto" is a pseudonym, and no one knows whether it refers to a real person or a group of people. In 2009 their ideas were released as open-source software. (Note that this is yet another example where the concept and organizing principle of the platform were simply gifted out of thin air; that's not a replicable strategy.) The Bitcoin software now exists as a platform and set of protocols for how to create, store, and use Bitcoins.

Bitcoins are sent from one user directly to another digitally. There is no bank at which to register and create an account. There are no banking hours. There is no $500 limit on same-day withdrawals, no $10,000 deposit that triggers a note to the tax authorities. The transactions look like this: Payer X wants to send Y Bitcoins to payee Z. This information is broadcast to everyone in the Bitcoin network. There is a very, very small Bitcoin transaction fee for this service that is dynamic (I'll talk about that in a bit). There is no centralized location or trusted authority who verifies or validates the amount of money you have or counts the money sent or received. So how does it work?

Records of the transactions are published by thousands of people simultaneously in a public ledger. Lots of people (anyone with a computer server can participate) simultaneously publish six times an hour all the transactions that happened in that time slot. This means that money can't be double-counted because the public ledger tallies up only the transactions that took place within those last ten minutes based on the previously published version. Attempts to report inaccurately would show up immediately as different from every other published version. Corruption is pretty much impossible due to the cryptographic algorithms employed (it would take longer than the life of the universe to crack) and theft is very difficult (but contingent on the security of where the owner chooses to store them). The publishing of the public ledger is called the "block chain," because it is a chain of published blocks of information. This innovative process—the block chain—is the foundation for what has wowed the technology community, and impresses me now that I've finally understood it.

The public record enables trusted transactions between strangers. Vetting and verifying is accomplished by the community together rather than by a central authority.

People are incentivized to publish the ledger (the underlying platform infrastructure) through a reward system. These rewards push people:

1. to collaborate in infrastructure building,
2. to have a long-term stake in the platform's success, and
3. finance the whole process.

People are paid in Bitcoins for publishing the ledger; the publishing process is called "mining." Mining is a complex technical dance among Bitcoin users to verify all the transactions. Bitcoin's security comes from this hard computational work: To make a fake block chain of any complexity would require thousands of times more computing power than exists in the entire world. Since these mines are all over the world, run by thousands of different individuals, all contributing their computing resources and labor to their enormous shared enterprise, Bitcoin is resilient and redundant, too (a characteristic of all Peers Inc organizations). This system manages to get people to cooperate in a situation where normally, without incentives, they wouldn't.

One of the challenges of many Peers Incs' efforts is reaching critical mass. We can all imagine how great something will be once everyone is using it, but how do you get from here to there? Some platforms are of little (or no?) value until they get big enough. Bitcoin figured out how to cross this chasm and how to finance this crossing. The size of the reward for publishing/mining declines over time, going from high to low. Cleverly, Bitcoin paid people who took the most risk—who participated in the beginning—more Bitcoins for mining than to people who did this same task later. Paying more early on attracts people when the platform has the least value. The reward structure effectively borrows value from the future (when an established Bitcoin currency will have value) to finance the infrastructure building of the nascent and risky idea (when there is very little value). This is genius.

Lastly, because what the Bitcoin people have earned will only be valuable if the whole Bitcoin enterprise succeeds, these early participants have every incentive to spread the good word and do what they can to make sure that it does.

The earliest assets leveraged are peers' excess capacity. This idea isn't unique to Bitcoin as you now well know. The benefits of this approach should be familiar to you: transformed economics, co-investment by the peers, potential to scale rapidly. In the earliest days of Bitcoin, Lyft, Airbnb, and Waze, the peer participants didn't buy new assets to participate because the value to them was too uncertain. As the platform grew and the value became proven, some peers did begin to acquire assets specifically for the new purpose. For Bitcoin, people have traded up from using their own personal computers to now employing very large, supercomputer-level resources.

The decentralized reward system makes payments based upon digitally measurable and verifiable outputs. We often pay for services this way: Cellphone use is paid by the minute or byte and Zipcar by the hour and mile using rates the company sets. Having a reward system that is adopted and applied by a decentralized group is more challenging and therefore more impressive. Can we allow for nuanced circumstances? How do we deal with arguments?

Innovators are now repurposing the block-chain methodology for a much wider range of activities and providing rewards dynamically based on more localized circumstances. An Israeli startup, LaZooz, is using the block chain to build a ridesharing network. People sign up and download the app, which measures distances travelled, and provides the reward in Zooz tokens accordingly. You can think back to my attempt at building a critical mass with GoLoco, and BlaBlaCar's success fueled in part by some luck (transit strikes and a volcanic eruption). By incentivizing people just for posting their trips, LaZooz is building the necessary posted ride infrastructure required to get to critical mass, adapting the block chain to cross the chasm.

It is LaZooz co-founder, Matan Field, who pointed out to me that we can and should think expansively about what can be automated and digitally recorded. It takes more than code and algorithmic solutions to build a successful platform. Building beautiful user interfaces and marketing and sales are also critical. LaZooz intends to incentivize these "softer" kinds of activities as well. Through social media, for example, we can easily count the number of comments made, or the number of people who "liked" our content. Matan, and other Bitcoin innovators and entrepreneurs, are pushing the envelope.

Much more content can be embedded in the transaction "Payer X wants to send Y Bitcoins to payee Z." See the Bitcoin transaction as a subject-verb-object command. All kinds of important data relating to the subject and object (name, address, ratings, contingencies), and all types of actions (rent, buy, barter, rideshare, publish) could be substituted in. Budding companies—LaZooz, Swarm, and Ethereum, to name three—are fleshing out this idea. Any kind of business or personal transaction needing standard contracts, for standard actions, with standard rules could all be sent, appended, and amended using the block chain. Every transaction can have its own special combination built using standard building blocks.

Rule-making and standards adoption is all accomplished through decentralized leader-free "voting" based on market signals. All of the transactions on the public ledger are there for all to see, and open source. In the potentiality of block-chain visionaries, the most useful programs, contracts, and methods will be the ones that are most copied, eventually becoming standards. The Bitcoin.org website explains how this is accomplished with Bitcoin:

> Nobody owns the Bitcoin network. . . . [It] is controlled by all Bitcoin users around the world. While developers are improving the software, they can't force a change in the Bitcoin protocol because all users are free to choose what software and version they use. In order to stay compatible with each other, all users need to use software complying with the same rules. Bitcoin can only work correctly with a complete consensus among all users. Therefore, all users and developers have a strong incentive to protect this consensus.[22]

While the block-chain protocol has necessarily evolved over the last six years, the evolution is driven by consensus, with the most suitable and widely adopted changes being the ones that win out over the alternatives. The block-chain process errs toward consensus and changes only for big improvements.

This chapter has been about exploring ways to finance platforms without the involvement of government or the private sector. Let me hand the narrative over to the editor of *The Coinsman*, who describes his 2013 trip to China to visit a huge data center containing some of the computers "mining" Bitcoins:

> Getting the opportunity to visit this mining operation was very eye-opening for me. Walking around the warehouse floor, I was struck with a feeling of awe that THIS is what keeps bitcoin alive. That even if someone wanted to bring down bitcoin, they'd have to outdo these guys and the dozens of other operations like this around the world. The decentralized nature of it all . . . that this

is just one operation among many, run by different operators in different countries around the world. This really drove home that bitcoin can't be killed by decree. Make it illegal in one country and people like this will keep hashing away in others.[23]

With the block chain, the Peers Inc future could be replaced by a Peers Peers one. Some people will be participants in the transactions; others will be builders and supporters of the infrastructure (the platforms). The expanded vision for block chain—its potential is being explored right now—dramatically reduces the volunteer coordinator problem because it has figured out a decentralized way to reward people for building the basic infrastructure on which everything else hangs.

PLATFORMS ARE LIKE GOVERNMENTS: WHOSE INTERESTS ARE BEING SERVED?

Every platform, regardless of how it is financed, is a bit like a small government. Each platform comes with its own rules of engagement, some as simple as protocol or standards, others with much more complicated rule sets defining precisely who can participate and how participation is possible. The larger the platform, the more this comparison with government feels apt.

I recently went to the Berkman Center for Internet and Society at Harvard University to hear Nicholas Gruen, an Australian economist, speak about a growing class of public goods that emerge from the private sector. He started his talk by giving the classic economic definition of a public good: goods that the government must provide because the private sector won't. In economic theory a public good is non-rivalrous (like a lighthouse, one person using it doesn't preclude anyone else from benefiting or diminish the benefits anyone else can get) and non-excludable (like national defense, everyone gets the benefit, whether or not they pay for it). Gruen then asked us to think about Google, Facebook, and Twitter. They are free and open to everyone. No matter how many people partake in them, they can't be used up. Here, I thought, was a striking insight: *The private sector is beginning to see that investments in maximally open platforms have the potential to deliver the greatest shareholder value.*

Then Gruen said something remarkable: "Private companies are delivering important public goods. Public goods are assembling themselves without the government."[24] Consider Bitcoin's creation of a currency, an activity that we really thought was in the government purview.

As Nicholas puts it, there is a spectrum of possibility as to how public goods get created, ranging from voluntary, opt-in "emergent public goods" to those that are protected through coercion (rules, regulations, and taxes). The idea of companies creating public goods is both exciting and terrifying—exciting because this means we don't have to rely only on government budgets or government will to produce public goods, and terrifying because, as we have noted, CEOs of private corporations and their investors aren't required to serve the public, don't have to care about social or environmental benefits, are often rewarded for short-term over long-term profits, and have little concern for the financial interests of those who are not shareholders.

A principle of Peers Inc is that each party should focus on what it does best. As we empower peers with more and more platforms, the higher-level, more complex skills and abilities and more expensive

PEERS (people, local NGOs, local companies)	**INC** (companies, institutions, governments)
Small investments	Large investments
Short-term sporadic efforts	Multiyear efforts
Delivery of small services	Integration & aggregation of many parts
Local knowledge	Deep sector knowledge
Specific unique expertise/offering	Diverse technical expertise(s)
Customization, specialization	Standard contracts & standardization
Creativity	Consistency
Personal social networks (trusted individual)	Brand promise (trusted company)
Local	Global

assets (once accessible only by the Incs) now become part of the smaller entity's (the Peers) tool kit. Today, this division of labor is illustrated in the figure on the previous page.

The big entity, the Inc (the large companies, institutions, and governments), should stick to doing what its size and scale uniquely qualify it to do and what the smaller Peers can't. These are typically big projects that take many years and lots of investment to accomplish and that require the integration of many types of skills and expertise. They also create standards in a situation where the peers can never assert their will because they are individually too inconsequential. All of these efforts are made available to the peers through the platform for participation. The Peers (people, local NGOs, and local companies) do what they do best: specialize, customize, localize, innovate, and interact with their own social networks.

But what is now represented by a sharp, clean, static line between the skills of the two sides is becoming blurry and shifting. Companies are finding it in their immediate interest to create public goods and to offer free products and services. Governments are turning to individuals to solve problems and become co-creators. Consumers are increasingly becoming empowered. And totally new ideas, like the block chain, are enabling Peers to coordinate their work—without coming up against the Volunteer Coordinator problem—to accomplish what was in the Inc's purview alone. Does this put some companies out of a job? Certainly we know that the rise of empowered peers has required some companies (in the hotel, taxi, mainstream media, and entertainment industries) to reenvision their roles and rethink where they add value. Allen Blue, one of LinkedIn's founders, speculated: "What is the value of the corporation in 25 years, as everything moves over to the individual side?"[25]

The millions of individuals contributing to, building, and governing the FOSS communities without the help of companies or governments do show what is possible right now with little direct involvement by either government or private capital. For the most part, FOSS is powered by communities of engineers building programming languages that they personally are interested in. While promise of Bitcoin/the block chain's novel uses are nascent, Wikipedia's hundreds of thousands of contributors—who are not engineers—show that we can build big things without the involvement of private capital. Building a start-up today costs a tenth of what it did when I founded Zipcar, thanks in large part to the assembled Web and its platforms, which make billing, customer management, electronic payment, website development and support, content management, mapping, and forums all simple plug-and-play extensions. Over the next ten years, we will see more platforms introduced as they become increasingly easier to build, quickly assembling component parts afforded by other platforms. I'd like to see more examples of important and successful platforms built by—and therefore controlled by—communities themselves. The ideas, imagination, and needs of the non-technical community need to be complemented with more love, attention, and excess capacity from the engineering community.

This chapter has focused almost entirely on the finance, control, and governance aspects of platform building. I've also highlighted the fact that nongovernmental platforms are now providing significant public goods and services. A curious reality of the Peers Inc model and the collaborative economy is that they are not really collaborative at all. These public goods and this currency creation do not require very much actual collaboration (laboring together) or co-operation (operating together). The platform is doing all the coordination so that none of us have to do it. This is the beauty of these platforms: Our simultaneous and asynchronous work produces highly collaborative results. As Nicholas Gruen wrote: "There is a class of public good that emerges from commercial life spontaneously—without any deliberate provision by government or even self-conscious collective action."[26]

Today the 1 percent control business, finance, infrastructure, and government. In 2010 the top 1 percent of Americans earned 12 percent of all the labor income; the top 10 percent earned 40 percent of labor income. In terms of ownership of capital, in that same year the top 1 percent of Americans owned 70 percent of the capital.[27] The productivity gains of the last few decades have gone disproportionately to the rich: Between 1979 and 2013, productivity grew 65 percent, while the hourly compensation of the workers who account for more than 80 percent of the private sector workforce grew just 8 percent.[28] In 2012, political action committees spent a billion dollars on political advertising; 73 percent of the money came from one hundred people.[29]

I don't know how to make the powerful practice of capitalism distribute wealth more fairly. I don't know how to ensure that governments err toward empowering people instead of empowering corporations. But I do know that Peers Inc platforms change the power balance and gain more value with each additional participant. I know that public goods and currencies can be created without the involvement of governments, and that platforms can be built and community value created (and protected against privatization) without the use of private capital. It is even possible to build rule-laden structures that are enforceable without a centralized force. So many new tools! It is up to us, and no one else, to build the world and the economy and society we want to see. Together we can engage millions of people to accomplish very big things, providing significant public benefits while retaining the rule-making governance and even ownership of the platforms within the creator communities.

TEN

Addressing Our Biggest Challenges

Climate Change and Sustainability Need Peers Inc

THE PEERS INC PARADIGM fascinates me not just because it's shaping the future of business. What is more important is that we've figured out what this model is and how it works exactly at our time of greatest need. The earth currently has 7 billion inhabitants, thirty megacities whose populations exceed 10 million, hundreds of cities harboring over a million inhabitants, and all the problems that come with urbanization—poverty, homelessness, congestion, and pollution. Add to this projections of a global average temperature increase of 4°C (7°F) by 2100 and population estimates as high as 11 billion.[1] If we continue with business as usual and leave these problems unaddressed, the future looks bleak. These challenges demand all the ingenuity we can muster. It is a question of life and death. For my money (and effort), there is only one way to solve these existential threats—climate change, lethal consumption of the world's finite resources, ecosystem collapse—and that's by investing in the Peers Inc approach: excess capacity, platforms, people.

Peers Inc allows us to use and reconfigure the tools, techniques, ideas, and people that we have here and now to solve entirely new kinds of problems. This kind of deep innovation bears an uncanny resemblance to what Mission Control at NASA had to do in 1970 when it applied the ingenuity of a team of engineers to save the crew of the Apollo 13 mission. If you weren't there watching with the world in awe as a solution to the crisis started to unfold (I personally don't remember that), then you probably saw the 1995 movie, in which Tom Hanks, in the role of mission commander, radios, "Houston, we've got a problem."

Fifty-six hours after launching and 200,000 miles from earth, the crew of the Apollo 13 spacecraft switched on the hydrogen and oxygen tank-stirring fans. Ninety-three seconds later, the three astronauts heard a loud bang. An oxygen tank had exploded, leading to a chain reaction of mechanical events that damaged and crippled so much of the craft that the astronauts found themselves in an unexpected life-and-death scenario. Solving the problem was complex: how to get these three men home despite inadequate fuel, oxygen, and battery power, while avoiding cooking them alive from a buildup of heat.

The spacecraft's CO_2 levels would soon become toxic. A solution needed to be found within twenty-four hours to avoid tragedy. The ground team circled a long flat worktable, pouring out several cardboard boxes of miscellaneous parts that matched those in the space module 200,000 miles away. In the movie, one team member picks up a square object and says, "We've got to find a way to make this fit into the hole for this"—he holds up a round object—"using nothing but that," he concludes, making a sweeping gesture toward the crowded table.

That's where we are with climate change. We have waited far too long. There is absolutely no time left. Global emissions need to peak by 2017 and move to net zero by 2050 if we want to avoid catastrophic—and we are talking truly catastrophic—effects of climate change. Think about how big the world is, and imagine the effort to thwart the momentum caused by 7.3 billion people living their daily lives based on the pervasive fossil fuel economy. CO_2 emissions must peak in a few years and start to decline thereafter! That means turning an annual 2.5 percent growth of CO_2 emissions into a year-over-year decline.

We must leverage existing excess capacity. We must find new value in existing objects, ideas, technologies, and behaviors. We only have time to reconfigure what we have on hand, right here, right now. We must build a platform for participation, because this is the only way we can scale any solution with the necessary speed. We must engage with peers worldwide, co-creating with us. Our problem can't be solved by a group of engineers and technicians with a box of parts. We are not talking about an emergency fix to a tiny space-craft; we are talking about reengineering the energy systems of our planet. This crisis is big and complex and involves the behavior of billions of us. We need to empower peers by opening up as many resources, data sets, and Inc capabilities as possible so that they can experiment, adapt, and evolve these solutions to fit every cor-ner of the globe. We need people co-investing simultaneously so that we can create and improve on solutions at an exponential pace.

SEE ONE, DO ONE, SHARE IT

Every year my extended family takes a vacation on an island off the coast of Maine. The result of glacial activity, it is composed of ele-mental gray granite, green pine trees, and the surrounding dark blue ocean. At the beginning of the tourist season, one particu-lar beach undergoes a transformation. In its natural state, swept clean by the winter's rough seas and storms, it is expansive and cov-ered with round polished rocks ranging from pea-size to boulder-size. And then, one early summer day, one person will build the first balanced stack of stones of the season. It stands alone, beauti-ful, inspiring, challenging.

Return to that beach two weekend days later, and what was a beach in its rocky wild form has been transformed into a landscape of dozens of rock cairns. With each passing day visitors see the ex-ample, the template for what is possible. The means of production lie at hand. One hour of pleasant painstaking experimentation later, you take a photo to capture and share your proud accomplishment, then continue on your hike.

See it, do it, share it—like the rocks on the beach of this Maine island, like videos on YouTube, like successful uses of GPS.

Photo: Robin Chase

Photo: Heidi Spencer

EVERYONE CAN PLAY:
FROM THE FORTUNE 100 TO RICKSHAW DRIVERS

There is room and need for everyone to play. Here are stories of all kinds of entities, across many sectors, using this formula for change.

In the corporate world, the huge consumer products multinational Unilever is an example of how the biggest companies are changing the way they do business to address sustainability. On any given day, more than 2 billion consumers in over 190 countries will use a Unilever product. With a whopping 174,000 employees, the company sells more than $63 billion worth of goods every year. Paul Polman, CEO since 2009, is on a mission to leverage the size and reach of Unilever to prove that companies can deliver on both sustainability and profitability. In 2011 he established a goal of doubling the company's revenue while delivering on aggressive social and environmental goals. "Business," said Polman, "must make an explicit positive contribution" to address issues of climate change.[2] Writing about the future of capitalism, he noted:

It will be a world where climate will change, water will be scarce, and food supplies will be insecure.

Business has a chance to become part of the solution to those challenges. Just as we need to ensure that we do not repeat the mistakes which led to the recent banking crisis, so there is an equal imperative to face up to the realities of a world where 9.5 billion people will put enormous strain on biophysical resources.

The challenge for business is to meet these needs in a sustainable fashion. Success will require completely new business models. It will demand transformational innovation in product and process technologies to minimize resource use, as well as the development of "closed-loop" systems so that one man's waste becomes another's raw material.

Interestingly too, the challenge is likely to encourage a much more collaborative form of capitalism. Companies will have to work with each other, not just with governments, nongovernmental organizations (NGOs), and civil society. Issues like deforestation and species extinction cannot be tackled by just one company acting alone; they will require collaboration within, and across, industry sectors. . . .

Just as important, the growth strategies that businesses pursue will have to be more inclusive.[3]

John Bartolone, Unilever's director of open innovation, tells me that everyone within the company does believe. "Sustainability is front and center—the biggest challenge we face. Unilever's grand challenges are the way we can help motivate others, thinking and solving these problems together. We need complete reworks of business models and products. It can only be done by the world working together."[4] Indeed, the goals of the Unilever Sustainable Living Plan that are within the company's control are on track to be met. The company has reached 300 million people (out of their goal of 1 billion) with health and wellness information. Thirty percent of Unilever's foods (by volume) reach the highest standards for nutrition.

In 2014 Unilever was recognized as the leader in the food, beverages, and tobacco category of the Dow Jones Sustainability Index.[5] Forty-eight percent of the raw materials the company used were sustainably sourced. In its own manufacturing, it has reduced CO_2 emissions by 32 percent and water use by 29 percent over 2008 levels.

But the goals that require consumer behavior change are not improving at the same rate. As a result, greenhouse gas emissions associated with consumption of Unilever products have increased by 5 percent and water use by 15 percent. The company has reduced its own packaging waste by 66 percent per ton, but that results in only an 11 percent reduction in the packaging that reaches consumers.[6]

And thus Unilever's list of twelve "wants," which, very much like Barcelona's list of problems (see Chapter 8), is open-ended and includes money to move meritorious ideas into pilot projects. Many of the challenges involve figuring out how to change consumer preferences and behavior or how to deliver products that produce less waste. How to better remove fatty grease stains out of dirty clothing? How might we use less water to achieve the same cleanliness when washing clothes? Preserve food naturally? Keep the color in herbs and vegetables longer? Improve health by consuming less salt, brushing teeth more, taking shorter showers, or using antiseptic cleaning agents?

The platforms for participation—the way Unilever is inviting and encouraging—are many, but seem to follow the same process: problems → pitch → pilot → launch, with a winnowing of the proposed solutions and expanding company support along that path. Problems are announced or solicited through Open Innovation Challenges online, weekend hackathons are held around the world, the establishment of a portal for entrepreneurs called The Foundry, and the starting up of two co-creation centers (Pitch London and Pitch New York City) where employees can propose their ideas. There is also the Academy, which allows start-ups and small companies to draw on Unilever's much greater resources. Early ideas are nurtured and shaped into a pitch that includes a business plan. The meritorious will receive $50,000 to follow through with a pilot. Unilever has also started an investment fund. All along the way, Unilever is offering access to its assets, including ultimately the vast reach of its marketing and distribution chains, to individuals and small companies who couldn't dream of doing this alone. These platform collaborations are primarily focused on solving consumer-side problems that the internal workings of Unilever could never solve alone.

In the two and half years since Unilever launched its Open Innovation platform, the company has received more than 3,500 idea submissions. It is just a matter of time until some of those ideas make it into the product or process pipeline.

When evaluating the first few years of its Sustainable Living Plan, Unilever concluded that in order to "go beyond what we can achieve in our own operations and with our suppliers, we are stepping up our engagement to work with governments, NGOs and others in our industry on these issues." One such collaboration is with the World Resources Institute and its new platform Global Forest Watch, which is profiled later in this chapter. In 2013, Unilever announced its plan to source all of the 1.3 million tons of palm oil it uses annually from sustainable sources within a year.[7]

Unilever has set a refreshingly high bar for what can be done, both internally and externally, to deliver solutions at scale. The company has set a template for action and serves as a role model for the corporate world, where there are still far too many businesses focused exclusively on maximizing profits for a small number of shareholders. What Unilever is proving is that pursuit of profit can coexist with efforts to move business away from the sorts of actions that are driving the world toward climate hell—and that it can be done today, starting this Monday morning.

The Peers Inc company Etsy, like Unilever, operates around the world, though on a much smaller scale: six hundred employees (the Inc) supporting the needs of more than 1 million creative makers (the peers). More than three-quarters of the sellers are women, and almost half have never sold their goods before opening up an online shop on Etsy. Etsy's mission is "to reimagine commerce in ways that build a more lasting and fulfilling world. We are committed to creating an economy that's fair, sustainable, and powered by people." With a significant amount of effort, the company became a B Corp in 2012. Chad Dickerson, Etsy's CEO, movingly described the process to me as one of the most difficult and important things he had accomplished in his life (admittedly, this was before he had his first child). That 2012 analysis of the company's governance and impact on its employees, community, and environment has provided a benchmark and a motivator for improvement. In the preamble of its first annual "Values & Impact" progress report, Etsy describes its values, which are similar to Paul Polman's: "To intercept the ecological and human crises that threaten us, we must redefine the ways in which capitalism operates. We believe that businesses are uniquely poised to create a sustainable and meaningful world."[8]

In its first year of focusing on these issues, Etsy made incredible strides. For its employees, Etsy increased financial transparency, job satisfaction, opportunity, and fun quotient, and was acknowledged in 2013 with an award from the Great Place to Work Institute. Etsy improved its gender balance by increasing the number of female employees by 8 percent (to 46 percent of all employees) and the number of female managers (which went from 15 percent to

40 percent)—impressive and non-trivial improvements in a company whose workforce is dominated by engineers. In terms of energy use, Etsy improved the productivity of its servers by delivering more gross sales per kilowatt hour—$515 per kilowatt hour in the third quarter of 2013, compared to $467 in the third quarter of 2012—and Etsy office electricity use per employee fell by about 19 percent. Etsy recycles 51 percent of its trash and reduced the volume sent to land-fills by 34 percent per employee. And since transportation has been so important to me for decades, I think it is significant and impres-sive that less than 10 percent of Etsy employees commute by car. Instead, nearly half commute by subway, and 30 percent commute by walking or biking. So many numbers and so much progress in one year! Here is the kicker: In 2013, which saw so much social and environmental progress, Etsy also grew its sales by 50 percent, to $1.35 billion. Out of 900 B Corps competing, Etsy won the Race to the Top Award for the biggest improvement in B Corp scores mea-suring social, governance, and environmental improvements.[9]

NGOs can serve as conveners, educators, researchers, doers—trusted third parties—all without the taint of profit-making self-interest or requirements. The World Resource Institute's Global Forest Watch provides another example of peer learning circling back to enhance the whole. The annual burning of forests and scrub-land for agricultural expansion in Southeast Asia creates a toxic haze that threatens to destabilize the region. In the dry seasons of 2013 and 2014, these fires raged out of control on the Indonesian is-land of Sumatra, scorching forests and afflicting more than 50,000 people with respiratory illnesses. The haze also shut down commer-cial activity in neighboring Singapore for some time, causing bil-lions of dollars of damage and igniting regional tensions. Tempers flared, and the debate about the fires dissolved into cross-border recriminations and blame as foreign ministers bashed each other over who was responsible.

Enter Global Forest Watch. True to form, GFW built a platform doing things that only an Inc could do. It negotiated with NASA to use satellite imagery from its MODIS and Landsat systems. Then GFW overlaid these aerial images of the world's forests with country and provincial boundaries and land use permits from many sources around the world, such as national ministries of forestry and agriculture, the UN Environment Programme, and that program's World Conservation Monitoring Centre. It engaged engineers to build a website that processes updates of the imagery every sixteen days, identifying areas where new forest clearing might be under way. It engaged designers who worked with test users and focus groups to create a site that is simple to use. And it raised $22 million to build the website and support the team for a number of years.[10] All these were things that the individuals on the ground could not do by themselves.

So what happened in Indonesia? The team at Global Forest Watch intervened by refocusing the debate on the data. Their online maps and analysis displayed in near real time the fire alerts from NASA satellites, which were refreshed every day on the site.[11] By overlaying those alerts onto maps of where palm oil and timber companies were operating, the team rapidly generated lists of which companies might be responsible for the burning, and published the analysis.

This is where the third miracle of Peers Inc—finding the right minds—came into play. The right people materialized. The needle flew out of the haystack. With the aid of more than two hundred media stories and a viral Twitter hashtag, #MelawanAsap ("stop the haze"), pressure mounted to hold the companies responsible. Corporate buyers from Europe and the Americas called their suppliers in Indonesia, and the government launched investigations against dozens of companies. Now, although the fires still remain an issue, there are new policy efforts to end them. Proposed legislation in Singapore would levy significant fines against companies found guilty of lighting haze-inducing fires. Indonesia has dedicated new resources to enforcing anti-burning laws. And hundreds of people continue to sign up to serve as local watchdogs for specific geographies through Global Forest Watch.

As always, the collaboration between peer and Inc optimized the best talents of each party to generate even bigger results. Neither entity could have accomplished the task without the other. Each side fed data to the other, improving the overall system. The person in the street has at his or her disposal the power of billions of dollars' worth of research and equipment, resulting from a partnership between the World Resources Institute, NASA, Google, the University of Maryland, and the United Nations Environment Programme. Global Forest Watch has combined the much-needed eyes on the ground with world-spanning hyperlocal knowledge and community networks. The sum of all this local vigilance plus the platform provided by Global Forest Watch equals an impact that is far greater than the sum of its parts: Local knowledge and global perspective combined to put real pressure on hundreds of different actors to solve the real problem. Constant feedback loops improve the system as a whole and make for dynamic action feedback loops. This is the essence of Peers Inc miracle #3: The right people will appear.

Another powerful example of the Peers Inc paradigm is 350.org. It was named after a number first exposed by James Hansen, one of the world's leading climate scientists, who wrote in 2008, "If humanity wishes to preserve a planet similar to that on which civilization developed and to which life on earth is adapted, paleoclimate evidence and ongoing climate change suggest that CO_2 will need to be reduced from its current 385 ppm to at most 350 ppm, but likely less than that."[12] In May 2013, however, we broke through 400 parts per million.[13] Under business as usual, we are on track to climb to even more tragic levels. Today, 350.org is a powerhouse in the environmental movement that is shaping conversations and motivating people worldwide, but its start was humble. A Middlebury College professor, Bill McKibben, and a handful of his students found some modest success with their first platform for participation—a five-day walk across Vermont to call for action on global warming. This led to Bill creating Step It Up, which demanded that the U.S. Congress move more quickly to curb carbon emissions. More success, but still a limited platform. In 2008, he and some of those same students founded 350.org, which builds its movement by creating platforms that will entice and engage people around the world to deliver the customized, specialized, localized content that 350.org cannot.

The first rallying platform was held in 2009 and had as its goal the depiction of the number 350 in simultaneous community events around the globe. Fifty-two hundred simultaneous demonstrations in 181 countries ensued, with 350.org orchestrating the global press, including images of the events displayed in Times Square, something difficult or impossible for any of those communities to do by themselves. In 2010, the organizing platform for participation was the 10/10/10 Global Work Party (7,000 events in 188 countries). December 2010 featured a planet-scale art project (twenty works, many visible via satellite).[14] In 2011 and 2012, 350.org launched a campaign against the proposed Keystone XL pipeline project, delaying approval of the pipeline and causing endless government debate in both Canada and the United States. In December 2012, 350.org launched its divestiture campaign, encouraging universities and other institutions to excise fossil fuel companies from their investment portfolios; this has brought about even more debate and soul-searching, as well as divestment, among wealthy individuals, universities, foundations, companies, counties, cities, religious institutions, and the press.[15] In response to the new demand, financial institutions are creating new index funds and new metrics are being discussed. The whole idea of "stranded assets"—fossil-fuel assets that are counted on company balance sheets but which may prove to be worthless—stems from 350.org's divestment push. Remember, 350 .org raises the issue, provides the fact sheets, and tracks progress, but it is the participating peers at universities and in boardrooms across the country and around the world who are carrying out the discussions. The most recent platform-for-participation triumph was the People's Climate March in the fall of 2014. Organizing for the Sunday before the UN Climate Summit, more than 1,500 organizations together enticed over 350,000 people to converge and march through Manhattan.[16] It was one of the largest demonstrations in U.S. history, rivaling the famous March on Washington in 1963, the nuclear disarmament march in 1983, and antiwar rallies.[17]

Rather than having a single focal leader and a mass-media-friendly slogan, the climate movement is made up of an overwhelming number of small groups. These small groups are like independent mini-movements, united by overarching shared goals but each approaching the problem at a scope, scale, and reach that best suits its capabilities. The free and open source software movement also shares this structure, with many independent software projects sharing licenses and code, working together for long-term global intellectual freedom. Paul Hawken believes the global climate movement to be the single largest human movement in history, and that it is still in its earliest phase.[18] The open-source movement has created incredibly valuable artifacts such as Wikipedia and Linux under licenses that make them available to the whole world for free: a historic charitable act. These "movements of movements" are the political expressions of the Peers Inc model.

There is a rising breed of forward-thinking entrepreneurs building scalable, sustainable, high-growth, values-driven companies. Their work makes me happy and restores my faith in humanity. Uh-oh, I now feel obliged, as my tech friends have taught me, to . . .

/rant on

I read a tweet, written by a millennial—"Why is it that all the brightest minds of my generation are focused on making people click?"—that nails my deep disappointment in some of the entrepreneurs I meet.[19] I want to say to them, "Where is your head at? Take it out of the sand. I know you are smart, capable, well-read, passionate, creative, and earnest. We have a few short years to change the world economy's trajectory to avert an unrecoverable collapse of the earth's ecosystems that will push our resilient human species into abrupt decline. Your own personal future is looking pretty damn bleak. We are in the middle of an existential crisis. Think you are safe in your wealthy-country enclave? Climate refugees will be everyone's problem. One hundred and fifty million people in Bangladesh live less than a meter above sea level. Thirty percent of the arable land in Africa will be unsuitable for farming by 2030. Many current wars are all about resource scarcity; there will be more of them. Desperate people are not passive. Money earned from the next Snapchat, Instagram, or clever advertising mechanism won't buy you the solace needed in this future. Go build something that makes a real difference and positively affects the lives of millions. And by 'positively,' I don't mean it helps them pass the time or check up on their friend's most recent I-consumed-this photo. You, with the fancy education and the desire to build something big, how do you convert your peers from producing eighteen tons of carbon per person per year in the United States (seven tons per capita in Europe) down to zero by 2050? Sooner, even. Build in readiness for the inevitable price on carbon. You'll be a prescient genius. Don't worry about the problems of the poor in other countries; let their entrepreneurs handle that. Address a market you know well: your own. Focus your brilliance, your creativity, your energy, your networks, your time on this problem. It's your chance to be a hero. Not many people or generations get a real shot at that. You do. Solve this problem and you will go down in history as a hero. And there will still be people writing and people reading history, so you will get your props. Otherwise, there will be no history. Just silence."

/rant off

I do meet plenty of entrepreneurs whose work I admire. Their young companies are changing value and power structures in ways that will support and build a humane, sustainable, low-carbon economy. Each of these companies has a platform that is poised for growth. Each relies on the diversity of the participating peers to deliver success. Each considers the peers partners. While none of them are explicitly reducing CO_2 emissions, they all have built a structure and a community that could easily lead the way. Here are four of those companies from different industries: agriculture, retail, community building, transportation.

In Paris, France, in 2011, Guilhem Chéron and Marc-David Choukroun co-founded La Ruche Qui Dit Oui. I'll translate that name for you at the right moment in the story. La Ruche is a farm-to-fork program, where the goal is to remove the middlemen between consumer and producer. The benefits to the consumers: fresher food, a direct connection to the producer, lower costs. The benefits to the producer: a higher price for their produce (fruits, vegetables, wines, jams and jellies, cheese, baked goods) and a closer tie to their consumers. So far, nothing new. The key business model innovation was the hive (*la ruche*). Anyone can create a hive. All that's needed is a Web browser, an Internet connection, and a place to manage food delivery and pickup. Producers tell hives in their area what they have, at what price, and at what minimum threshold quantity they are willing to make a delivery. The hive coordinators communicate with the hive members (neighbors, friends, and anyone else they can rally) about what's on offer, and manage the pickup out of their house/location. Most hive coordinators turn out to be stay-at-home moms. Now here is the key sentence: At the moment that a particular hive's demand has grown past the minimum threshold for product delivery, "la ruche dit oui"—the hive says yes to the producer: Yes, we want it! Like any good platform, this one makes things simple and easy for everyone.

The producers get an online profile page (like a store), no unsold products, flexibility to offer (or not) goods week over week, an accounting report and analysis tools, and payment guaranteed within fifteen days. The price to the farmer for this? One-sixth of the proceeds—16.7 percent—which is divided fifty-fifty between hive coordinator (8.35 percent) for her efforts, and the platform (8.35 percent).[20] *Et voilà!*

Three years later, there are currently 550 hives across France, Spain, Germany, Belgium, and the United Kingdom, with 3,000 active producers. In 2014, sales were around €25 million ($32 million), a very nice start. My guess is that the Ruche's platform is now working well and that it's time for some great growth! Guilhem tells me the Ruche has made a real difference to many small local farmers for whom the additional income is critical to being able to maintain their farms. With the support from a Peers Inc–type structure, their farms are viable; without it, they wither. They are drawing support and energy from the network, like grapes from the vine. It has also proven to be a fulfilling economic activity for many isolated stay-at-home women (80 percent of the network is female). Lastly, there have been new neighborly connections made within the hives; I get invitations to all the wine and cookie tastings at the hive nearest where I used to live in Paris.

To conclude, Guilhem tells me this little love story. He had just returned from the largest gathering for the French network over a lovely weekend in September. One of the hive coordinators introduced his girlfriend to Guilhem, saying, "I met her in my hive; she was a client. One day she had forgotten to pick up her eggplants, so I delivered them myself." Paul Polman of Unilever is looking for ways to sustain small local farms; Guilhem is building one answer.

Retail comprises 12 percent of the United States' GDP and likely a similar percentage around the world.[21] How we consume matters. The website The Grommet notes, "We truly believe that every purchase is an act of citizenship. That's why we launch undiscovered products and help them succeed. Our Grommets aren't just things. Grommets are products with a purpose invented by people with stories."[22] Each weekday, The Grommet launches one product at noon Eastern Time. Their goal is to level the playing field. In the old regime, massive retailers have controlled which products live or die. The Grommet does things differently. From the two hundred ideas the staff sees weekly, they choose five "heroic, innovative and inspiring" products. For each one, they help the maker tell his or her story by creating an original video—you could almost think of it as a movie trailer that creates interest in the full picture. The stories they craft include a deep understanding of the values behind a product, and in particular the ones that The Grommet's 2-million-strong community cares about: green and social enterprises, job creation both in the United States and abroad, preserving craft, new technologies, supporting underrepresented and crowdfunded entrepreneurs. Not every Grommet reflects all these values, and some of them are even contradictory; but as a whole the companies promoted by The Grommet represent a positive force in the economy and a simple, clear way for ordinary people to vote with their dollars.

The Grommet's platform does for makers what is nigh impossible for them to do as individuals: instantaneously create competencies in the functions big consumer-products companies have taken years to build. As Jules Pieri, The Grommet's founder, describes it: "We help them navigate the tricky waters of pricing their product, shaping its messages and reaching influential consumers, media outlets and re-tailers. What we do in one day would literally take them years to achieve and many of these companies would not survive without our community's jumpstart."[23] Launched in 2008, The Grommet saw its revenues grow 900 percent between 2012 and 2014. "At this point, we have such a large community that within one hour of launch we know exactly what America thinks of this previously unheard of company and product. We literally move markets with this community of curious, optimistic, and engaged people." Fifty-seven percent of Americans self-identify as makers, and with the increasing accessibility of maker spaces, crowdfunding, 3-D printing, and access to manufacturing resources, this group will continually advance from DIY/project-based makers to self-determined businesses. Jules concluded, "I know we are capturing some pretty massive main-stream sentiments around empowerment, making, entrepreneur-ship, and a forceful rejection of the same-old-ways big businesses have operated."

The Grommet is still probably too consumption-oriented for my taste. It hasn't embraced the circular economy; most of the stuff purchased will still find its way into landfills eventually and not be used up. But The Grommet does embody the values that I think we need to embrace and which the Peers Inc model excels at: giving consumers a much better understanding of the supply chain, giving them more visibility into the products they are buying, letting them make purchases based more on values they care about and less on marketing shortcuts and retail distribution chains that are making the decisions for them. And, like La Ruche Qui Dit Oui and Etsy, The Grommet is supporting the makers in a shorter supply chain, giving them more economic authority, autonomy, and money.

Meetup was launched in 2002, but I probably didn't meet Scott Heiferman, its co-founder and CEO, until 2006. By then I was already dazzled. Like me, Scott was fascinated by community and created Meetup to help people get together in real life. He wanted people to sit face-to-face and actually talk, eat, drink, climb, dance, listen, travel, play cards, knit, and make music together. At a confer-ence, I watched Scott's quiet delight as he pointed to the huge screen behind him on which rapidly scrolled a list of meetings around the world that were starting at that moment. Thousands of meetups take place every day in 180 countries around the world. In London on Wednesday, October 8, 2014, before 1:00 p.m., I could attend Berkeley Square Speakers (six attending), BRX City Business Networking Breakfast (four attending), Entrepreneur and Investor Network (ten attending), Monthly Online Marketing Support (only one spot left), Creative Hub's How to Survive the Film Industry (fifteen attending), Digital London (four attending), Mummy Meetup (seven Marvellous Mummies going), Open Coffee (twenty-two entrepreneurs going), Ruby Business (eighteen attending), or Pivotal London Tech Talks, with the day's theme Bitcoin: Will It Transform the World? (thirty attending). The New York Tech Meetup is the largest, with 40,000 members; Foursquare and Tumblr debuted on its stage, networks and relationships created there spurred the civil rights battle against the restrictive Internet legislation SOPA and PIPA (see Chapter 7), and it convened the Red Cross, the Federal Emergency Management Agency, the City of New York, local NGOs, elected officials, and hackers to provide tech relief after Hurricane Sandy struck the metro area. New York City—where Meetup the company is headquartered—is the meetup capital of the world, with 1 million people (that's one in every eight New Yorkers) participating. Meetup is building face-to-face community at scale.

We've talked a lot about Uber and Lyft, both services that are serving the wealthiest among us. In India, one company is striving to provide a platform that serves the daily transportation needs of a much broader sector of the population. Much more like Lyft than Uber, G-Auto is improving the lives of both vehicle owners and passengers and using a platform to accomplish this as cost-effectively as possible. In India, there are auto rickshaws plying the streets of most cities, filling the enormous unmet demand for low-cost transport in the absence of adequate public transit. Most auto rickshaws are independently owned and owner-driven. I have a love-hate relationship with the rickshaws. The love part: The rickshaws are basically a motorcycle in front and two wheels with a wide covered seat in the back. They are fuel-efficient. They turn on a dime. They accommodate three adults squeezed in together, or six precariously balanced schoolchildren. They carry goods—I've seen them piled high with hay bales or refrigerators, taking vendor and goods to market. They are literally everywhere. The hate part: Well, there is a lot to hate, and most transportation wonks, city officials, and drivers of personal cars, buses, and trucks hate them; even their own passengers hate them at times. All of the auto rickshaws' failings can be corrected, however. Nirmal Kumar, G-Auto founder and CEO, rebuts the haters: "On the contrary, [the industry] gives revenue in the millions to the government through taxes and generates a livelihood to millions of the poor and downtrodden."[24] In Nirmal's world (and mine), auto rickshaws can be one of the best, most versatile urban vehicles on the planet.

The platform-and-peers model can do for auto rickshaws what it does for other sectors: organize them, offer scale economies where interested, increase economic control for both supply- and demand-

Nirmal Kumar, founder and CEO, G-Auto. Photo: G-Auto

side peers, and improve quality. G-Auto took off in 2009 with a small fleet of fifteen auto rickshaws in Ahmedabad and has grown to 15,000 rickshaws across Ahmedabad, Delhi, Gandhinagar, Surat, and Rajkot. Four and a half million passengers use its services every month. G-Auto has worked closely with local municipalities, and the government of India has formally recommended that all the states of India replicate the initiative in their cities for the benefit of commuters.[25] Particularly remarkable, and not necessarily obvious to the non-Indians among us, is that there has long been a lack of governmental support for this industry, which tends to be operated by members of the lowest castes. Why has G-Auto succeed in avoiding this trend? Because G-Auto is taming the chaotic auto rickshaw market to the benefit of everyone.

G-Auto leveraged technology with agility, and did so in advance of the rest of the transport sector. In addition to a call center and a website, its mobile app enables people to book, call, and track the vehicle. The technology has reduced the incidence of refusal, overcharging, and fare haggling, and has brought a great degree of safety to passengers by disclosing the identity of drivers both before and after hiring the autos. Additionally, passenger feedback mechanisms ensure better driver behavior. Drivers no longer take long, unnecessary detours to increase the fare, keep passengers waiting in the backseat while they fill up at a gas station, or feign having inadequate change. As a company, G-Auto encourages all kinds of auto rickshaw use: ad hoc or routine scheduled pickups, rickshaw sharing, long-distance trips, and even a six-hour "Heritage Tour" package for tourists with specially trained drivers. All of this is really great for the passengers.

But there is another reason I love Nirmal and G-Auto. Consider that auto rickshaws evolved from pulled rickshaws: hard manual labor and a means of making money for those who had no skills other than strength. Rickshaw drivers are for the most part poor, poorly educated, living day to day on a low income, and working long hours. Yes, they have this amazing asset, but the life is a hardscrabble one. G-Auto brought real, relevant technology to bear on rickshaw owners' previously very low-tech lives. G-Auto sends the closest and most recent bookings to the appropriate drivers, manages their daily bookings, sends a text message to customers with the bill amount, and updates invoice status to the G-Auto server. It is the first company in India to provide metered auto rickshaw service at airport and train stations (in Ahmedabad) through a privately owned booking counter. It has arranged low-cost leases so that drivers can upgrade from filthy two-stroke engines to cleaner vehicles that use compressed natural gas (CNG) and has negotiated a discount with the largest CNG distributor in Ahmedabad. All of this supports the economic life of the drivers. But wait, there's more! All participating drivers receive free personal accident and life insurance, driver training, an educational allowance for their children, and a uniform. G-Auto negotiated with doctors and diagnostic centers to provide cheaper medical consulting and diagnosis services to the families of all 15,000 auto rickshaw drivers. Wow, wow, wow! G-Auto is practically pulling rickshaw drivers into the Indian middle class—it's not just changing their income, it's changing their station in life.

Nirmal has much bigger plans. "India has more than 5 million auto rickshaws carrying 250 million passengers every day, mostly in urban areas. No single mode of transportation has the capacity to carry this volume of passengers," he tells me. He adds that there are twenty cities in India with potential similar to Ahmedabad's, and the company's goal is 100,000 auto rickshaw drivers by 2017 and 1 million by 2020. Why not? We've seen the potential for the Peers Inc model to scale fast. Developing-world markets where well-established monopolies do not exist (like New York's taxi medallions or London's cabs) can potentially leapfrog to new organizational models faster than the countries where these models were invented. They can go directly to a Peers Inc structure without having to pass through the stage of building giant monopolistic industrial-style providers first. And Nirmal doesn't intend to stop with India and its population of 1.3 billion. G-Auto can improve the lives of passengers and drivers alike in Sri Lanka, Pakistan, Thailand, Philippines, Indonesia, and Bangladesh, where auto rickshaws are equally popular. Nirmal concludes, "G-Auto can transform the unorganized nature and lack of reliability of this sector. We will evolve it to become a trusted provider of paratransit services throughout Asia." I hope he succeeds. I can also imagine G-Auto and its thousands of peer owner/drivers providing almost instant and very low-cost public transit services with just a few government additions: dedicated traffic lanes and pickup/drop-off locations for the busiest routes, and the leasing of new jumbo auto rickshaws with parallel benches in the back that can accommodate up to eight passengers. Instead of the $1 billion per linear mile needed to build a subway system or the $13 million per mile to build a bus transit system, this peer rapid-transit system could be delivered at some tiny fraction of the cost and time and give satisfying employment to millions of drivers.

All four companies I've profiled here, like most Peers Inc organizations, have resilience and community-building potential as by-products. We are going to need these as we move into this future of more extreme weather events and more resource conflict. Peers Inc solutions are naturally resilient because of the baked-in redundancy, but without the sort of costs that redundant systems usually impose on organizations seeking resilience. But we need to work harder and proactively on this community building. One of the lessons learned the hard way is that community is the first responder following climate-related disasters. The neighbors who are still on the ground or in communities nearby are the ones that can offer the first, best help.

A couple of months before Hurricane Sandy struck the New England coast, I was part of a roundtable at the annual conference of the Urban Land Institute, along with Shaun Donovan, then U.S. secretary for housing and urban development. I presented the Peers Inc framework to the audience of a few thousand. A day or so after Hurricane Sandy hit the Eastern seaboard, I received a call from Shaun. Could the excess capacity hidden in metro New York be tapped to find temporary housing for the thousands of people affected? I connected his office with others in the sharing economy to see what might be done. I'll admit that I failed to tap into the potential of excess capacity in cars because of insurance issues. But Airbnb did spring into action—1,400 Airbnb hosts in the New York metro area offered up rooms for free to those who needed them.[26] The Airbnb website wasn't structured for zero-cost rooms, and frankly, the connection between displaced families and Airbnb hosts was not well communicated. Some matches were made and real families benefited, but most rooms went empty. Still, the idea of using existing communities and platforms to respond to disasters took hold.

Lessons were learned, and in 2013 Airbnb launched a disaster response initiative that makes it easy for Airbnb hosts to provide space for people in need when disasters strike.[27] Since then, hosts have opened their door to displaced residents in response to emergencies around the world, including in San Diego in response to major fires; in Serbia, Bosnia, and Croatia for people affected by the Balkan floods; in London, Sardinia, and Colorado after serious flooding hit those regions; in Kefalonia after an earthquake hit the island; in Toronto and Atlanta following severe ice storms; and in the Philippines following Typhoon Haiyan.

In response to a disaster, Airbnb emails hosts in the affected area to see if they want to participate. Listings can be set to "free," and Airbnb waives its own fees. All the transactions are still supported by Airbnb's usual guarantees. A small amount of investment from Airbnb providing those guarantees helps to make an enormous amount of accommodation available, supported by the work done all the way through the development of the platform. It's an efficient way for people to volunteer support, but it needs the Peers Inc model to coordinate and provide accountability. This new Airbnb disaster response group is kept apprised of disaster response updates. When it partners with a city or state in advance of anticipated disasters (now there's a crazy thought!), Airbnb can use its standard communication tools to prepare hosts by sending out emergency preparedness materials and inviting them to training programs. We are still in the early days of this idea, but I expect these platforms to increasingly be tapped and more widely used during emergencies. BlaBlaCar was effectively an ad-hoc and real-time emergency transportation service for those stranded throughout Europe by the 2010 volcano eruptions in Iceland.

Another peer-built platform came to the rescue after Hurricane Sandy in a neglected neighborhood that had neither electricity nor phone service and spotty Internet connectivity. The Red Hook Initiative, run by a group of young tech leaders-to-be from this neighborhood in Brooklyn, had previously installed a wireless mesh communications network. Their network bridged those without access to those who did, and connected them all together for local emergency updates.

I've loved mesh networking for a very long time now, championing it not just for its potential for emergency services but also for its promise to provide very low-cost wireless connectivity to people around the globe. Mesh networks are a terrific solution for wireless in congested or remote places, helping connect up the Internet of Things. They also give us the possibility of individual real-time billing for road and electricity use, key to creating the right incentives to stop dirty energy consumption. A mesh works like this: Instead of your phone call being routed through a satellite or a cell tower and then back to your friend across town (or just across the street), it could go directly, perhaps hopping once over a friendly neighbor's phone or server to get to its destination. Data that are local stay local: your calls, texts, and photos to friends and colleagues; the news from the media that someone pulled off the Internet this morning and everyone is reading; and the hours of operation and addresses for area schools, services, and businesses can all go just a few hops from house to house in your neighborhood, rather than being transmitted to San Francisco and back for every new reader. There's no need to build new infrastructure; we connect up our existing wireless devices and routers. There's no monthly fee; by contributing our own server and devices to the network, we leverage idle capacity. There's complete privacy; your data isn't being routed through a company's network or possibly to the NSA. This story isn't yet a reality as I've told it here (although GuiFi.net in Spain has more than 20,000 peer nodes), but we are getting very close.[28] In January 2013, the first robust open-source build-your-own mesh network software platform was released, taking us one step closer to being able to turn the smartphones and laptops of everyone in the world into one giant network, without the need for additional infra-structure and—better yet—without a monthly subscription fee.[29]

Joshua Breitbart, a senior fellow at the New America Founda-tion's Open Technology Institute who co-created the open source software that helps the Red Hook mesh operate, said: "The general narrative of Silicon Valley is, build an app and change the world. [But t]here should be room to say, 'Build an app and change my neighborhood.'"[30] Expanding on that sentiment, I say: Build an app that changes so many neighborhoods, it changes the world. Mesh networking does just that. It multipurposes routers and devices and leverages excess capacity, creating something that otherwise seems impossible; it shares resources, relying on a distributed network of peers to grow and scale.

An article in *the New York Times* about the Red Hook initiative explained the pull: "Because the devices speak to one another, they are more than a series of 'hot spots' with Internet access; the mesh remains a network whether or not it is connected to the Internet. And that independence is its main attraction—in Berlin, where a tech collective shares Internet access to save money; in rural Spain, where one of the largest mesh networks covers areas ignored by tele-coms; in Tunisia, where the State Department has spent millions establishing a mesh network to experiment with a local network im-pervious to government censorship."[31]

A mesh network in Tunisia? Located 140 kilometers from Tunis, the coastal community Sayada decided that it wanted to have an alternative to government-controlled media, telecommunications, and spectrum. The old regime had been well known for its censorship and widespread surveillance practices. Local residents, ranging in age from six to eighty, and CLibre, a Sayada-based free technology association, held a four-day workathon to construct a network that covered 70 percent of the town. Collaboratively designed and built, the wireless network serves as a platform for locally hosted content, such as Wikipedia and Open Street Maps, and will include locally created content. Technology and organizing expertise came from the Open Technology Initiative, which worked with CLibre to help the local community organizers use an open-source self-guided kit, the Commotion Construction Kit. Total cost for the wireless routers, local server, and installation hardware was less than $2,500, but it was the excess capacity—donated rooftops and community labor—that made it affordable. Over time, the network is extensible without permission and as needed.

Hey, reader, have you perhaps noticed a giant gap in this chapter? We covered efforts by big business and by start-ups, by NGOs, by groups of people working together, and by individuals acting alone. Government is the gorilla missing from this story. Some governments, particularly at the local level, have been moving slowly, cautiously, with snail-like incremental efforts. But I can't close this chapter on how Peers Inc structures are the response of choice without mentioning a price on carbon, again. I closed the last chapter with it. A price on carbon is the ultimate, largest, and most far-reaching platform for participation we could develop. Excess capacity resides in the fact we are going to buy goods and services and houses and infrastructure anyway; adding a carbon tax multipurposes the value of that spending, and the carbon price can help inform our choices. It does the platform's role: A price on carbon organizes the efforts of all the stakeholders and every purchaser, and it simplifies our decision making by incorporating it directly into the price. This is an action that governments alone can do (the Inc), sticking to what they do best. In their myriad and diverse ways all around the world, participating peers will do what they do best—adapting this price signal to their own unique circumstances. I was talking with an economist who made me see the price on carbon in a whole new light: It is as if the world were to suddenly discover a new, incredibly valuable asset. Poof—a new trillion-dollar marketplace is created out of thin air. Each of us has the ability to trade on the value out of this new resource. Much like Bitcoin, it would be a new gold rush.

The collaborative Peers Inc economy is exactly what we need to respond to the size, scale, and urgency of problems facing the planet. The crisis of climate change, sustainability, water scarcity, deforestation, housing, sustainable transportation, education, and poverty will all require Peers Inc solutions if we are to find solutions soon enough. We need resilience, redundancy, community, and cost-effective and well-used resources. We also need the new platforms for participation that can quickly scale, be adapted locally, and be informed by individual innovation with learning integrated into the whole. We need all of this now (actually, we needed it yesterday, or at least at some point long before we reached 350 ppm). Let's design platforms that leverage existing assets (speed), do what is required to maximize participation (exponential learning), and rely on peers for local adaptation. If we are to deliver on our goal of emissions reaching a peak by 2017 and declining thereafter, there is no time for inaction.

As Nirmal of the amazing G-Auto wrote me when I told him how much I admired his work, "Thank you for the appreciation. I need to do a much greater volume to become a star. The world is so vast and my work is like just a tiny sand particle in the ocean."

We are all particles in this ocean. I'm counting on you, personally, to help make this happen: your talents, your experiences, and your passions. Mine certainly can't know or touch the daily life you know so well. We need the diversity that reflects our world. We can't do it without you.

My friend Christiana Figueres, head of the UN Climate Change Convention, writes me: "Climate change is not a one-person, one-community, one-city or one-country issue. It is an everyone issue. We are all called upon to contribute to the solution, and to do so urgently."

ELEVEN

What Happens Next?

The Collaborative Economy

THIS BOOK is a dare.

It is a challenge not only to entrepreneurs but also to all those who want to change the game by creating platforms that share power and value with the people who give them life. It is an ode to the individual, who when she gets access to the resources she needs to create something becomes an innovative, irreplaceable producer. Most of all, it is an expression of the hope that together we can become the collaborative generation who builds an economy that does not ask us to pit owner against laborer or producer against consumer. Instead we share everything we can, because that is the only viable path forward.

Over the last two centuries, the industrial economy rewarded a specific type of capitalist. To survive and thrive involved becoming just a smidge smaller than a monopoly, controlling the market while avoiding regulation. Control was maintained by exclusive ownership of intellectual property, trade secrets, copyrights, equipment, and employees. Why? Because factories, tools, and other expensive means of production demanded organizations large enough to extract their full potential. Products and services were standardized because high volumes led to economies of scale and the ability to offer lower-priced products. Higher volumes also meant increased market share.

Then the Internet happened.

Those old barriers to entry—large privately held assets and closed intellectual property—no longer result in the greatest value. They are dated strategies, unable to match the potential that exists in shared assets, which will always deliver better returns and empower multitudes who represent infinitely larger intellectual pools. And so around the world power is shifting from the lumbering, closed, centralized entities to the nimble, adaptive, distributed Peers Inc framework. This is how Peers Inc organizations started rewiring capitalism.

Where the industrial economy concentrates power and wealth, the collaborative economy succeeds by distributing it. So for those in power, enjoying the fruits of the status quo, this change will be especially hard. The old guard will fight to protect what it has from an uncertain future. The industrial economy, its regulations, and its biggest companies will not transform overnight. But we will end up by going down the Peers Inc path—of that I have no doubt.

Why?

I have observed that in the new collaborative economy, where we are networked and resources are highly accessible, the following are almost always true. The four principles on the next page will carry us inevitably to the collaborative economy.

The real question is how we prepare our workforce, our government, and ourselves for this new, inevitable economic order. We cannot afford a long period of delay, conflict, and resistance to this fundamentally more ecologically efficient new world. Platforms will be the successful companies of the future, in both ecological and economic terms. So it is imperative for us to confront how value will be shared between platforms and peers.

On a brilliant Sunday in March I met up with my good friend Carlos Romero. It was the kind of day people who live in the Bay Area revel in and use to make us New Englanders jealous. Carlos picked me up in an ancient brown pickup truck held together with duct tape. I placed my feet carefully for fear they would go through the floorboards, and he told me he usually travels by transit or bike, but free parking lets him keep this beater for the few times a year he has to move heavy objects.

THE PRINCIPLES OF THE COLLABORATIVE ECONOMY

1. *Open accessible assets > closed assets*

   Open assets deliver more value than closed assets because they are more efficiently used and let us continually uncover new valuable uses.

2. *More networked minds > fewer walled-in minds*[1]

   More people are smarter than fewer people, but only when they are networked together.

3. *Benefits of openness > problems of openness*[2]

   Collectively, the upside opportunities of innovation and shared learning are much larger than the downside problems, such as bad behavior, which we can identify and address with ratings, comments, and trust networks.

4. *I get > I give*[3]

   As individuals, each person who contributes assets to a platform necessarily gets more than she gives. This is how Wikipedia, potluck dinners, and taxes that pay for public libraries and national defense work.

We drove up and out of the Oakland valley. Just before we reached the top of the low hills—the dense suburbia all around us now overlooking the water, with beautiful views—we turned right, following the ridge down to a parking lot in a dense redwood forest. We were in Chabot Regional Park, a remarkable hidden slip of land. As we walked along the path, the only vistas are along the wild north-south axis, exposing a length of the untouched valley and blue hills beyond. It felt like a world long gone by, yet I knew it was nestled in a very real cityscape.

As we climbed, Carlos interrogated me about my optimistic Peers Inc predictions. He has spent twenty years in economic development, organizing new immigrants, and building subsidized housing in the Bay Area. I told Carlos about the world I envisioned, with a workforce of economically empowered and passionate freelancers supported by a porous set of platform companies providing scaffolding for distributed value creation and making efficient use of existing assets.

His take on what Peers Inc might look like from the perspective of the low-skilled marginalized worker was not so rosy. Carlos saw wages falling to the lowest possible levels, as a nearly infinite supply of freelance labor meant there would always be someone willing to work at a lower rate. He saw freelancers as workers without collective bargaining power, benefits, or safety nets. He saw that platforms can easily become monopolies. Consumers would have no choices. Peers would do the work, while the platform owners got all the money and retained all the control—same as it ever was, but perhaps even worse, since more people will find themselves in tenuous unprotected jobs, outsourced from their full-time-with-benefits ones. Increased unemployment. Increased income inequality.

Once out of the primeval landscape and back into the real world, this dialogue stayed with me. I share Carlos's concerns. Some of these undesirable outcomes will, and are, playing out. Governments could quickly get on the wrong side of this transition. If governments force adherence to outdated regulations and create new regulations that protect the largest companies, we won't build the platforms needed to adapt to climate change and sustainability requirements fast enough, and the legacy companies will still tumble down, albeit more slowly. If governments cling to an outdated understanding of employment, we will have an increasingly vulnerable workforce. Carlos and I spoke extensively about the need to extend worker protections and social safety nets to cover this new way of working and new type of workforce (see Chapters 7 and 8). We have a choice to make. We can transfer the huge gains from productivity that will result from the Peers Inc platforms and elevate the standards of living for everyone . . . or not.

As to whether successful platforms all become monopolies, I touched on this in Chapters 6 (building a platform from scratch), 8 (government's role), and 9 (platform financing). In the real world many things we would expect to become monopolies because of increasing returns at scale—from dating sites through to car rental itself—never actually do. They remain diverse because people want different things, and because of this, platforms continue to evolve. The key point of this book is to reveal the Peers Inc framework for thinking and taking action: Identify excess capacity, build a platform for participation, enable peers—and emphasize the collaboration. In the same way delectable pasta requires both boiling water and hard flour-based shapes, platforms and peers are nothing without each other. Denial of that reality by either party won't end well.

In the collaborative economy, peers are resourced and networked too. And while platforms may create more powerful companies and leverage existing platforms to build others more quickly, the peers too become more powerful through platform empowerment and the layering of connections (miracle #3, accessing the right minds).

Unlike industrial capitalism, in the collaboration economy money can't buy you everything. When more transactions are local, social intangibles—friendships, local and cultural knowledge, understanding of special exceptions and circumstances—matter more. And while the industrial economy signals status through the acquisition and display of physical goods, in the collaboration economy we aren't worried about ownership because things are at our fingertips when we need them and status is derived from reputation and the size of one's networks.

While industrial capitalism evolved to put the corporation's survival at the center, the collaborative economy thrives by putting people at the center—both customers and suppliers. Even mainstream economists are recognizing that measuring success and value creation through monetary growth alone is insufficient. The Peers Inc paradigm, with its different structure and means of value creation, will play an important role in transitioning world economies to a new value system and a new way of measuring prosperity.

Over the last two years I've done a lot of talking with taxi drivers in countries around the world about the quality of their work environment and their life. Uber has raised a staggering $3.3 billion in venture capital, much of it budgeted to fend off its many competitors (and lobby local governments for regulatory change). It has investors like Google, with deep pockets and a broad user base. In mid-2014, Google Maps, the top app worldwide, reaching 54 percent of all smartphones, started including in its directions the option for travel by Uber in addition to the generic options of car, transit, bike, and walking.[4]

Despite all of these advantages, the opinions I have heard from drivers and media stories about the company's extreme disregard for its drivers suggest that the drawbacks could prove fatal. Drivers are a fundamental and critical input in Uber's success. Yet an opinion piece in *GQ* magazine opined that "Uber operates more like a pimp than a boss."[5] I tested the line out on my Uber driver in San Francisco. "Exactly," he replied, "Pimp, not partner." A *Times of India* article from September 2014 highlighted a similar problem there. A general manager at Uber's office in Delhi said, "Our drivers are entrepreneurs who run their own businesses with no reporting structure to Uber, hence there is lesser need to be in constant touch." But a Delhi-based Uber driver was quoted as saying, "We've been told to call only on a Friday between 5–6 p.m. to get our concerns addressed. And I've never been able to get through to the manager between those hours."[6]

Given that Uber has many competitors, you have to believe that peers will choose platforms that work with them and for them. The opt-in employment on a Peers Inc platform means easy in *and* easy out. The balance of power between individuals and corporations is changed. That said, some platforms are undeniably monopolies. The ones that will succeed over the long term are the ones that give power to the peers, enabling self-governance in matters related to their side of the bargain (remember Elinor Ostrom's eight design principles for a long-lived commons, discussed in Chapter 6).

Our past emphasis on ownership stemmed from our fear of scarcity. But the more we experience the availability, viability, and superiority of pooled resources, the more we will trust ourselves to share rather than own, give when we get, and teach when we learn. Imagine the feeling of potential in a world where so much is easily accessible in a huge shared network. Even things that were once considered "rivalrous"—where one person's use would diminish another's ability to enjoy it—are actually *not* rivalrous when you put them into a big enough pool. Zipcar is the proof of this.

I started this book with a basic understanding and admiration of what the Peers Inc framework can deliver. As I researched and wrote, I discovered the potential for the three miracles: excess capacity that lets us scale at exponential speeds, platforms that produce exponential learning, and diverse peers that give us real-time access to the right minds. But as I tracked the incentives for each stakeholder (in Chapters 6 through 9), I changed my thinking in a way that took me by surprise. Here are my conclusions:

- Governments must create and open up assets for value extraction by all.
- We need to tax heavily at the platform level because most everything will be turned into a platform and we want to keep fluidity within the peers.
- Government regulations need to protect autonomous individuals against the power of the platforms and benefits need to be tied to people and not jobs.
- Everyone should be an independent contractor to give maximum flexibility and resilience to both companies and workers to match the rate of change.
- We must have a minimum basic income so that the enormous productivity gains are spread throughout the economy instead of increasing unemployment.
- We should emulate the potential and promise of the free and open-source software movement and the block chain to create and govern platforms by communities themselves.

We live on a planet with more than 7 billion people and rapidly diminishing resources. When I think seriously about where we are in the world today, several things bring me to tears: the horrible suffering of millions of blameless people around the world because of extreme climate events; young adults who are actively weighing whether they should have children; the 50 percent of species that will go extinct because of us by 2100; the loss of human potential to press forward with its understanding of the universe and the magnificence of creativity, culture, tradition, and family. Will we ruin the planet that is our home and our ability to thrive on it just as we are on the brink of so much potential? We are in a time-constrained race.

We need Peers Inc because sharing of physical assets requires the least amount of stuff to sustain the greatest number of people.

We need Peers Inc because virtual assets can be endlessly recombined to create new ideas and give new pleasures without diminishing the original asset in any way.

We need Peers Inc because we need new minds with new approaches and different life experiences to tackle seemingly insurmountable problems in fresh ways.

We need Peers Inc because to respond to the rapid rate of change in the world today, we need millions of people iterating on a variety of platforms so that we can learn at the fastest possible speed, find those with the best results, and spread their work.

In the collaborative economy, growth doesn't require us to expand production and consumption of physical goods. Instead, growth occurs when each individual peer joins a platform and contributes—in the form of existing assets and intellectual capital—and gains access to something many times larger than what was contributed. When public or private assets are newly pooled, it allows us to extract more value out of previously inaccessible excess capacity. This too increases wealth. More physical stuff isn't generated, but more stuff is made available and useful by being connected. More ideas, assets, and people are at hand for endless recombinations. There may be a limit to this process, but it is far above our current standard of living, and will rely on vastly fewer material resources!

This is Airbnb + Zipcar + Lyft + G-Auto + La Ruche + LinkedIn + Facebook + OKCupid + SoundCloud + Spotify + Twitter + openData + eLance-oDesk + Peerby + Yerdle + Etsy + Fiverr + mesh networks + GPS + smartphone apps + YouTube + Tumblr + BitTorrent + Meetup + MOOCs + Ciclovía + co-housing + co-working + Open Street Maps + shared public spaces + flash mobs + virtual choirs + The Johnny Cash Project.

In order to find ourselves in the world we want to live in, we can't sit passively. David Bollier eloquently delivers this call to action in his book *Think Like a Commoner*: "We can begin to imagine ourselves as commoners [participants in a global commons]. We can begin to become protagonists in our lives, applying our own considerable talents, aspirations and responsibilities to real-life problems. We can begin to act as if we have inalienable stakes in the world into which we were born. We can assert the human right and capacity to participate in managing resources critical to our lives."[7]

And this is happening already: G-Auto moves 4.5 million passengers monthly in clean CNG-powered vehicles steered by drivers whose lives are better. BlaBlaCar moves 2 million people a month in shared personal car trips. Each and every day 15,000 Meetups will take place. More content is uploaded to YouTube monthly than the three major television networks produced over a period of sixty years, and more than a million creators from over thirty countries earn money from their videos. WhatsApp's 50 billion daily messages sent using existing data plans saved users $4 billion worth of SMS and MMS fees in 2013. Duolingo provides free language instruction to 50 million people around the world. More than 40 million people purchase products on Etsy, and most of the transactions—$1.35 billion worth in 2013—represent new income to the more than 1 million Etsy sellers from two hundred different countries.

Zipcar is my personal experience that sharing improves people's lives and the environment simultaneously. In aggregate, for every Zipcar on the street, fifteen people either avoided buying a car or sold theirs because they now had access to the shared fleet. With 870,000 members and 10,000 cars, that means that 150,000 personal cars are no longer being stored on city streets and in driveways. Boston, New York, Washington, D.C., and Chicago have all seen declines in car registrations of between 7 and 10 percent since Zipcar entered their markets. Zipcar members weigh the full cost of going by car against their other options—walking, biking, or taking transit. The result is that Zipcar members drive about 80 percent fewer miles than they would if they owned their own car. That adds up to about 4.1 billion miles not driven and 1.7 million metric tons of CO_2 not emitted in 2014.

Take everything you've learned in this book and layer on a new meaning to Peers Inc. It is also People Incorporated: people incorporated into the dialogue, people incorporated into the value creating, people incorporated into the economy, people creating new organizations and entities among themselves and as unique individuals.

In the middle of 2003, Zipcar received an email sent to info@zip car.com, apropos of nothing. Here is the entire email, minus the sender's name: "Have I told you lately that I love you?"

Dare to be an individual, an entrepreneur, a businessperson, a change maker, a policy maker, a leader who shares. Dare to let go of ownership and invest in networked communities and accessible assets. Let's create the world we want to live in.

Continue the conversation at www.peersincorporated.com.

ACKNOWLEDGMENTS

I want to acknowledge those whose thinking is very much aligned with my own and whose ideas have bolstered, expanded, and challenged my framing for Peers Inc: Chris Anderson, Yochai Benckler, Peter Corbett, Brett Frischmann, Lisa Gansky, Stephen Johnson, Karim Lakhani, Tim O'Reilly, David Reed, Don Tapscott, Doc Searls, Bruce Schneier, Clay Shirky, Jeremiah Owyang, JP Rangaswami, Jeremy Rifkin, Eric Von Hippel, Jonathan Zittrain, and many others. We are all seeing the same things but coming at them from different angles.

Three people made this book much stronger and went well beyond what you might ask of a friend—Vinay Gupta, Willy Karam, and Cameron Russell. Thank you for your important and precise edits and additions.

Enormous thanks to those who spent many hours of their precious free time to read, comment, write, research, and cajole: Lawrence Barriner, Roxane Googin, Annemarie Grey, Anastasia Leng, Doc Searls, Juliet Schor, Thomas Stevenson, and Tim Woods.

Special thanks to David Weinberger, who worked closely with me in the beginning for no personal reward, and who introduced me to Lisa Adams, my kind and patient agent. John Mahaney, my editor at PublicAffairs, seemed to know when to encourage and when to press for change. A sincere group shout-out to the many people who discussed and challenged these ideas as I tested them out in the world, and who supported me with kind words of encouragement over the last few years. Every bit of that, even just a few words, helped get this work done.

And thank you Roy, without whom none of this would be possible.

NOTES

CHAPTER 1: "HELLO, ZIPCAR. THIS IS ROBIN."

1. Carol Tice, "Zipcar: Two Moms, a Business Idea, and $68 in the Bank," *Entrepreneur*, June 1, 2012, www.entrepreneur.com/article/223692.

2. Karim R. Lakhani, "The Core and the Periphery in Distributed and Self-Organizing Innovation Systems," PhD dissertation, Sloan School of Management, Massachusetts Institute of Technology, 2006, http://dspace.mit.edu /handle/1721.1/34144.

3. During the trial period before the company formally launched, when Craig first drove a Zipcar, here is what would happen once he'd made that online reservation: He would walk over to my house, where Beetle Betsy was parked out front on the street. He would walk up the side yard and up the steps on to my back porch to find the glider. Under the pillow were the car keys. He'd walk back to the car, unlock the door, and then fill out a form that was left in the glove box: start time, stop time, start odometer, stop odometer. When he was done he'd park back in front of my house, leave the filled-out form in the glove compartment, lock the car door, and return the key to under the pillow.

4. Ruth Eckdish Knack, "Pay as You Park: UCLA Professor Donald Shoup Inspires a Passion for Parking," *Planning*, May 2005, http://shoup.bol.ucla.edu /PayAsYouPark.htm.

5. See the spreadsheet by Jeremiah Owyang at https://docs.google.com /spreadsheets/d/12xTPJNvdOZVzERueyA-dILGTtL_KWKTbmj6RyOg9 XXs/edit#gid=1884009904.

CHAPTER 2: EXCESS CAPACITY

1. "Owning and Operating Your Vehicle Just Got a Little Cheaper According to AAA's 2014 'Your Driving Costs' Study," AAA NewsRoom, May 9, 2014, http://newsroom.aaa.com/2014/05/owning-and-operating-your-vehicle-just-got-a-little-cheaper-aaas-2014-your-driving-costs-study.

2. "AT&T Corporation," Wikipedia, http://en.wikipedia.org/wiki/AT%26T _Corporation.

3. Ibid.

4. "Skype," Wikipedia, http://en.wikipedia.org/wiki/Skype.

5. Craig Newmark, "What Was the True Genesis of Craigslist?," Quora .com, January 22, 2012.

6. "About Craigslist," www.craigslist.org/about/open_source"AT&T Corporation.

7. "iPhone Unlocked: AT&T Loses iPhone Exclusivity, August 24, 2007, 12:00PM EDT," Engadget, August 24, 2007, www.engadget.com/2007/08/24 /iphone-unlocked-atandt-loses-iphone-exclusivity-august-24-2007.

8. "Apple Sticks with Jailbreaking-Is-Evil Warning," *ComputerWorld*, February 6, 2013, www.computerworld.com/article/2494626/apple-ios/apple-sticks -with-jailbreaking-is-evil-warning.html.

9. Pelle Snickars and Patrick Vonderau, eds., *Moving Data: The iPhone and the Future of Media* (New York: Columbia University Press, 2013).

10. Sarah Perez, "iTunes App Store Now Has 1.2 Million Apps, Has Seen 75 Billion Downloads to Date," TechCrunch, June 2, 2014, http://techcrunch.com /2014/06/02/itunes-app-store-now-has-1-2-million-apps-has-seen-75-billion -downloads-to-date.

11. Zoe Fox, "The Average Smartphone User Downloads 25 Apps," Mashable, September 5, 2013, http://mashable.com/2013/09/05/most-apps-download -countries.

12. Luis von Ahn, "Massive-Scale Online Collaboration," TEDxCMU talk by Luis Von Ahn, April 2011 (transcribed December 2011), www.ted.com /talks/luis_von_ahn_massive_scale_online_collaboration/transcript ?language=en.

13. Ruth Eckdish Knack, "Pay as You Park: UCLA Professor Donald Shoup Inspires a Passion for Parking," *Planning*, May 2005, http://shoup.bol.ucla.edu /PayAsYouPark.htm.

14. Gabriel Lewenstein, "Bogotá Ciclovía," ADB KA Case Study, Institute for Transport and Development Policy, December 20, 2013, https://go.itdp.org /pages/viewpage.action?pageId=38109749.

15. Analysis from Wikipedia, "List of Largest Consumer Markets," http://en
.wikipedia.org/wiki/List_of_largest_consumer_markets, using the UN's National Accounts Main Aggregates Database, http://unstats.un.org/unsd/snaama
/selbasicFast.asp.

16. "Building China: The Role of Cement in China's Rapid Development,"
TheEnergyCollective.com, March 5, 2014, http://theenergycollective.com/robert
wilson190/347591/building-china-role-cement-chinas-rapid-development.

17. Dan Sperling, *Two Billion Cars: Driving Towards Sustainability* (New York:
Oxford University Press, 2009).

CHAPTER 3: PLATFORMS FOR PARTICIPATION

1. Liana Baker, "Alibaba Issues Additional Shares to Raise IPO Total to
$25 Billion," *Reuters*, September 22, 2014.

2. Michael De La Merced, "As Its I.P.O. Nears, Alibaba Gets Ready for a
Splashy Debut," *New York Times*, September 5, 2014.

3. "Reinventing the Wheel: Like Zipcar for Bikes," Urbandaddy.com,
March 15, 2011, www.urbandaddy.com/mia/leisure/12745/DecoBike_Like
_Zipcar_for_Bikes_Miami_MIA_Flamingo_Lummus_Product.

4. Dana Blankenhorn, "Private Health Reform Is MinuteClinic for Everyone," Smartplanet.com, February 2, 2010, www.smartplanet.com/blog/re
thinking-healthcare/private-health-reform-is-minuteclinic-for-everyone.

5. "Online Lens Rentals for Canon and Nikon (D)SLR," *Photography Things*
(blog), September 27, 2006, http://blog.romanzolin.com/index.php?blog=2
&cat=27&paged=2.

6. John Biggs, "Snapgoods: Like Zipcar for Gadgets," TechCrunch, July 26,
2010, http://techcrunch.com/2010/07/26/snapgoods-like-zipcar-for-gadgets.

7. Julie Donnelly, "'Zipcar for Hospital Gear Startup Moves to Boston
from Fla.," Bizjournals, January 9, 2014, www.bizjournals.com/boston/blog
/health-care/2014/01/zipcar-for-hospital-gear-startup.html?page=all.

8. "For Sail: Like Airbnb for Boats," Urbandaddy, June 16, 2014, www
.urbandaddy.com/dal/leisure/31148/GetMyBoat_Like_Airbnb_for_Boats
_Dallas_DAL.

9. Juliet Rylah, "HovelStay Is Like Airbnb for Adrenaline Junkies on
a Budget," Laist, October 28, 2014, http://laist.com/2014/10/28/hovelstay
_specializes_in_adventurou.php#photo-8.

10. James Robinson, "Rover.com Like Airbnb for Your Dog," SFGate,
April 25, 2013, www.sfgate.com/pets/article/Rover-com-like-Airbnb-for-your
-dog-4460469.php.

11. Personal correspondence with Peter Corbett.

12. Ibid.

13. Ibid.

14. Peter Corbett and Vivek Kundra were indeed the first to flesh out what standardized open data for government would look like from an implementation perspective. At little less than a year before Corbett and Kundra met up, Tim O'Reilly of O'Reilly Media and Carl Malamud of Public.Resource.Org had hosted a meeting of thirty people interested in framing what "open government" might look like.

15. World Resources Institute, "Aqueduct Water Risk Atlas," www.wri.org/resources/maps/aqueduct-water-risk-atlas.

16. "Ethiopia Toto Agriculture Portal," Data.gov, April 25, 2013, www.data.gov/food/applications/ethiopia-toto-agriculture-portal.

17. Personal correspondence with Nick Sinai, White House deputy CTO.

18. Kristin Burnham, "Facebook's WhatsApp Buy: 10 Staggering Stats," *Information Week*, February 21, 2014, www.informationweek.com/software/social/facebooks-whatsapp-buy-10-staggering-stats-/d/d-id/1113927.

CHAPTER 4: PEER POWER

1. Alyson Shontwell, "Tons of Women Are Using Lulu, an App That Rates Men, and Guys Are Going Nuts," *Business Insider*, March 1, 2014, www.businessinsider.com/lulu-app-for-iphone-2014-3?op=1.

2. Ronald Weitzer, "Legalizing Prostitution: From Illicit Vice to Lawful Business," *NYCPress,* 2012, page 22.

3. "A Personal Choice," *The Economist*, August 9, 2014, www.economist.com/news/leaders/21611063-internet-making-buying-and-selling-sex-easier-and-safer-governments-should-stop.

4. Will Yakowicz, "3D Robotics, Flying High with Drones," *Inc.*, June 24, 2014, www.inc.com/will-yakowicz/35-under-35-jordi-munoz-co-founder-3d-robotics.html.

5. "Peter Steiner (cartoonist)," Wikipedia, http://en.wikipedia.org/wiki/Peter_Steiner_(cartoonist).

6. Farhad Manjoo, "Grocery Deliveries in Sharing Economy," *New York Times*, May 21, 2014.

7. "Nasty Gal's Sophia Amoruso: #GIRLBOSS | Disrupt NY 2014," interview by Alexia Tsotsis, May 7, 2014, YouTube, https://www.youtube.com/watch?v=i7WCwyaVXxU.

8. "Freelancing in America: A National Survey of the New Workforce," study commissioned by the Freelancers Union and Elance-oDesk, 2014, http://fu-web-storage-prod.s3.amazonaws.com/content/filer_public/c2/06/c2065a8a-7f00-46db-915a-2122965df7d9/fu_freelancinginamericareport_v3-rgb.pdf.

9. "Redefining Entrepreneurship: Etsy Sellers' Economic Impact," an Etsy report based on the online Etsy Sellers Survey, 2013, https://blog.etsy.com/news/files/2013/11/Etsy_Redefining-Entrepreneurship_November-2013.pdf.

10. Taylor Soper, "From Doctor to Dog Sitter: Why This MD Left the Hospital to Take Care of Four-Legged Friends," GeekWire.com, November 11, 2013, www.geekwire.com/2013/doctor-dog-sitter-md-left-hospital-care-fourlegged-friends.

11. "We Are Peers," Peers Tumblr page, http://peersstories.tumblr.com/?src=peers-feature.

12. Susan Adams, "Unhappy Employees Outnumber Happy Ones Two to One Worldwide," Forbes.com, October 10, 2013.

13. Ossi Rahkonen, Mikko Laaksonen, Pekka Martikainen, Eva Roos, and Eero Lahelma, "Job Control, Job Demands, or Social Class? The Impact of Working Conditions on the Relation Between Social Class and Health," *Journal of Epidemiology and Community Health* 60, no. 1 (2006): 50–54.

14. Jodi Kantor, "Working Anything but 9 to 5," *New York Times*, August 13, 2013, www.nytimes.com/interactive/2014/08/13/us/starbucks-workers-scheduling-hours.html?module=Search&mabReward=relbias%3As&_r=0.

15. June 11, 2014, 6:21 a.m., https://twitter.com/LaszloTheDog/status/476715770299162624.

16. Leena Rao, "Reid Hoffman Tells Charlie Rose: 'Every Individual Is Now an Entrepreneur,'" TechCrunch, March 5, 2009, http://techcrunch.com/2009/03/05/read-hoffman-tells-charlie-rose-every-individual-is-now-an-entrepreneur.

17. Erik Sherman, "Kansas Supreme Court: FedEx Ground Drivers Not Contractors," Forbes.com, November 3, 2014, www.forbes.com/sites/eriksherman/2014/10/03/kansas-supreme-court-fedex-ground-drivers-not-contractors.

18. Neil Irwin, "The Benefits of Economic Expansions Are Increasingly Going to the Richest Americans," *The Upshot* (blog), *New York Times*, September 26, 2014, www.nytimes.com/2014/09/27/upshot/the-benefits-of-economic-expansions-are-increasingly-going-to-the-richest-americans.html?rref=upshot&_r=1&abt=0002&abg=1.

19. http://en.wikipedia.org/wiki/Joy%27s_Law_%28management%29.

20. "Crowdsourcing Apps and Government Innovation," talk given by Peter Corbett, iStrategyLabs CEO, fedscoop, ca. 2011, http://vimeo.com/25385952.

21. Will Bradden, "Henri, Paw de Deux," http://www.youtube.com /watch?v=Q34z5dCmC4M.

22. Vi Hart, "Wind and Mr. Ug," 2011, https://www.youtube.com/watch?v =4mdEsouIXGM.

23. DC Toy Collector, "Giant Princess Kinder Surprise Eggs Disney Frozen Elsa Anna Minnie Mickey PlayDoh Huevos Sorpresa," https://www.youtube .com/watch?v=R91WnllMcNA.

24. Marco della Cava, "SoundCloud's Growth Tempts Suitors," *USA Today*, May 20, 2014.

25. Ibid.

26. Josh Dean, "Is This the World's Most Creative Manufacturer?," Inc.com, October 2013.

27. Ibid.

28. Steve Lohr, "Quirky to Create a Smart-Home Products Company," *New York Times*, June 22, 2014.

29. "Garthen Leslie," Quirky.com, https://www.quirky.com/Drgldm.

30. "Appirio's Crowdsourcing Community Creates Breakthrough Solutions to Support the Advancement of Space Science and Protect Planet Earth / Protecting Earth from Asteroids and Finding Anomalies in Saturn's Rings Are Just a Few Ways [TopCoder] Is Helping NASA," Appirio press release, August 7, 2014.

31. Ibid.

32. Personal correspondence with Karim Lakhani.

33. Josh Ong, "Lyft Puts New York Launch on Hold to Pursue Regulator Approval," *TNW Blog*, July 11, 2014, http://thenextweb.com/insider/2014/07/11 /lyft-delays-new-york-launch-regulators-move-block-ridesharing-service.

34. TripAdvisor Fact Sheet, www.tripadvisor.com/PressCenter-c4-Fact _Sheet.html.

CHAPTER 5: BRINGING IT TOGETHER

1. "Investor Relations," HiltonWorldwide.com, http://ir.hiltonworldwide .com/investors/default.aspx.

2. "Accor," Wikipedia, http://en.wikipedia.org/wiki/Accor.

3. This number is from personal communication with Founder CEO Frédéric Mazzella.

4. Kristin Burnham, "Facebook's WhatsApp Buy: 10 Staggering Stats," *Information Week,* February 21, 2014.

5. Facebook Shareholder presentation, February 19, 2014, http://files .shareholder.com/downloads/AMDA-NJ5DZ/2971143669x0x727110/3b516115 -909d-4044-b758-d1742a46a135/Facebook_02_19_14.pdf.

6. Duolingo website, www.duolingo.com.

7. Roumen Vesselinov and John Grego, "Duolingo Effectiveness Study," report published by Duolingo, December 2012, www.duolingo.com/effectiveness -study.

8. Ibid.

9. http://www.epicurious.com/recipes/food/views/Pasta-with-Lentils-and -Kale-238092occ.

10. Dr. P. J. Buxton, OBE FRCR, personal correspondence.

11. Sandra Levy, "Mobile Safety Net App Helps People with Diabetes Connect," Healthline, July 15, 2014, www.healthline.com/health-news/diabetes -mobile-app-helps-diabetes-patients-connect-071514.

12. Feminista Jones, "Is Twitter the Underground Railroad of Activism?," Salon.com, July 17, 2013, www.salon.com/2013/07/17/how_twitter_fuels_black _activism.

13. U.S. Agency for International Development, "Fighting Ebola: A Grand Challenge for Development," www.usaid.gov/grandchallenges/ebola.

14. Walter Isaacson, "Where Innovation Comes From," *Wall Street Journal*, September 26, 2014, www.wsj.com/articles/a-lesson-from-alan-turing-how -creativity-drives-machines-1411749814.

15. "Vint Cerf Pt. 1," *The Colbert Report*, July 15, 2014, http://thecolbertreport .cc.com/videos/08a2dg/vint-cerf-pt—1.

16. Gordon Rosenblatt, "Google's Biggest Competitor Is Amazon," Medium .com, October 18, 2014, https://medium.com/@gideonro/the-google-amazon -slugfest-8a3a07a1d6dd.

17. Intergovernmental Panel on Climate Change, "Climate Change 2014: Synthesis Report," November 1, 2014, https://www.ipcc.ch/report/ar5 /syr.

18. World Bank, "Turn Down the Heat: Why a 4°C Warmer World Must Be Avoided," report for the World Bank by the Potsdam Institute for Climate Impact Research and Climate Analytics, November 1, 2012.

19. Ibid.

20. Intergovernmental Panel on Climate Change, "Climate Change 2014: Synthesis Report."

21. Jim Robbins, "Building an Ark for the Anthropocene," *New York Times*, September 27, 2014.

22. "London Congestion Charge," Wikipedia, http://en.wikipedia.org/wiki /London_congestion_charge.

23. "Living Sustainably," Cornell University, https://living.sas.cornell.edu /live/community/sustainability.cfm.

24. U.S. PIRG Education Fund, "Millennials in Motion: Changing Travel Habits of Young Americans and the Implications for Public Policy," October 14, 2014, www.uspirg.org/reports/usp/millennials-motion.

25. INET Logistics, "The Next Gold Mine: The Industrialisation of Road Freight Transport," www.inet-logistics.com/en/news/inet-in-the-news/news /the-next-gold-mine_-the-industrialisation-of-road-freight-transport.

26. uShip website, www.uship.com.

27. Center for Climate Change and Environmental Forecasting, U.S. Department of Transportation, "Transportation and Greenhouse Gas Emissions," http://climate.dot.gov/about/transportations-role/overview.html.

28. Heather Clancy, "GM, HP, Walmart and Others Demand Simpler Buying of Renewables," GreenBiz.com, July 11, 2014.

29. Yuliya Chernova, "The Economics of Installing Solar," *Wall Street Journal*, September 17, 2012, http://online.wsj.com/articles/SB10000872396390444506 004577615662289766558.

30. Karen Seto, Burak Güneralp, and Lucy R. Hutyra, "Global Forecasts of Urban Expansion to 2030 and Direct Impacts on Biodiversity and Carbon Pools," *Proceedings of the National Academy of Sciences* 109, no. 40 (2012).

CHAPTER 6: FROM SCRATCH

1. Stephen Levy, "Levy: Is Carpooling with Strangers the Way of the Future?," *Newsweek*, April 22, 2007.

2. "Google Buys YouTube for $1.65 Billion," NBCNews.com, October 10, 2006.

3. "No Plan Survives First Contact with Customers—Business Plans Versus Business Models," SteveBlank.com, April 8, 2010, http://steveblank.com/2010 /04/08/no-plan-survives-first-contact-with-customers-%E2%80%93-business -plans-versus-business-models.

4. "The Most Popular Operating Systems," www.linfo.org/operating _systems_list.html.

5. Personal correspondence with Jack Hughes.

6. Personal correspondence with Frédéric Mazzella.

7. "The Battle for Power on the Internet," a Bruce Schneier TEDx talk, September 25, 2013, www.youtube.com/watch?v=hod_QDgl3gI.

8. "From Zero to $5 Billion: The Lending Club Story," http://blog .lendingclub.com/wp-content/uploads/2014/07/LC-0to5B-Infographic.jpg.

9. E. Scott Record, "Lending Club Shares Soar in Biggest IPO by California Firm This Year," December 11, 2014, www.latimes.com/business/la-fi-lending-club-ipo-20141212-story.html.

10. Ibid.

11. Amy Cortese, "Loans That Avoid Banks? Maybe Not," *New York Times*, May 3, 2014.

12. "Peer-to-Peer Lending: Banking Without Banks," *The Economist*, March 1, 2014.

13. Aaron Vermut, "Marketplace Lending Takes the Main Stage," December 11, 2014, http://blog.prosper.com/2014/12/11/marketplace-lending-takes-the-main-stage/.

14. "About Us," LendingClub.com, www.lendingclub.com/public/about-us.action.

15. Office of New York State Attorney General Eric Schneiderman, "Airbnb in the City," October 2014, www.ag.ny.gov/pdfs/Airbnb%20report.pdf.

16. Personal interview with Chip Conley, September 13, 2014.

17. Edward Cone, "Decoding the Professionalization of Linux," CIO Insight Blogs, April 21, 2008, http://blogs.cioinsight.com/it-strategy/decoding-the-professionalization-of-linux.html.

18. Personal correspondence with Doc Searls.

19. See Chapter 9 for an in-depth analysis of the power and politics behind platform creation.

20. "Facebook Payments," Facebook.com, https://developers.facebook.com/docs/payments.

21. Nick Bilton, "Why Are People So Upset with Twitter? Let's Grab a Bite," *Bits* (blog), *New York Times*, August 24, 2012.

22. John Koetsier, "AppGratis: Last Week Apple Approved Our App—This Week They Pulled It," VB News, April 9, 2013, http://venturebeat.com/2013/04/09/appgratis-last-week-apple-approved-our-app-this-week-they-pulled-it.

23. "Uber Drivers Form Association Similar to Union," Kirotv.com, May 18, 2014, http://m.kirotv.com/news/news/uber-drivers-form-association-similar-union/nfy6x.

24. Avi Asher-Schapiro, "Against Sharing," *Jacobin Magazine*, September 19, 2014, www.jacobinmag.com/2014/09/against-sharing.

25. Personal correspondence with Emily Castor.

26. Comments of Etsy, Inc. before the Federal Communications Commission, July 8, 2014, https://blog.etsy.com/news/files/2014/07/Etsy-Open-Internet-Comments-7.8.14.pdf.

27. "Motley Fool CEO Tom Gardner Talks with LinkedIn Founder Reid Hoffman," October 13, 2014, www.fool.com/investing/general/2014/10/13/motley-fool-ceo-tom-gardner-talks-with-linkedin-fo.aspx.

28. "Airbnb: What Are Groups?" https://www.airbnb.com/help/article/496.

29. Personal conversation with Cory Ondrejka, July 2014.

30. "Drupal," Wikipedia, http://en.wikipedia.org/wiki/Drupal.

31. "Acquia Fastest-Growing Private Company in North America on Deloitte's 2013 Technology Fast 500," press release, November 13, 2013, www.acquia.com/about-us/newsroom/press-releases/acquia-fastest-growing-private-company-north-america-deloittes-2013.

32. Adam Kramer, Jamie Guillory, and Jeffrey Hancock, "Experimental Evidence of Massive-Scale Emotional Contagion Through Social Networks," *Proceedings of the National Academy of Sciences of the United States of America* 111, no. 24 (2014).

33. Danah Boyd, "What Does the Facebook Experiment Teach Us?" Medium.com, July 1, 2014, https://medium.com/message/what-does-the-facebook-experiment-teach-us-c858c08e287f.

CHAPTER 7: FOR THE PEOPLE

1. Jeffrey K. McGee, "Global Positioning System Selective Availability: Legal, Economic, and Moral Considerations," School of Advanced Military Studies, U.S. Army Command and General Staff College, Fort Leavenworth, KS, November 23, 1999.

2. "Military Satellite System to Go Public," CNN.com, March 29, 1996.

3. "Improving the Civilian Global Positioning System (GPS)," speech by President Bill Clinton, May 1, 2000, http://clinton3.nara.gov/WH/EOP/OSTP/html/0053_4.html.

4. "Global Positioning System," Wikipedia, http://en.wikipedia.org/wiki/Global_Positioning_System.

5. Barbara van Schewick, "Network Neutrality and Quality of Service: What a Non-Discrimination Rule Should Look Like," Center for Internet and Society, June 11, 2012.

6. "Minitel," Wikipedia, https://en.wikipedia.org/wiki/Minitel.

7. Jack Clark, "NHS Tears Out Its Oracle Spine in Favour of Open Source," TheRegister.com, October 10, 2013, www.theregister.co.uk/2013/10/10/nhs_drops_oracle_for_riak.

8. Stephen Crocker, "How the Internet Got Its Rules," *New York Times*, April 6, 2009.

9. Andrew Leonard, "You're Not Fooling Us, Uber! 8 Reasons Why the 'Sharing Economy' Is All About Corporate Greed," Salon.com, February 17, 2014.

10. Lisa Fleisher, "Thousands of European Cab Drivers Protest Uber, Taxi Apps," *Wall Street Journal*, June 11, 2014.

11. Megan McArdle, "Why You Can't Get a Taxi," *The Atlantic*, May 2012.

12. "Taxicab," Wikipedia, http://en.wikipedia.org/wiki/Taxicab.

13. "Taxicabs of the United Kingdom," Wikipedia, http://en.wikipedia.org /wiki/Taxicabs_of_the_United_Kingdom#cite_note-The_Knowledge-3.

14. Jeff Bercovici, "Uber's Ratings Terrorize Drivers and Trick Riders. Why Not Fix Them?" Forbes.com, August 14, 2014.

15. Andy Kessler, "Brian Chesky: The 'Sharing Economy' and Its Enemies," *Wall Street Journal*, January 17, 2014.

16. "Freelancing in America: A National Survey of the New Workforce," 2014, independent study commissioned by the Freelancers Union and Elanceo-Desk, http://chaoscc.ro/wp-content/uploads/2014/09/freelancinginamerica_re port-1.pdf.

17. Søren Mark Peterson, "Loser-Generated Content: From Participation to Exploitation," *First Monday* 13, no. 3 (2008), http://firstmonday.org/article/view /2141/1948.

CHAPTER 8: EMBRACING THE CHANGE

1. "Creative Destruction Whips Through Corporate America," INNO-SIGHT Executive Briefing, Winter 2012.

2. Barry Libert, Yoram Wind, Megan Beck Fenley, "What Airbnb, Uber, and Alibaba Have in Common," *Harvard Business Review*, November 20, 2014, https://hbr.org/2014/11/what-airbnb-uber-and-alibaba-have-in -common.

3. Dan Bieler, "The Collaborative Economy Will Drive Business Growth and Innovation," Forrester.com, May 19, 2014, http://blogs.forrester.com/dan _bieler/14-05-19-the_collaborative_economy_will_drive_business_innovation _and_growth.

4. Dries Buytaert, "The Business Behind Open Source," July 24, 2014, http://buytaert.net/the-business-behind-open-source.

5. Eric von Hippel, *Democratizing Innovation* (Cambridge, MA: MIT Press, 2005).

6. "Free Rider Problem," Investopedia, www.investopedia.com/terms/f /Free_rider_problem.asp.

7. Barton Gellman and Greg Miller, "U.S. Spy Network's Successes, Failures and Objectives Detailed in 'Black Budget' Summary," *Washington Post*, August 29, 2013.

8. "Army Launches Software Application Development Challenge 'Apps for the Army,'" Army CIO/G-6, http://ciog6.army.mil/ArmyLaunchesSoftware ApplicationDevelopmentCha/tabid/68/Default.aspx.

9. Elizabeth Montalbano, "Army Challenges Public to Build Apps," *Information Week*, May 3, 2011, www.informationweek.com/applications/army-challe nges-public-to-build-apps/d/d-id/1097502?.

10. "Army Launches Software Application Development Challenge."

11. GlaxoSmithKline, "Open Innovation," GSK.com, www.gsk.com/en-gb /research/sharing-our-research/open-innovation.

12. "Creating a Greater Choice of Tools: Procurement for the 21st Century; Citymart," talk given by Sascha Haselmayer, Citymart CEO, at the CfA Summit, 2014, https://www.youtube.com/watch?v=E1mQW80YCzE&index=22&list =PL65XgbSILalWFStqV0z0N9pvftstJ8AAh.

13. Ibid.

14. Personal interview with Sascha Haselmayer.

15. Personal correspondence with Sascha Haselmayer.

16. "Five Cities Selected as Winners in Bloomberg Philanthropies 2014 Mayors Challenge," Bloomberg.org, September 17, 2014, www.bloomberg.org/press /releases/five-cities-selected-winners-bloomberg-philanthropies-2014-mayors -challenge.

17. Christophe Vidal, "My Little Pony—Spitfire," on Shapeways website, www.shapeways.com/model/2207519/my-little-pony-spitfire-asymp-70mm-tall .html?materialId=26.

18. Elon Musk, "All Our Patents Are Belong to You," TeslaMotors .comblog, June 12, 2014, www.teslamotors.com/blog/all-our-patent-are-belong -you.

19. Personal correspondence with John Hagel and John Seely Brown.

20. "Financial Performance," J-Sainsbury.co.uk, www.j-sainsbury.co.uk/inves tor-centre/financial-performance.

21. "Crowdsourced Green Mondays: Sainsbury's," report reviewing Sainsbury's 20x20 Sustainability Plan, www.thecrowd.me/sites/default/files/Wisdom _of_the_Crowd.pdf.

22. "Alex Cole: Talking to Customers About Sustainability and the Value of Values," J Sainsbury plc blog, September 19, 2014, www.j-sainsbury.co.uk/blog /2013/11/alex-cole-talking-to-customers-about-sustainability-and-the-value-of -values.

23. Thomas Spanyol, "Sainsbury's ASA Challenge Goes to Judicial Review," December 22, 2014. www.marketinglaw.co.uk/advertising-regulation/sainsburys -asa-challenge-goes-to-judicial-review?cat_id=1.

24. "Rethinking Retail in the Collaborative Economy," talk given by Véronique Laury, Castorama CEO, OuiShare Fest, June 9, 2014, ww.youtube.com/watch?v=nDkrBfaP8bg.

25. Kevin Delaney, "Google in Talks to Buy YouTube for $1.6 Billion," *Wall Street Journal*, October 7, 2006.

26. Curt Woodward, "MA Warns Ride-Sharing, Car-Sharing Drivers of Insurance Risks," Xconomy.com, June 26, 2014, www.xconomy.com/boston/2014/06/26/ma-warns-ride-sharing-car-sharing-drivers-of-insurance-risks.

27. Scott Austin, "How Does Airbnb's $10 Billion Valuation Size Up?," *Digits* blog, *Wall Street Journal*, March 20, 2014.

28. Roxane Googin, "The Techonomy, Get Used to It," *High Technology Observer*, September 27, 2012.

29. Paul Krugman, "The Rich, the Right, and the Facts: Deconstructing the Income Distribution Debate," *The American Prospect*, Fall 1992.

30. Kurt Badenhausen, "US Slides Again as Denmark Tops Forbes Best Countries for Business," December 17, 2014, www.forbes.com/sites/kurtbadenhausen/2014/12/17/u-s-slides-again-as-denmark-tops-forbes-best-countries-for-business/.

31. OECD Stat extracts, Level of GDP per capita and productivity, 2013, http://stats.oecd.org/Index.aspx?DataSetCode=PDB_LV.

32. http://en.wikipedia.org/wiki/List_of_countries_by_tax_rates.

33. World Happiness Report, 2103, published by the United Nations Sustainable Development Solutions Network, http://unsdsn.org/wp-content/uploads/2014/02/WorldHappinessReport2013_online.pdf

CHAPTER 9: WHO HAS THE GOLD?

1. Neil Irwin, "The Benefits of Economic Expansions Are Increasingly Going to the Richest Americans," *The Upshot* (blog), *New York Times*, September 26, 2014.

2. "Airbnb," CrunchBase.com, www.crunchbase.com/organization/airbnb.

3. Financial statements, WhatsApp, years ended December 31, 2012 and 2013, filed with the SEC, www.sec.gov/Archives/edgar/data/1326801/000132680114000047/exhibit991auditedwhatsappi.htm.

4. Grant Gross, "FCC's Wheeler: US Needs More High-Speed Broadband Competition," *PC World*, September 4, 2014.

5. Michael Porter and Mark Kramer, "Creating Shared Value: Redefining Capitalism and the Role of the Corporation in Society," *Harvard Business Review*, January 2011.

6. Trade School, "About," http://tradeschool.coop/about.

7. Ibid.

8. Kickstarter, "Stats," www.kickstarter.com/help/stats.

9. Accenture, "The 'Greater' Wealth Transfer: Capitalizing on the Intergenerational Shift in Wealth," 2012, www.accenture.com/us-en/Pages/insight-capitalizing-intergenerational-shift-wealth-capital-markets-summary.aspx.

10. Adrianne Jeffries, "If You Back a Kickstarter Project That Sells for $2 Billion, Do You Deserve to Get Rich?" TheVerge.com, March 28, 2014, www.theverge.com/2014/3/28/5557120/what-if-oculus-rift-kickstarter-backers-had-gotten-equity.

11. Greg Belote, "What If Oculus Crowdfunded for Equity? A 145x Return," WeFunder, March 26, 2014, https://wefunder.me/post/42-what-if-oculus-crowdfunded-for-equity.

12. "Top 20 Open Source Licenses," BlackDuckSoftware.com, www.blackducksoftware.com/resources/data/top-20-open-source-licenses.

13. David Wheeler, "GPL, BSD, and NetBSD—Why the GPL Rocketed Linux to Success," blog post, September 1, 2006, www.dwheeler.com/blog/2006/09/01/#gpl-bsd.

14. "Creative Commons," Wikipedia, http://en.wikipedia.org/wiki/Creative_Commons.

15. Timothy Lee, "The Open Source Model Is About Organization, Not Who Signs Your Paycheck," techdirt.com, April 15, 2008, www.techdirt.com/articles/20080423/082724929.shtml.

16. Edward Cone, "Decoding the Professionalization of Linux," *CIO Insight Blogs*, April 21, 2008, http://blogs.cioinsight.com/it-strategy/decoding-the-professionalization-of-linux.html.

17. Bruce Schneier, "Heartbleed," blog post, April 9, 2014, www.schneier.com/blog/archives/2014/04/heartbleed.html; Paul Mutton, "Half a Million Widely Trusted Websites Vulnerable to Heartbleed Bug," Netcraft.com, April 8, 2014, http://news.netcraft.com/archives/2014/04/08/half-a-million-widely-trusted-websites-vulnerable-to-heartbleed-bug.html.

18. "Core Infrastructure Initiative," Wikipedia, http://en.wikipedia.org/wiki/Core_Infrastructure_Initiative.

19. Michael Carney, "GitHub CEO Explains Why the Company Took So Damn Long to Raise Venture Capital," pando.com, June 20, 2013, http://pando.com/2013/06/20/github-ceo-explains-why-the-company-took-so-damn-long-to-raise-venture-capital.

20. "Benevolent Dictator for Life," Wikipedia, https://en.wikipedia.org/wiki/Benevolent_dictator_for_life.

21. "Crypto-Currency Market Capitalizations," http://coinmarketcap.com.

22. "Who Controls the Bitcoin Network?," Bitcoin website, https://bitcoin.org/en/faq#who-controls-the-bitcoin-network.

23. Bitsmith, "Inside a Chinese Bitcoin Mine," *The Coinsman*, August 11, 2014, www.thecoinsman.com/2014/08/bitcoin/inside-chinese-bitcoin-mine.

24. "Government as Impresario: Emergent Public Goods and Public Private Partnerships 2.0," talk given by Nicholas Gruen as part of a luncheon series at the Berkman Center for Internet and Society, January 14, 2014, http://cyber.law.harvard.edu/events/luncheon/2014/01/gruen.

25. Personal correspondence with Cory Ondrejka, July 18, 2014.

26. Gruen, "Government as Impresario."

27. Kunal Jasty, "A Piketty Primer: 'Capital' in 10 Graphs," RadioOpenSource.org, April 29, 2014, http://radioopensource.org/capital-in-10-graphs.

28. Elise Gould, "Why America's Workers Need Faster Wage Growth—and What We Can Do About It," Economic Policy Institute, August 27, 2014.

29. Evan Osnos, "Embrace the Irony," *New Yorker*, October 13, 2014.

CHAPTER 10: ADDRESSING OUR BIGGEST CHALLENGES

1. World Bank, "Turn Down the Heat: Why a 4°C Warmer World Must Be Avoided," report for the World Bank by the Potsdam Institute for Climate Impact Research and Climate Analytics, November 1, 2012; Robert Kunzig, "A World with 11 Billion People? New Population Projections Shatter Earlier Estimates," *National Geographic News*, September 18, 2014, http://news.nationalgeographic.com/news/2014/09/140918-population-global-united-nations-2100-boom-africa/.

2. "Our Approach to Sustainability," Unilever.com, www.unilever.com/sustainable-living-2014/our-approach-to-sustainability.

3. Paul Polman, "The Remedies for Capitalism," McKinsey.com, www.mckinsey.com/features/capitalism/paul_polman.

4. Personal correspondence with John Bartolone, September 26, 2014.

5. Charlotte Malone, "Unilever and Siemens Among Companies Named Sustainability Leaders," Blue & Green Tomorrow, September 15, 2014, http://blueandgreentomorrow.com/2014/09/15/unilever-and-siemens-among-companies-named-sustainability-leaders.

6. "Our Approach to Sustainability," Unilever.com.

7. Peter Evans, "Unilever Commits to Sustainable Palm Oil by End of 2014," *Wall Street Journal*, November 12, 2013, http://online.wsj.com/articles/SB10001424052702304644104579193841716811338.

8. Etsy Values and Impact Annual Report, 2013.

9. Ibid.

10. World Resources Institute website, www.wri.org.

11. "Indonesia Forest Fires," a group of blog posts, World Resources Institute, www.wri.org/blog-tags/8705.

12. J. Hansen et al., "Target Atmospheric CO_2: Where Should Humanity Aim?" *Open Atmospheric Science Journal* 2 (2008): 217–231.

13. Robert Kunzig, "Climate Milestone: Earth's CO_2 Level Passes 400 ppm," *National Geographic News*, May 9, 2013.

14. "350.org, Global Work Party," Wikipedia, http://en.wikipedia.org/wiki/350.org#10.2F10.2F10_Global_Work_Party.

15. "Divestment Commitments," Fossil Free, http://gofossilfree.org/commitments.

16. Independent Press, "100 Summit Unitarians Joined Thousands in People's Climate March," NJ.com, September 27, 2014, www.nj.com/independentpress/index.ssf/2014/09/100_summit_unitarians_joined_t.html.

17. Jesse Jenkins, "How Does the People's Climate March Stack Up Against the Largest Protest Rallies in U.S. History?" The Energy Collective, September 22, 2014, http://theenergycollective.com/jessejenkins/584611/how-does-peoples-climate-march-stack-against-largest-protest-rallies-us-history.

18. Paul Hawken, *Blessed Unrest: How the Largest Movement in the World Came into Being, and Why No One Saw It Coming* (New York: Viking, 2007), www.blessedunrest.com/.

19. Jeff Hammerbacher @hackingdata.

20. "Participer à une Ruche," La Ruche Qui Dit Oui website, www.laruchequiditoui.fr/member/home.

21. Jonathan House, "Five Takeaways from the New GDP-by-Industry Report," *Real Time Economics* (blog), *Wall Street Journal*, April 25, 2014, http://blogs.wsj.com/economics/2014/04/25/five-takeaways-from-new-gdp-by-industry-report/.

22. "Tech & Gadgets," The Grommet website, www.thegrommet.com/tech-gadgets.

23. Personal correspondence with Jules Pieri, September 26, 2014.

24. Personal correspondence with Nirmal Kumar.

25. Ibid.

26. "Airbnb Disaster Response," https://www.airbnb.com/disaster-response.

27. Ibid.

28. Guifi.net website, https://guifi.net/en.

29. Veniam, the company I most recently co-founded, is building the networking fabric for the Internet of Moving Things. Combining cellular, Wi-Fi and vehicle-to-vehicle communications, Veniam turns every vehicle into a hotspot, as well as collector and conveyor of sensor data for smart cities and ports.

30. Noam Cohen, "Red Hook's Cutting-Edge Wireless Network," *New York Times*, August 22, 2014.

31. Ibid.

CHAPTER 11: WHAT HAPPENS NEXT?

1. Bill Joy, Linus Torvalds, and Eric Raymond have all been given credit for this observation.

2. Nicholas Gruen articulated this idea to me.

3. David Reed inspired me with this sentence from his blog: "Each member of the Internet who contributed to the mutual enterprise gained connectivity disproportionate to the member's contribution." David Reed, "If the Stimulus Is the New Black, I'm Betting on Red," *The PI Blogs*, MIT Communication Futures Program, April 1, 2009, http://cfp.mit.edu/cfp-pi/?p=15%20.

4. Marcello Mari, "Top Global Smartphone Apps: Who's in the Top 10," *Global Web Index Blog*, http://blog.globalwebindex.net/Top-global-smartphone-apps.

5. Mickey Rapkin, "Uber Cab Confessions," *GQ*, March 2014.

6. Harsimran Julka and Aditi Shrivastava, "Discontent Rises Amongst Uber Drivers in India Against Its Global Policies," *Times of India*, September 3, 2014, http://timesofindia.indiatimes.com/tech/tech-news/Discontent-rises-amongst-Uber-drivers-in-India-against-its-global-policies/movie-review/41630766.cms.

7. David Bollier, *Think Like a Commoner* (New York: New Society Publishers, 2014).

INDEX

Credit: Andrew Elliott

ROBIN CHASE is co-founder of Zipcar, Veniam, and founder of Buzzcar and GoLoco, all businesses that have disrupted and innovated the transportation sector. She was named one of *Time*'s 100 Most Influential People in the World, and has been featured in the *New York Times*, NPR, *Wired*, *Newsweek*, and *BusinessWeek*. She lives in Cambridge, Massachusetts.

PublicAffairs is a publishing house founded in 1997. It is a tribute to the standards, values, and flair of three persons who have served as mentors to countless reporters, writers, editors, and book people of all kinds, including me.

I. F. STONE, proprietor of *I. F. Stone's Weekly*, combined a commitment to the First Amendment with entrepreneurial zeal and reporting skill and became one of the great independent journalists in American history. At the age of eighty, Izzy published *The Trial of Socrates*, which was a national bestseller. He wrote the book after he taught himself ancient Greek.

BENJAMIN C. BRADLEE was for nearly thirty years the charismatic editorial leader of *The Washington Post*. It was Ben who gave the *Post* the range and courage to pursue such historic issues as Watergate. He supported his reporters with a tenacity that made them fearless and it is no accident that so many became authors of influential, best-selling books.

ROBERT L. BERNSTEIN, the chief executive of Random House for more than a quarter century, guided one of the nation's premier publishing houses. Bob was personally responsible for many books of political dissent and argument that challenged tyranny around the globe. He is also the founder and longtime chair of Human Rights Watch, one of the most respected human rights organizations in the world.

•   •   •

For fifty years, the banner of Public Affairs Press was carried by its owner Morris B. Schnapper, who published Gandhi, Nasser, Toynbee, Truman, and about 1,500 other authors. In 1983, Schnapper was described by *The Washington Post* as "a redoubtable gadfly." His legacy will endure in the books to come.

Peter Osnos, Founder and Editor-at-Large